50% OFF Online SHRM-CP Pr

Dear Customer,

We consider it an honor and a privilege that you chose our SHRM-CP Study Guide. As a way of showing our appreciation and to help us better serve you, we have partnered with Mometrix Test Preparation to offer you **50% off their online SHRM-CP Prep Course.** Many SHRM-CP courses are needlessly expensive and don't deliver enough value. With their course, you get access to the best SHRM prep material, and you only pay half price.

Mometrix has structured their online course to perfectly complement your printed study guide. The SHRM-CP Prep Course contains **in-depth lessons** that cover all the most important topics, over **950 practice questions** to ensure you feel prepared, and **more than 450 digital flashcards**, so you can study while you're on the go.

Online SHRM-CP Prep Course

Topics Covered:

- Behavioral Competencies
  - *Leadership*
  - *Interpersonal*
  - *Business*
- Technical Knowledge
  - *People*
  - *Organization*
  - *Workplace*
  - *Strategy*

Course Features:

- SHRM-CP Study Guide
  - Get content that complements our best-selling study guide.
- 6 Full-Length Practice Tests
  - With over 950 practice questions, you can test yourself again and again.
- Mobile Friendly
  - If you need to study on the go, the course is easily accessible from your mobile device.
- SHRM-CP Flashcards
  - Their course includes a flashcard mode consisting of over 450 content cards to help you study.

To receive this discount, visit their website: mometrix.com/university/shrm/ or simply scan this QR code with your smartphone. At the checkout page, enter the discount code: **APEXSHRM50**

SCAN HERE

If you have any questions or concerns, please don't hesitate to contact them at universityhelp@mometrix.com.

FREE

Free Study Tips Videos/DVD

In addition to this guide, we have created a FREE set of videos with helpful study tips. **These FREE videos provide you with top-notch tips to conquer your exam and reach your goals.**

Our simple request is that you give us feedback about the book in exchange for these strategy-packed videos. We would love to hear what you thought about the book, whether positive, negative, or neutral. It is our #1 goal to provide you with quality products and customer service.

To receive your **FREE Study Tips Videos**, scan the QR code or email freevideos@apexprep.com. Please put "FREE Videos" in the subject line and include the following in the email:

    a. The title of the book

    b. Your rating of the book on a scale of 1-5, with 5 being the highest score

    c. Any thoughts or feedback about the book

Thank you!

SHRM CP Exam Prep 2022-2023

2022-2023

SHRM Certification Study Guide Book
with Practice Test Questions
[Updated for the New Outline]

Matthew Lanni

Written and edited by APEX Publishing.

ISBN 13: 9781637753309
ISBN 10: 1637753306

APEX Publishing is not connected with or endorsed by any official testing organization. APEX Publishing creates and publishes unofficial educational products. All test and organization names are trademarks of their respective owners.

The material in this publication is included for utilitarian purposes only and does not constitute an endorsement by APEX Publishing of any particular point of view.

For additional information or for bulk orders, contact info@apexprep.com

Table of Contents

Test Taking Strategies

1. Reading the Whole Question

A popular assumption in Western culture is the idea that we don't have enough time for anything. We speed while driving to work, we want to read an assignment for class as quickly as possible, or we want the line in the supermarket to dwindle faster. However, speeding through such events robs us from being able to thoroughly appreciate and understand what's happening around us. While taking a timed test, the feeling one might have while reading a question is to find the correct answer as quickly as possible. Although pace is important, don't let it deter you from reading the whole question. Test writers know how to subtly change a test question toward the end in various ways, such as adding a negative or changing focus. If the question has a passage, carefully read the whole passage as well before moving on to the questions. This will help you process the information in the passage rather than worrying about the questions you've just read and where to find them. A thorough understanding of the passage or question is an important way for test takers to be able to succeed on an exam.

2. Examining Every Answer Choice

Let's say we're at the market buying apples. The first apple we see on top of the heap may *look* like the best apple, but if we turn it over we can see bruising on the skin. We must examine several apples before deciding which apple is the best. Finding the correct answer choice is like finding the best apple. Although it's tempting to choose an answer that seems correct at first without reading the others, it's important to read each answer choice thoroughly before making a final decision on the answer. The aim of a test writer might be to get as close as possible to the correct answer, so watch out for subtle words that may indicate an answer is incorrect. Once the correct answer choice is selected, read the question again and the answer in response to make sure all your bases are covered.

3. Eliminating Wrong Answer Choices

Sometimes we become paralyzed when we are confronted with too many choices. Which frozen yogurt flavor is the tastiest? Which pair of shoes look the best with this outfit? What type of car will fill my needs as a consumer? If you are unsure of which answer would be the best to choose, it may help to use process of elimination. We use "filtering" all the time on sites such as eBay® or Craigslist® to eliminate the ads that are not right for us. We can do the same thing on an exam. Process of elimination is crossing out the answer choices we know for sure are wrong and leaving the ones that might be correct. It may help to cover up the incorrect answer choice. Covering incorrect choices is a psychological act that alleviates stress due to the brain being exposed to a smaller amount of information. Choosing between two answer choices is much easier than choosing between all of them, and you have a better chance of selecting the correct answer if you have less to focus on.

4. Sticking to the World of the Question

When we are attempting to answer questions, our minds will often wander away from the question and what it is asking. We begin to see answer choices that are true in the real world instead of true in the world of the question. It may be helpful to think of each test question as its own little world. This world may be different from ours. This world may know as a truth that the chicken came before the egg or may assert that two plus two equals five. Remember that, no matter what hypothetical nonsense may be in the question, assume it to be true. If the question states that the chicken came before the egg, then choose your answer based on that truth. Sticking to the world of the question means placing all of our biases and assumptions aside and relying on the question to guide us to the correct answer. If we are simply looking for answers that are correct based on our own judgment, then we may choose incorrectly. Remember an answer that is true does not necessarily answer the question.

5. Key Words

If you come across a complex test question that you have to read over and over again, try pulling out some key words from the question in order to understand what exactly it is asking. Key words may be words that surround the question, such as *main idea, analogous, parallel, resembles, structured,* or *defines.* The question may be asking for the main idea, or it may be asking you to define something. Deconstructing the sentence may also be helpful in making the question simpler before trying to answer it. This means taking the sentence apart and obtaining meaning in pieces, or separating the question from the foundation of the question. For example, let's look at this question:

> Given the author's description of the content of paleontology in the first paragraph, which of the following is most parallel to what it taught?

The question asks which one of the answers most *parallels* the following information: The *description* of paleontology in the first paragraph. The first step would be to see *how* paleontology is described in the first paragraph. Then, we would find an answer choice that parallels that description. The question seems complex at first, but after we deconstruct it, the answer becomes much more attainable.

6. Subtle Negatives

Negative words in question stems will be words such as *not, but, neither,* or *except.* Test writers often use these words in order to trick unsuspecting test takers into selecting the wrong answer—or, at least, to test their reading comprehension of the question. Many exams will feature the negative words in all caps (*which of the following is NOT an example*), but some questions will add the negative word seamlessly into the sentence. The following is an example of a subtle negative used in a question stem:

> According to the passage, which of the following is *not* considered to be an example of paleontology?

If we rush through the exam, we might skip that tiny word, *not,* inside the question, and choose an answer that is opposite of the correct choice. Again, it's important to read the question fully, and double check for any words that may negate the statement in any way.

7. Spotting the Hedges

The word "hedging" refers to language that remains vague or avoids absolute terminology. Absolute terminology consists of words like *always, never, all, every, just, only, none,* and *must.* Hedging refers to words like *seem, tend, might, most, some, sometimes, perhaps, possibly, probability,* and *often.* In some cases, we want to choose answer choices that use hedging and avoid answer choices that use absolute terminology. It's important to pay attention to what subject you are on and adjust your response accordingly.

8. Restating to Understand

Every now and then we come across questions that we don't understand. The language may be too complex, or the question is structured in a way that is meant to confuse the test taker. When you come across a question like this, it may be worth your time to rewrite or restate the question in your own words in order to understand it better. For example, let's look at the following complicated question:

> Which of the following words, if substituted for the word *parochial* in the first paragraph, would LEAST change the meaning of the sentence?

Let's restate the question in order to understand it better. We know that they want the word *parochial* replaced. We also know that this new word would "least" or "not" change the meaning of the sentence. Now let's try the sentence again:

> Which word could we replace with *parochial,* and it would not change the meaning?

Restating it this way, we see that the question is asking for a synonym. Now, let's restate the question so we can answer it better:

> Which word is a synonym for the word *parochial?*

Before we even look at the answer choices, we have a simpler, restated version of a complicated question.

9. Predicting the Answer

After you read the question, try predicting the answer *before* reading the answer choices. By formulating an answer in your mind, you will be less likely to be distracted by any wrong answer choices. Using predictions will also help you feel more confident in the answer choice you select. Once you've chosen your answer, go back and reread the question and answer choices to make sure you have the best fit. If you have no idea what the answer may be for a particular question, forego using this strategy.

10. Avoiding Patterns

One popular myth in grade school relating to standardized testing is that test writers will often put multiple-choice answers in patterns. A runoff example of this kind of thinking is that the most common answer choice is "C," with "B" following close behind. Or, some will advocate certain made-up word patterns that simply do not exist. Test writers do not arrange their correct answer choices in any kind of pattern; their choices are randomized. There may even be times where the correct answer choice will be the same letter for two or three questions in a row, but we have no way of knowing when or if this might happen. Instead of trying to figure out what choice the test writer probably set as being correct, focus on what the *best answer choice* would be out of the answers you are presented with. Use the tips above, general knowledge, and reading comprehension skills in order to best answer the question, rather than looking for patterns that do not exist.

FREE Videos/DVD OFFER

Achieving a high score on your exam depends on both understanding the content and applying your knowledge. **Because your success is our primary goal, we offer FREE Study Tips Videos, which provide top-notch test taking strategies to help optimize your testing experience.**

Our simple request is that you email us feedback about our book in exchange for the strategy-packed videos.

To receive your **FREE Study Tips Videos**, scan the QR code or email freevideos@apexprep.com. Please put "FREE Videos" in the subject line and include the following in the email:

a. The title of the book

b. Your rating of the book on a scale of 1-5, with 5 being the highest score

c. Any thoughts or feedback about the book

Thank you!

Introduction to the SHRM-CP

Function of the Test

The Society for Human Resource Management Certified Professionals (SHRM-CP) exam was designed as a way for Human Resource (HR) professionals to earn a certification that leads to professional distinction as committed leaders and experts in the human resources field. The Society for Human Resource Management developed the exam and certification process as a means for HR professionals to gain a competitive advantage in today's economy by conveying that they have obtained a certain level of skill and knowledge.

The SHRM-CP exam is intended for HR professionals who deliver HR services and functions, design and administer HR policies, and act as the point of contact in their organization for staff and stakeholders.

Candidates must satisfy certain eligibility requirements prior to being permitted to sit for the exam. Those with an HR-related graduate degree must be currently serving in an HR role. With a non-HR graduate degree or a bachelor's degree in HR, the candidate must have at least one year of employment in an HR role. With a non-HR bachelor's degree, the candidate needs a minimum of two full years of employment as an HR professional. Lastly, if the candidate has less than a bachelor's degree, three or four full years of employment as an HR professional is mandatory, depending on whether collegiate coursework towards an HR degree has been completed or not. It is important to note that one "year" of employment experience requires at least 1,000 hours specifically dedicated to HR-related work functions.

Test Administration

The SHRM-CP exam is a computer-based exam offered during two testing windows in the calendar year: winter and spring. There are application deadlines for each testing window. These deadlines and the dates during which the testing windows are open are available on the SHRM website (www.shrm.org). Test candidates must fill out an application form, which includes fields where the information substantiating the satisfaction of the exam eligibility requirements must be provided.

Candidates can register to take the exam at over 8,000 Prometric testing centers in 160 countries worldwide. For candidates in the United States, registration can be completed online at prometric.com/shrm or via phone at (888) 736-0134. Before registration is possible, candidates must receive their Authorization to Test (ATT) letter that contains their eligibility ID, which is required for registration.

A Testing Accommodations Request form is available on the SHRM website for test takers who need accommodations for documented disabilities. Supporting documentation must be submitted alongside this form.

Test Format

The SHRM-CP exam is administered via computer. The exam lasts four hours and contains 160 multiple-choice questions. Of these, 95 are knowledge questions and 65 are situational judgment questions. The knowledge-based questions evaluate mastery of factual, HR-related information in three categories, each with subcategories:

- Leadership: Leadership and Navigation, and Ethical Practice

- Interpersonal: Relationship Management, Communication, and Global and Cultural Effectiveness
- Business: Business Acumen, Consultation, and Critical Evaluation

The situational judgment questions assess the test taker's judgment and decision-making skills by presenting a realistic work-related scenario and four potential solutions. Test takers are tasked with selecting the answer choice that represents the most effective solution offered. A panel of experienced HR professionals is responsible for establishing the correct response for each work-related scenario.

Included in the 160 questions are 30 unscored field-test questions. These items are used solely to determine their effectiveness and potential to become scored questions on future exams. These questions are distributed randomly throughout the exam so that test takers are unaware that they are unscored.

The table below details the distribution of questions by content and type on the SHRM-CP exam:

Behavioral Competencies	Question Type
Leadership (13%)	Situational Judgement (40%)
Business (18.5%)	Foundational Knowledge (10%)
Interpersonal (18.5%)	
HR Knowledge Categories	**Question Type**
People (16%)	HR-Specific Knowledge (50%)
Organization (17%)	
Workplace (17%)	

Scoring

Of the 160 questions on the exam, 130 are scored. Test takers can earn a raw score of 0-130 on the exam, with each correct response earning one point. Incorrect responses are not penalized. Raw scores are then scaled from 120-200. To pass, test takers must achieve a scaled score of 200. It is important to note that 200 doesn't represent a "perfect score;" rather, SHRM simply does not report scores above 200 because they have determined the benchmark for competency to be set at 200. Those test takers who meet the minimum scaled score of 200 have done enough to demonstrate their competency in the field.

As soon as test takers submit their exam responses, they receive a provisional passing status on the screen. Approximately four weeks after the test window has closed, official results become available on the test taker's online portal. Test takers who successfully pass the exam receive an official letter of congratulations, a lapel pin, and their SHRM-CP credential certificate in the mail.

The pass rate for the SHRM-CP varies between different testing windows, but it generally falls around 70%.

Study Prep Plan for the SHRM-CP

**Breathe**

Reducing stress is key when preparing for your test.

Build

Create a study plan to help you stay on track.

**Begin**

Stick with your study plan. You've got this!

1 Week Study Plan

Day 1	Day 2	Day 3	Day 4	Day 5	Day 6	Day 7
Behavioral Competencies	Business	Functional Areas	Organization Knowledge	Workplace Knowledge	Practice Test	Take Your Exam!

2 Week Study Plan

Day 1	Day 2	Day 3	Day 4	Day 5	Day 6	Day 7
Behavioral Competencies	Interpersonal	Business	Analytical Aptitude	Functional Areas	Employee Engagement and Retention	Learning and Development

Day 8	Day 9	Day 10	Day 11	Day 12	Day 13	Day 14
Organization Knowledge	Employee and Labor Relations	Workplace Knowledge	Risk Management	Practice Test	Answer Explanations	Take Your Exam!

30 Day Study Plan

Day 1	Day 2	Day 3	Day 4	Day 5	Day 6	Day 7
Behavioral Competencies	Ethical Practice	Interpersonal	Negotiation	Communication	Global Mindset	Business

Day 8	Day 9	Day 10	Day 11	Day 12	Day 13	Day 14
Consultation	Analytical Aptitude	Practice Questions	Functional Areas	Employee Engagement and Retention	Learning and Development	Administering Programs to Support Knowledge Transfer

Day 15	Day 16	Day 17	Day 18	Day 19	Day 20	Day 21
Total Rewards	Organization Knowledge	Organizational Effectiveness and Development	Workforce Management	Employee and Labor Relations	Developing Workplace Policies, Handbooks, and Codes of Conduct	Technology Management

Day 22	Day 23	Day 24	Day 25	Day 26	Day 27	Day 28
Workplace Knowledge	Diversity and Inclusion	Risk Management	Corporate Social Responsibility	U.S. Employment Laws and Regulations	Practice Questions	Practice Test

Day 29	Day 30
Answer Explanations	Take Your Exam!

Behavioral Competencies

Leadership

Leadership and Navigation

Leadership has many aspects: influencing people, directing work, engaging employees, and motivating individuals to reach their goals and accomplish the vision of the organization. Leadership also takes many forms, both formally and informally. Leaders can best deploy the human capital of an organization through information recognition, communication of the organization's strategic goals and vision, and engagement of employees in their performance evaluations and development. Understanding the many ways that leadership can be exhibited and how the workforce responds to each kind of leadership is an excellent way for Human Resources professionals to navigate the organization and make an impact.

Navigating the Organization

It is important for HR professionals to engage with the leadership of the organization, but not just at the highest levels or "C-suite." Leaders exist at every level in an organization, and every leader has an essential role in engaging employees in the organization. When a concerted effort is made to understand how each leader directs, engages, motivates, and encourages others, HR professionals can encourage and develop this behavior. Additionally, modeling leadership can encourage the newer employees to develop their own leadership skills for future leadership opportunities, both informal and formal. Executive leadership should recognize the informal leadership that is shown throughout the organization, as these behaviors are integral to achieving strategic goals.

Formal and Informal Work Roles, Leader Goals and Interests, and Relationships Among Employees
HR professionals are the subject matter experts in understanding work roles and how individual contributions align with the departmental and organizational goals and strategic plans. Each employee has a formal job description with specific tasks and responsibilities; however, employees may also have informal duties that are assigned as needed or requested as a volunteer. Employees also belong to a formally structured group or team with a manager providing direction, guidance, and leadership. Additionally, employees also belong to informal groups such as the group of new hires that went through orientation together or a group of employees that went through a leadership training together. HR professionals should engage with employees to understand these dynamics so that the best methods can be deployed to motivate employees. From training and coaching to accomplishing strategic goals that are aligned with the organization's mission, an understanding of how employees do their jobs will assist executive leadership in ensuring that the employees have the right tools and resources while leading them in the most effective manner possible.

Facilitating Communication and Decision Making
One vital skill of HR professionals is the ability to facilitate effective communication with others. This includes tailoring messages to all employees across the organization, from a mechanic to an accountant, from an information technology analyst to the CEO. Additionally, HR should be able to use these communications to engage employees in the organization's ultimate goal(s). Ensuring that employees understand the task and their role in accomplishing it is a skill that HR professionals should work to develop. It is also important to remember a message's audience and to shape communication to that specific audience.

An Organization's Processes, Systems, and Policies

HR professionals often engage the organization in initiatives such as performance evaluations, benefits enrollment, job description reviews, compensation studies, and other efforts. To ensure successful implementation of any initiative, it is important for HR to understand how the organization works internally and among work groups. Each organization has its own unique culture, processes, systems, and policies that affect the way information is disseminated to employees. In order to be effective, HR should have an awareness of these elements. One strategy may work well at one organization but not at the next, so it is important to learn how an organization functions before working on an important initiative.

Organization's Political Environment and Culture

Politics surround every organization in different ways. One does not have to work for a public agency such as a city, county, or state to understand how politics and culture affect an organization. HR professionals should engage with their peers, both inside and outside the organization, to understand what drives the political and cultural landscape in the organization. Having this awareness will enable an HR professional to address employees' needs.

Vision

After a scan of a company's external and internal environments has taken place, the executive team can turn their focus to developing the vision statement, mission statement, and values to guide the company over the long term.

Vision Statement

A **vision statement** is a concise, forward-thinking statement that reflects organizational confidence and long-term aspirations regarding how a company will achieve more than economic success. Some questions that can be addressed in a vision statement are: How does this company fit into the world? How would it positively change the world? Institutionally, how does the company plan to deliver its product or service less expensively and more efficiently than its competitors? Ultimately, vision statements serve the purpose of boosting trust and confidence, as well as creating an image that the company is engaging in a task larger than itself.

Mission Statement

A company creates a mission statement to detail how it will work toward obtaining its vision. A **mission statement** tells employees what the company does, where the company is going in the mid to long term, and how the company is different from other organizations. A company's mission statement should stay constant throughout the company's life cycle.

Items that may be addressed in a company's mission statement include:

- Where does the company compete geographically?
- What are the company's top products or services?
- Who are the company's customers?
- What is the company's competitive advantage?
- How responsive is the company to environmental concerns?
- Does the company consider its employees to be valuable assets?
- Is the company committed to financial stability?

Values

A company's values—such as integrity, open-mindedness, respect, safety, and teamwork—communicate to employees the standards to which they are expected to adhere while conducting business. **Values** are the things that are most important to a company, which is why they should be deeply ingrained in the corporate culture and demonstrated in employees' daily business interactions with stakeholders and customers. HR can play an important role in reinforcing a company's values through leading by example and communicating them to employees.

Organizational Structure

Organizational structure is used to help companies achieve their goals by defining the hierarchy of employees and allocating resources through decisions surrounding the following factors:

- **Chain of command**: This clarifies to whom employees report. It is the continuous line of authority from senior-level managers to employees at the lowest levels of the company.

- **Centralization**: A company where lower-level employees carry out the decisions made by senior-level managers is highly centralized. The opposite of this is **decentralization** or employee empowerment.

- **Span of control**: This refers to the number of employees a manager can effectively supervise. This can be affected by such things as a manager's skills, the physical proximity of the employees, the employees' characteristics, and the complexity of the work being performed.

- **Formalization**: An organization with standardized jobs, allowing for little discretion over what is to be done because the work is guided by rules, has a high degree of formalization. The opposite of this is low formalization, where employees have more freedom to decide how they can complete their tasks.

- **Work specialization**: This is also known as **division of labor** and refers to the degree to which a company divides tasks into separate jobs that are completed by different employees. This allows employees to become very proficient in a specialized area, such as painting or framing.

- **Departmentalization**: This comes into play when a company divides up its work by the specialization of its departments. Companies are known to departmentalize by function, product, geography, or division.

Functional Structure

This is the most common type of organizational structure in which jobs are according to function, such as finance, IT, sales, purchasing, and HR. Efficiencies are gained from grouping together individuals with common knowledge and skills. This type of organizational structure is good for a company that has one product line that can benefit from specialization. However, employees can have a limited view of the company's goals, and there can be poor communication across the various functional areas.

Product Structure

This is a type of organizational structure where jobs are grouped by product line. For example, a product organizational structure for a transportation company might be grouped by rail products, mass transit products, and recreational and utility vehicle products. Organizing by product allows managers to become experts in their industry and for specialization in certain products and services. However, employees can have a limited view of the company's goals, and there is a duplication of functions within each product line.

Geographic Structure

This is a type of organizational structure where jobs are grouped according to geographic location. For example, a company's sales directors for various regions (Eastern, Western, Midwestern, and Southern) may each be responsible for the business functions in their areas and report to the company's vice president of sales. This type of structure is the best way to serve the unique needs and issues that may arise in different geographic markets. Since most decisions are made at the location level, decision making is decentralized. However, employees may feel isolated from other organizational areas, and there is a duplication of functions within each geographic region.

Division Structure

This is a type of organizational structure where jobs are grouped by industry or market. A divisional organizational structure also experiences decentralized decision making and is similar in nature to the geographic structure.

Matrix Structure

Employees report to two managers in this type of organizational structure. Typically, one manager has functional responsibility, and the other manager has a product line responsibility. Employees have a primary manager they report to and a second manager they also work for on specified projects. In order for a matrix structure to be successful, there must be a high degree of trust and communication among the employees involved. This type of structure is a good way to share resources across functions.

Managing HR Initiatives

Project Requirements

Once senior leadership has established the strategic goals for the organization, HR professionals put together the departmental goals that directly align with the overall goals. For each of the departmental goals, it is necessary to define the project, identify the timeline and resources, determine which employees will be responsible for each component, and describe what success will look like and how it will impact the organization, department, and employees. To ensure project efficiency, HR professionals should understand the skills needed for the project and the employees who excel at these skills. Understanding the needs and matching them with the employees who can best meet those needs are essential skills for HR professionals.

Project Goals and Milestones

HR professionals should engage the employees in the process of establishing and tracking the project goals and progress timeline. **Project goals** are separate objectives that are dependent on each other to ensure full accomplishment of the overall goal. It is important to celebrate when accomplishments are achieved on time, under budget, and within resource allocations. It is also important to celebrate individual employees and their contributions to the project. Project goals should be set to align with the **SMART** philosophy—an acronym that stands for the qualities of goals: specific, measurable, achievable, realistic, and time-targeted. By ensuring that each project goal is SMART, employees will have a clear understanding of the deliverables.

Project Budgets and Resources

Projects can require an immense amount of money and resources. HR professionals should understand the budget, which could include labor costs, hours needed to perform the work required, overtime, and other employee-related budget costs. Resources must also be managed, such as computers, printers, office furniture, tools, marketing documents, printing materials, and other associated costs. Budgets are typically set at the beginning of a project and for the most part should be adhered to; however, budgets should also be flexible if possible. As changes or setbacks occur, it is important to discuss them, especially if the budget needs to be increased.

Overcoming Obstacles

Some projects have setbacks that can affect the project's timing or overall success. HR professionals should encourage employees to have discussions when these obstacles occur. Engaging in conversation and brainstorming with others can foster new ideas and possible solutions. When a project's goals are SMART, employees are quicker to identify the issues that need to be focused on and resolved. It is important to identify potential concerns early so that employees can be proactive.

Resources to Maintain HR Projects

After a project has been approved and the outcome established, it is important to understand the resources necessary for success, not only in the initial accomplishment of the project but also in maintaining it afterward. The life of a project can include being updated to adjust to current needs of the organization. Understanding this maintenance need is vital to properly identifying resources during the budget process. HR professionals can tap into previous successful projects to identify which resources were used and in which amounts. Using too many resources would lead to waste and diminish the overall return on investment. Using too few or inappropriate resources would lead to the project not being successful. Projects should strive to use the appropriate amount and type of resources to be successful, which will maximize the overall return on investment while keeping to the project plan.

Resource Allocation Inconsistency

Projects have milestones identified along a specific timeline. When milestones are not being met, it is necessary to review the goals and timing to ensure that the appropriate resources are allocated. In order for certain objectives to be accomplished, employees with certain skill sets may be needed to assist with the project. Consideration should also be given to the length of time provided to accomplish a goal. Both of these areas—resource allocation and timing—need to be reviewed when a milestone is not met. Timelines may have originally been unrealistic, or they may have been set without having a true understanding of how long certain things take. It is important to allow flexibility in the project milestones and timing so that adjustments can be made as appropriate while keeping the project on target.

Changing Goals

One very important skill of an HR professional is the ability to adapt to an organization, its leadership, and its employees as they evolve. No organization is static. The workforce changes, leadership and executives change, and the objectives of the organization change. Adaptability is also important when managing a project because there will always be changing variables. Understanding employees' specific skill sets will allow an HR professional to assign them to specific tasks necessary to address an emergent issue. This will allow the entire team to engage in the project, resolve issues, keep the project on track, and achieve success.

Influence

Building Credibility as an HR Expert

All professionals, including those in human resources, need to establish credibility both inside and outside their organization. There are many ways to accomplish this, including formal education in the field of business. Formal education could include obtaining a bachelor's degree with concentrations in human resources–related fields, master's degrees in human resources management, or certification programs such as this one. There are also training and certification programs specific to certain HR fields, such as investigations, benefits, compensation, and labor relations. These programs can provide formal training to those who want to expand their skills. Experience also enables professionals to communicate their credibility in the field. Having both the education and experience enables HR professionals to be productive when reviewing organizational needs and providing resolutions for issues. Referring to successful projects with previous employers and the roles that were performed is essential in conveying the subject matter expertise to an organizational team at the leadership, peer, and subordinate levels.

Buy-In Among Organizational Stakeholders

There are various ways to promote engagement and commitment to HR initiatives; however, the single most effective method is to bring stakeholders together and communicate the benefits of the proposed initiatives and how they will provide value to each area of the organization. Stakeholders will want to know "what's in it for me?" By communicating this information early in the process, HR professionals can better engage with the organization. Additionally, it is important to ask each stakeholder what accomplishments they would want to see. This helps HR professionals to understand each department's needs. Many departments may have similar needs or goals that need to be accomplished; by having this knowledge in the beginning of the process, HR professionals can best align the project's milestones, accomplishments, and overarching objectives with the needs of specific departments as well as the entire organization.

Motivating HR Staff to Support HR Vision and Goals

Motivating the HR staff is not an easy task for an HR leader. Each individual has their motivation for coming to work each day, meeting standards on the job, and going above and beyond expectations. Some employees are motivated simply by a paycheck, while others are motivated by formal recognition and accolades. It is vital for a successful HR leader to understand the needs of each member of the HR staff and how to properly motivate and engage them. The first step is ensuring that the employees have the appropriate skills to be successful in their assigned job.

If there is a gap between the skills needed and the individual's abilities, motivation will suffer, as the employee will mostly be in a state of struggle. Providing the proper guidance, training, education, and leadership can assist employees who are in this situation. The next step is to determine what motivates each individual and then work to provide that motivation. Ensuring that employees understand the organization's vision and goals, as well as HR's vision and goals, is an excellent way to help employees see how they contribute to the bigger picture. When employees know how their individual success contributes to the departmental and organizational success, they are more likely to be motivated to achieve their objectives.

Advocating for the Organization

HR professionals must understand how to appropriately balance the needs of the organization and the needs of the employees. Actions, programs, projects, and goals must support the organization while also supporting the employees, who are ultimately responsible for the organization's achievement of its goals. Balancing the needs of the organization and the employees can be complicated; often the needs of one side do not align with those of the other side. HR professionals must ensure that employees are treated fairly, and they must also ensure that the organization is providing fair wages, appropriate benefits, and other rights and entitlements provided under federal and state laws such as leaves of absence, worker's compensation, healthy workspaces, ergonomic capabilities, and other programs.

Ethical Practice

Organizations are held accountable to high legal standards; however, an organization exhibits their ethical practices when policies, procedures, and expectations go beyond legal requirements. What an organization does when no one is looking establishes the organization's true ethical identity. Employees who incorporate this ethical identity into daily practices continue to promote, facilitate, and enable an ethical culture in the organization. When an organization establishes and requires ethical practices, positive relationships are facilitated and maintained between the organization and its employees, customers, shareholders, and others. Ethical practices are a fundamental keystone in the human resources department when establishing policies and procedures. HR must ensure that legal requirements are met and complied with, and also that the policies and procedures are ethical in nature. Organizations must also ensure ethical practices in areas such as advertising, pricing, contract administration, and sales.

Personal Integrity

The most meaningful leadership quality is **personal integrity**, which is being honest with oneself and determining actions based on personal values and beliefs. Human resources must ensure that integrity is at the foundation of all policies and procedures, including the reporting of unethical behavior. Ensuring confidentiality is important as well. Employees must feel safe reporting an unethical practice or behavior, knowing it will not have a negative impact on their employment. HR professionals who have strong personal integrity can work to ensure that this principle is woven throughout the policies that employees must abide by.

Consistency Between Espoused and Enacted Values

"Practice what you preach" is a saying that could not be more appropriate to describe how HR professionals should behave. All employees should be held accountable for their actions, not just some based on a supervisor's opinion. HR professionals that are consistent with the application of policy and practice are more likely to ensure a fair, engaged, and productive workforce. If employees do not trust the HR professionals, they are less likely to report unethical behavior or other issues that must be investigated and handled appropriately. If an HR professional does not practice what they preach, then, regardless of how good the HR policies are, employees will not hold a high level of respect for them, and unethical behavior may be more likely throughout the organization.

Demonstrating Accountability

One indicator of strong integrity and work ethic is admitting when a mistake has been made and taking responsibility for the error, including making corrections and fixing the issue. Additionally, an employee should install measures to ensure that the mistake is not made again in the future. Not only does taking responsibility show an individual's personal integrity, but it also displays a level of growth and development. Admitting to having done something wrong is not easy, and when an employee does make this admission, it should be handled appropriately, with the employee being allowed the opportunity to grow from the mistake.

Recognizing Personal Biases

HR professionals are responsible for ensuring that appropriate training and development opportunities are available to all employees. While some training opportunities are specific to an employee's position or level in an organization, many training opportunities should be made available to all employees, regardless of the function or scope of their role. Examples of training that should be available to everyone are communication, computer skills, leadership, time management, and diversity and inclusion. Many diversity and inclusion training programs incorporate sessions related to biases—both conscious and unconscious—so that employees can work to become self-aware of their own beliefs and opinions while working to address them. Becoming self-aware of an issue or belief and then working to address these issues or beliefs is a vital component to personal growth and development.

Serving as a Role Model of Personal Integrity and High Ethical Standards

HR professionals are role models to the organization. From coming to work on time, taking the appropriate and required breaks, displaying respect to others, adhering to policies and procedures, working to accomplish goals that translate to organizational success, and upholding strong ethical standards, HR professionals must exhibit the traits and behaviors that all employees should demonstrate. It is also vital to ensure that the leadership of the organization exhibits these same standards since employees model the behavior of their superiors and those at the highest levels of the organization. If employees routinely see their manager coming late or taking long breaks, they will begin to model this behavior; however, if employees see their managers working diligently to accomplish their tasks on time and in a professional manner, arriving on time and taking appropriate breaks, they too will work to exhibit this behavior.

Professional Integrity

Professional integrity is displayed through an organization's ethics and how employees practice each of the following: truth, honesty, social responsibility, good behavior, obedience to law, and refusal to ever mislead. There are numerous models of business ethics; the following model is easy to understand and apply. Integrity and ethics should not be complicated; do the right thing when no one is watching. If we all adhere to this simple principle, we are behaving ethically, fairly, and with integrity. Unfortunately, this is not as easy as it sounds, and Human Resources professionals often have to address behavior that is unethical, unfair, and inappropriate.

Not Taking Adverse Actions Based on Personal Biases

HR professionals should never take action against an employee based on personal bias, whether conscious or unconscious. If this is something that an HR professional cannot avoid, then they should consider another line of work. Ensuring fair and ethical treatment of all employees is the foundation of ethical human resources practices. Adverse actions based on personal biases could include discipline, demotion, or any other action that would have a negative impact on an employee and their employment situation. HR professionals should consider the facts, context, and detailed information gained through insightful and thorough investigation while adhering to legal and regulatory standards. Only when this is done should an HR professional move forward with actions to address inappropriate behavior.

Maintaining Privacy

Confidentiality is important to an organization, especially when an employee is reporting unethical or inappropriate behavior. HR professionals have a duty to protect this confidentiality when appropriate and legally mandated; however, in some circumstances, confidentiality cannot be maintained. It is therefore important to ensure that employees understand this. In cases such as physical abuse or other criminal matters where law enforcement would need to be involved, an HR professional cannot maintain confidentiality; however, all efforts should be taken to maintain privacy for the employees involved, including those reporting the behavior and those involved in the behavior. Ensuring a level of privacy can enable an unbiased and fair investigation, which in turn ensures that the whole situation is understood and appropriate actions can be taken.

Using Discretion Around Privacy

In many cases, HR must involve stakeholders in issues that must be addressed at the highest levels of the organization. In these circumstances, it is crucial to ensure that these stakeholders understand privacy and confidentiality and how they apply to the issues at hand. HR should work to ensure that all individuals know how and when to use attorney-client privilege, as well as which matters can and cannot be discussed outside of closed-door sessions. Employment matters and personal information are almost always protected by confidentiality and should be strictly monitored to ensure that the organization is not put into a risky situation and that liability is not increased.

Current Knowledge of Ethics Laws, Standards, Legislation, and Emerging Trends

One of the most important functions of an HR professional is to ensure an up-to-date knowledge of the laws, standards, legislations, and trends that could impact the organization's HR policies and procedures. New bills that are introduced into the state assembly or senate could have significant impacts that need to be addressed. An example of this is the recent Assembly Bill 5 in the state of California. This bill changed the definition of an independent contractor and required agencies to utilize a new method of determining whether an independent contractor should be designated an employee, therefore gaining the rights and benefits as an employee. HR professionals need to understand the changes that are being made and ensure that policies and procedures align with these changes. Without this, an organization could be put at risk in a variety of ways, including costly lawsuits.

Leading HR Investigations

Human resources is the department responsible for leading investigations into employees. These investigations should be completed in a thorough, timely, and unbiased manner. When an employee comes forward to report a concern, HR should immediately take a statement from the individual, asking clarifying questions and delving into the specifics to ensure that all details of the alleged concern are clear. HR should then begin taking statements from all other employees who are either identified in the initial complaint or are deemed by HR to be credible and necessary to speak to. Details such as dates, times, witnesses, and any other pertinent information should be properly investigated. HR should always conduct these investigations in an efficient, productive, and timely manner to ensure that if a violation of policy has occurred, it can be corrected immediately.

Possible actions include discipline, up to and including termination; policy changes; training initiatives; or other actions that properly remedy the concern brought up. HR should also communicate with the employee who raised the concern to indicate that the investigation has been concluded and appropriate actions will be taken. HR professionals should be careful to relate only appropriate information. For example, if an employee is disciplined as a result of the investigation, it should not be discussed with other employees.

Establishing Credibility

As an HR professional, it is of utmost importance that employees view you as credible and trustworthy. If you don't follow through on what you say, employees will be less likely to trust you and come to you for advice and counsel. By engaging employees in process and discussion, HR professionals can build a relationship with employees beyond just a job description. These strong and proactive relationships mean that employees are more likely to seek out HR before issues arise, which enables timely discussion and action. When HR follows up with employees on minor matters or basic questions, employees realize they can trust the HR professionals on more serious matters. Trust can be established by being sincere, reliable, and actively engaged in discussions with employees.

Organizational Ethics and Integrity Policies

On occasion, HR becomes aware of issues with current policies based on investigations or concerns raised by an employee. Regardless of how HR becomes aware of an issue, it is the responsibility of HR to ensure that all ethics and integrity policies are appropriate, clear, specific, and relevant to the employees and the work being done. If changes are necessary, HR should bring these concerns to the executive leadership, along with any proposed recommendations. Executive leadership should have the ability to communicate additional insights or information that HR should consider as well. Another important thing to consider is having buy-in from leadership, which can ensure buy-in from all employees when there is a policy change that has far-reaching impacts, such as an ethics and integrity policy change. Policy changes may impact how work is done on a day-to-day basis, and other policies may need to be reviewed as well to ensure alignment. There should not be any contradictions between two policies, especially with the ethics and integrity policies.

Managing Political and Social Pressures

An important focus of HR should be the results of HR programs, practices, and policies throughout the organization. Every program has consequences, positive and negative. The goal of HR should be to minimize negative consequences and maximize positive ones. When political or social factors are involved, HR should always consider the impacts of a program before implementing and enforcing it. There may be unknowns, but when HR attempts to address all potential impacts, a plan can be put together to address these issues. An excellent tool to work through this would be the SWOT analysis tool.

The acronym **SWOT** stands for strengths, weaknesses, opportunities, and threats; looking at these can assist HR in developing an action plan.

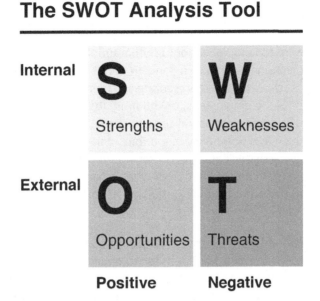

Providing Honest and Constructive Feedback

Having difficult conversations with employees is hard—especially when it has to do with questioning an individual's ethics, integrity, or behavior. It is important for HR professionals to listen actively, ask insightful and probing questions, and ensure that employees know there is a sincere need to resolve any matter quickly, even if it is just a misunderstanding. Being clear, to the point, engaged, and specific is important to ensure that all parties are on the same page. An employee who needs to receive a message should get it in writing, addressed specifically to them. Sometimes employees need to hear a message that they simply do not want to hear; however, if HR strives to ensure clarity, honesty, and specificity, employees generally will accept the message with understanding and a need to grow and learn from the experience.

Ethical Agent

All HR professionals are responsible to act as ethical agents by ensuring that employees at every level and in every position understand the policies and procedures that guide the organization. Beginning with onboarding and new employee orientation, HR must set the tone and ensure that the expectations of the organization are fully communicated and understood. Employees must know their rights, obligations, and expectations when it comes to following policy, reporting those who do not follow policy, and encouraging others by modeling appropriate behavior.

Empowering Employees to Report Unethical Behavior

HR should ensure that all policies and procedures are available to employees from their first day on the job. Many organizations provide a hard copy of the employee handbook and require employees to read through it, ask questions, discuss the requirements, and sign an acknowledgement receipt. In this way, HR can be confident that employees are aware of the policies and expectations of the organization. One of the policies that should be fully communicated is how to report inappropriate behavior by another employee. This policy should include the process, privacy rights, and expectations of no retaliation for coming forward. Employees should be able to voice concerns without fear of retaliation, either by the organization or other employees. However, it is important to understand that if false complaints are submitted, the employee may be disciplined. Depending on the current culture in an organization, it may be important and necessary to create an anonymous reporting method or purchase a third-party service for reporting complaints.

Mitigating the Influence of Bias

An employee may come forward to complain about another employee, a supervisor, or a leader of the organization, and the HR professional may have a concern about their own bias in this situation. This could be for several reasons, such as the HR representative is friends with the employee, they have inside information or knowledge about the employee(s) or situation, the complaint is against their supervisor, or they simply do not know enough about the actual context of the situation. In these cases, it is best to be open and honest about the issue and potentially hire a third-party investigator to handle the complaint and formal investigation process. This will accomplish several things: 1) ensure a fair and unbiased investigation; 2) provide an accurate representation of what is occurring; and 3) enhance credibility and trust in HR for acknowledging this potential bias and taking action to address it.

Maintaining Transparency

Human resources should consistently ensure that employees know where to find information related to programs, practices, and policies. From internal websites to emailed brochures, HR should strive to make information available in multiple forms. New employees should receive all the policies and procedures, whether electronically or via hard copy. Current employees should receive communications on where to find current, new, or updated information. Updated information should always be communicated immediately to employees. While there are requirements to post brochures and posters for employees to read about their rights, it is important to communicate in various ways to ensure that employees have information readily available.

Communicating Ethical Risks and Conflict of Interest

Many HR departments prepare reports to provide to leadership. These reports may be done monthly, quarterly, or annually. These reports should include the organization's demographics, new hires, vacancies, complaints, investigations, and other information deemed important for the leadership to know. In addition to demographics information, HR should also ensure that leadership is aware of possible ethics violations or conflicts of interest. Leadership will need to know that issues have been handled expeditiously and that policy changes have been reviewed and addressed. When HR is first notified of a potential ethical risk, leadership should immediately be notified to ensure that appropriate actions can take place. Some of the policy changes may require the approval of leadership prior to being implemented. Additionally, if the changes are substantial, it may be in the organization's best interest to have the message come from leadership to ensure top-to-bottom understanding of responsibility surrounding the policy change.

Ensuring Access to Ethical Standards and Policies

Organizations typically communicate a vision, mission, and values statement on their websites and in recruitment brochures. This information is usually a candidate's first look at the organization's processes and its expectations for employees. This impression is further solidified when a candidate begins working for the organization and is presented with the policies, procedures, and information from the employee handbook. Employees should receive communications about the organization's vision, mission, and values throughout the year and understand how their role aligns with accomplishing these three objectives. It is important that employees hear from leadership about expectations and how these were met.

Diversity, Equity, and Inclusion

Diversity, Equity, and Inclusion (DE&I) in the workplace refers to the need for individuals to be treated fairly and with respect. This also includes the need for workers to have equal access to opportunities and resources within the work environment. Lastly, DE&I includes individuals being able to use their particular backgrounds and experiences to contribute to the organization's success and to feel an overall sense of community and belonging within their workplace.

Creating a Diverse and Inclusive Culture

The key to creating a diverse and inclusive culture is cultivating a workplace environment in which everyone feels wanted, respected, and supported. Ensuring these workplace characteristics directly contributes to and increases everyone's sense of belonging within that organization. HR professionals play a significant role in increasing and maintaining a diverse community within a workplace.

In doing so, the HR professional advocates for representation of candidates regardless of race, gender, sexual orientation, ethnicity, religious beliefs, country of origin, education, and abilities. In addition to advocating for a diverse workplace community, the HR professional is also responsible for confronting evidences of bias, stereotyping, harassment, microaggressions, and any form of exclusion that might be present within an organization.

Depending on the organization(s) the HR professional is working for, they will need to be able to communicate the benefits of DE&I to the supervisors and employees. They will also need to be able to communicate the benefits of interpersonal risk taking, mutual respect and trust, and advocate for the voice of the team members within an organization.

Ensuring Equity Effectiveness

Equity effectiveness refers to providing fair treatment in accessibility, opportunity, and advancement for everyone within a workplace. The HR professional must contribute to the development and growth of this fair treatment. They should always be looking for ways to enhance the equity policies within the organization. The HR professional should incorporate benefits and programs that encourage a diverse workplace population. They will need to communicate with supervisors about any sort of issues of behavioral performance of DE&I differences.

Connecting DE&I to Organizational Performance

HR professionals must communicate and demonstrate how DE&I can help achieve goals and objectives for the organization. They communicate the organizations DE&I efforts to stakeholders, both internal and external. They execute effective strategies and initiatives to help achieve the goals of the organization. They also assess metric results for an organizations DE&I efforts and relay that information to show the company's productivity in the world of diverse and inclusive work environments.

Interpersonal

Relationship Management

The Oxford dictionary defines **relationship management** as "the supervision and management of relationships between a company and its external partners, especially its clients." This simple definition is acceptable, but it should be expanded to include the relationships between individuals. Relationships among and between employees and supervisors need to be cultivated to be successful at the organization, department, and team levels. Successful relationship management can be broken down into three elements: 1) understanding the needs of the other party; 2) creating solutions that address those needs; 3) delivering the solutions.

Networking

Networking is a fundamental component of relationship management as it is the interconnection between individuals. Networking enables individuals to exchange ideas, share insights, solicit advice and feedback, and relate to others in various ways. Working in a vacuum does not foster diverse ideas, whereas networking enables discussion, creative thinking, and the exchange of ideas. The saying "two heads are better than one" is the concept behind effective networking. Networking can be informal or formal, and it can occur inside and outside an organization. Networking often happens organically when two professionals get together, even just to have coffee. It also encourages social support structures so that employees can support others that may be having similar difficulties in their roles. Nurturing these networking relationships is important, regardless of the organization to which an employee belongs.

Professional Contacts

HR professionals should strive to create a network of contacts from various organizations and in various roles. HR is often tasked with crafting unique and creative solutions to issues in an organization. Having a network of professionals enhances the resources available. Relationships with current and former coworkers across functions such as operations, finance, logistics, compliance, legal, manufacturing, marketing, and human resources allows an individual to ask questions of people who have different perspectives and unique opinions. All the information that is gained through trustworthy sources can then be used to craft a resolution to an issue. Contacts who have worked on similar challenges may have insights from their experience. This information is invaluable as it can be used to address issues before they arise, in hopes that they can be avoided.

External Partners

HR professionals should also strive to maintain a network of customers, vendors, and suppliers. Vendors offer services such as payroll, investigations, worker's compensation administration, benefits administration, and leave administration. Sometimes a change of vendor is needed, and having a network of cost-effective companies will be a huge resource. Referrals are a great way to learn more about a vendor, but when that knowledge is first-hand, one can make a faster and better decision based on actual history.

Professional Colleagues

Throughout an HR professional's career, there will be opportunities to attend workshops, training events, and conferences. Taking advantage of these opportunities not only provides the ability to learn in the HR field, but it is also a good way to network with other HR professionals. Having a network of talented HR professionals will be an asset in multiple ways. First, when there is a problem, the knowledge available in this group of people can prove priceless. Second, when recruiting for and hiring top HR talent, the network group can provide an excellent candidate pool and can also refer recruiters to an excellent candidate pool. Finally, this network is useful when the HR professional looks for their own new opportunities. The names of HR professionals who can attest to one's work ethic, knowledge, and skill set would be fantastic references to put on a resume.

Relationship Building

Building relationships is vital to success, personally and professionally. While building relationships is not easy or fast, here are twelve tips to follow:

- Genuinely get to know the other person.
- Find similar interests or challenges.
- Work to build trust.
- Speak positively.
- Support the other person's choices.
- Share knowledge and insight.
- Be positive.
- Engage with others frequently.
- Avoid cliques and be inclusive.
- Don't complain to the boss.
- Be honest and encouraging.
- Express thankfulness.

Once relationships are established, it is important to nurture them to ensure that they continue to develop while being supportive beyond the initial needs of the individuals.

Mutual Trust and Respect

Consistency is one of the most important factors in gaining others' trust and respect. When an employee consistently shows reliability, commitment, competency, sincerity, and integrity, regardless of the situation, trust is built between individuals. Maintaining these traits is vital to continue building and keeping trust. Being honest is critical to this process as well. If an individual is unsure about something or needs to adjust the plan to address issues or deficiencies, it is important to communicate openly so that the trust is not eroded.

Reciprocal Exchanges

A give-and-take approach is necessary to build relationships and garner trust. Employees need to practice giving advice as much as asking for advice. If an employee is always asking from others and never reciprocating, others will eventually stop providing guidance and support when asked. One analogy used for demonstrating this concept is gift giving. If an individual consistently gives a gift for occasions such as birthdays, anniversaries, and holidays, but the other party does not reciprocate the custom, eventually the gift-giving individual will stop. This can have a huge impact on the relationship and begin to erode trust and respect. It is important to be aware of how one gives and takes in a professional relationship.

Wellbeing of Colleagues

Building trust requires one to be sincere and show genuine concern for the wellbeing of others. When you apologize for making a mistake, you are showing sincerity to others. Paying a compliment for a job well done also shows sincerity, as does being honest about your own strengths and weaknesses while offering or asking for help. By being sincere, HR professionals can assure individuals that their contributions are valued.

Establishing a Positive Reputation

When an HR professional creates and maintains a strong reputation inside and outside their organization, the result is a good relationship that yields high productivity. Striving to do the right thing, providing constructive feedback, apologizing for mistakes, going above and beyond, actively listening to others, and having patience will all work to establish a strong professional reputation. Such a reputation will allow an

HR professional to engage this network when there is a problem, concern, or question. Referrals are also an important by-product of positive reputations.

Acknowledging Stakeholder Voices

Being an HR professional also means being a business partner to the organization. One role that business partners play is to engage every stakeholder and ensure them that their concerns are heard. An effective way to ensure success is to engage all stakeholders early in the process. Actively listening to each individual will allow HR professionals to gauge each concern and assure individuals that their concerns are being addressed. Sometimes it is not possible to remedy a concern, but it is important to listen and then tell the employee why you are moving forward without a specific resolution. Sometimes, when employees know that they have been heard, it can be more important than finding a specific resolution to the matter.

Leveraging Common Interest Among Stakeholders

Communicating with all stakeholders about their concerns enables the HR professional to show all parties that their interests are the same as those of others in the organization. This insight will encourage stakeholders to work together and engage available resources. When stakeholders know the benefits and the impacts in the initial phases of a process, they are more likely to help. Additionally, it is important to ensure that benefits are identified for the whole organization, not just one department. While some projects may be department-specific, it is important to ensure a holistic view. This enables different perspectives, goals, and resources to be added to the project plan. This, in turn, can result in benefits for everyone, not just a specific group, department, or team.

Managing Working Relationships

While managing projects and communications throughout the organization, it is also important that HR professionals manage working relationships with their supervisors. It is important to engage in weekly one-on-one meetings, send email status reports, and ensure that work is being completed effectively, efficiently, and in a timely way. By communicating this information frequently, the HR professional can assess resources that may be needed to continue with particular projects. If deadlines are not being met, it is important to relay this information and indicate the reason(s) why. Supervisors and managers can then address these issues once they are made aware of the needs.

Teamwork

Andrew Carnegie, an industrialist who made his fortune in the steel industry, defined **teamwork** as "the ability to work together toward a common vision." Teamwork can occur at all levels of an organization and is vital to achieve goals. On a small scale, teamwork can mean working through a simple change that may only affect a few employees. On a large scale, teamwork can mean working through strategic changes that will affect the entire organization. Communication is the key to ensuring that teamwork is effective. Team members must fully understand their roles and how their contributions affect the entire team. They must also understand the holistic goals, the strategy to accomplish these goals, and the timeline.

Building Engaged Relationships with Team Members

Supporting team members and providing resources are important to maintaining work relationships. Listening to and being aware of what each individual is working through is also important so that everyone is engaged and fully participating in the tasks necessary to accomplish the goals. Every individual should be participating, and it is important that HR know what each employee can provide to the holistic needs of the team. It is easy to bring a group of people together physically but much more difficult to bring them together to work cohesively. By being engaged, proactive, respectful, honest, and open, HR professionals can work to establish a successful teamwork dynamic.

Fostering Open Communication

Asking questions, engaging individuals, and providing updates and status reports help to ensure a collaborative and open exchange of ideas and solutions. HR can be instrumental in providing this resource and enabling all parties to work better together. HR often has a deep understanding of individual and group skill sets, and being able to make the best use of these resources is what sets HR professionals apart from others. When the team has information and is allowed to ask questions, brainstorm with each other, and help build the solutions, teamwork is being fully utilized to its maximum benefit. Only then will individual contributors be able to collaborate as a team and deliver larger and more complex solutions.

Supporting a Team-Oriented Organizational Culture

Organizational culture is defined as the shared beliefs, values, philosophies, and assumptions within an organization. There can be various cultures within an organization—division, department, workgroup, and teams—but in general, all separate cultures should align with the higher-level cultures.

There are four primary culture types: clan, adhocracy, hierarchy, and market. Each culture has different benefits to an organization relative to flexibility, stability, control, focus, and strategy. The **clan culture** focuses on collaboration with leaders that are facilitators, mentors, and team builders. The clan culture is built on a foundation of employee development and participation at all levels of the organization. The **adhocracy culture** focuses on creativity with leaders who are innovators, entrepreneurs, and visionaries. The adhocracy culture is built on a foundation of innovation, vision, and new resources. The **hierarchy culture** focuses on control and process with leaders that are organizers, coordinators, and monitors. The hierarchy culture is built on a foundation of control and efficiency through the use of stable and consistent processes. The **market culture** focuses on competition with leaders that are hard driven, competitors, and producers. The market culture is built on a foundation of aggressive competitiveness and customer focus.

When HR professionals identify, or are made aware of, concerns and issues within an organization's culture, it is important to fully understand the issues and provide recommendations to leadership that fully address these issues. It may be a good idea to incorporate elements from different organizational cultures into an organization's holistic philosophy. Each organization, department, and team will naturally create and maintain a culture within the individual work groups. It is important to ensure that the overall culture and philosophies flow downward and upward to each level, allowing smaller groups to nurture a culture that aligns within the overall organizational culture. To change or strengthen the culture of an organization, Human Resources professionals should follow a standard process to ensure effective and productive results.

First, it is important to understand the values and personalities of the leadership. Transformational leadership can reshape and change a culture but must take ownership and be held accountable for initiating change at the highest levels of the organization. Once the leadership style is understood, it is important to align the facts and information to determine the changes needed to initiate a cultural change at each level of the organization. Once the recommendations have been proposed and accepted for implementation, it is important to align these recommendations with rewards and incentives that support the changes. Employees who understand how and when their behavior will be rewarded and incentivized will be more likely to embrace and support the changes being implemented.

Strengthening organizational culture will occur when leadership supports workforce stability and communicates to employees regularly and frequently. Communication is key to any initiative and communication plans can determine success or failure of a program. Finally, HR professionals should incorporate the culture and cultural initiatives into the recruitment process. Newly hired employees should understand the organization and the culture prior to accepting an offer of employment. Ensuring that there is a cultural fit for both the organization and employee is vital to the employment experience and retaining the most qualified individuals.

Creating cultural change is difficult and does not happen quickly. When HR professionals implement a strong, well-thought-out process that is supported by leadership and communicated clearly and frequently, employees will feel empowered to incorporate these changes at an individual level and within the workgroups and teams.

Project Teams

One of the most exciting things about being an HR professional is the ability to work with HR employees and non-HR employees. HR has a unique ability to bring others together, regardless of their differences, and align them to work toward a common goal. HR professionals get to see other programs in the organization, work with other employees, and engage in different ways of thinking. Working with employees outside of HR enables amazing growth and learning opportunities that can expand one's way of thinking. Additionally, this growth can enable HR professionals to see things in a different light and make improvements to existing programs based on this new knowledge.

Leading a Team

Teamwork is truly effective when a talented and thoughtful individual is identified to lead the team. Embracing leadership and effectively working to maximize others' strengths can be rewarding. It can also provide an opportunity to highlight leadership skills to the executive management team, which can provide future professional prospects such as promotions, recognition, and incentives such as bonuses. Leadership opportunities provide the ability for a team, department, and organization to be successful as well as the leader who is working to bring the entire team together and work as a cohesive unit. This is not easy work, but the rewards can be substantial.

Filling Team Roles

An HR leader will have many roles and responsibilities when developing the dynamics and characteristics of a team. One of the most important is to identify the skills necessary to achieve goals. An HR leader must be realistic when assigning specific employees to certain roles to ensure that each employee is utilizing their strengths and abilities to accomplish the assigned tasks. It is equally important to understand when a team does not have enough of a particular skill. A leader can develop a plan to access this skill from an external resource or to have an identified employee trained in this skill.

Conflict Management

There are many definitions of conflict management, most of which are complex and extensive; however, **conflict management** can be summed up in one simple statement: increase the positive while decreasing the negative. While conflict management is a simple concept in theory, it can be an extremely difficult process to engage, facilitate, and resolve. Managing conflict is a fundamental skill set that most HR professionals should obtain, as conflict will occur when dealing with many different personalities, backgrounds, professions, and individuals in general. There are multiple styles of conflict management, and each HR professional should have several different ways to handle conflict so that they can assess the situation and appropriately apply the technique that will address the issues quickly and effectively.

Resolving Conflicts

There are numerous ways to manage conflict and mediate an appropriate resolution so that all parties involved are engaged in the process while understanding the concerns and needs of each. The **Thomas–Kilmann Conflict Mode instrument (TKI)** is a questionnaire that elicits different modes of handling conflict. The modes of the TKI show the relationships between high and low levels of cooperation and assertiveness. The conflict styles of the individuals can provide a road map to the HR professional on how best to assess and resolve the conflict. The TKI shows that if an individual is highly assertive and minimally cooperative, they are more likely to be competitive. The HR professional should design a conflict management process to address this individual's competitiveness. If the other individual is less assertive and highly cooperative, they are more likely to be accommodating. Understanding these dynamics between the two individuals involved can assist the HR professional in bringing the two parties together in a compromise to resolve the conflict.

Thomas–Kilmann Conflict Mode instrument

	Low ⟶ Cooperative ⟶ High
High / Assertive / Low	Competing — Collaborating — Compromising — Avoiding — Accommodating

Addressing Conflict

When there is conflict, the HR professional helps with finding the root cause of the conflict, what enables it to continue, and how to resolve it. One technique that can be used to find the root cause is called "**the Five Whys**," which involves repeating the question "why" at least five times. With each successive answer, the question is repeated, revealing deeper causes. If the true reason is not identified and addressed, then the conflict will never be resolved. Unless the root cause is determined, the HR professional may find themselves addressing surface issues, not the root. When the root cause is found, the HR professional determines a plan to address the concerns, move forward, and resolve the issues for all employees involved.

Facilitating Difficult Interactions

Engaging employees in difficult conversations can be part of the conflict resolution process. While employees do not have be the best of friends, it is vital to the health of the organizational culture that employees respect each other and work together with integrity, focusing on the common goal. In a single organization there will be as many personalities, work styles, communication methods, and backgrounds as there are employees. No two people are ever the same, and it is important for HR professionals to understand this when working to resolve conflict. Ensuring that employees work to appreciate the differences of others is one of the hardest functions of human resources.

Encouraging Productive Conflict

Clear and open communication is the only thing that will help two conflicted individuals work to resolve their issues and reach a solution. A trained Human Resources professional can help work through a fair and honest process while providing opportunities for each individual to express their thoughts and feelings. Asking questions throughout this process can also assist in encouraging the parties to think about the situation, their behaviors, their feelings, and what they can do to work through the issues. If the matter is complex and requires multiple conversations, it is important to provide each employee with questions to think about before meeting again. HR can assist in a process to resolve conflict, but it is up to the employees involved to address the issues and resolve the matter effectively to move forward.

Serving as a Role Model for Positive Conflict

Conflict can also serve as the impetus for creative thinking, productive discussions, and brainstorming. In some cases, encouraging employees in a conflict style exercise will challenge employees to move beyond their usual ways of thinking and doing things. Organizations must continually evolve to stay ahead of the competition. Using conflict to move the barometer can be a great way to challenge the normal standards. When HR serves as the leader in these situations, using positive reinforcement while challenging and encouraging, employees can start to think outside of the box and come up with innovative solutions while feeling protected and safe.

Resolving Conflict that is Harmful

While some conflict is positive, negative conflict can be harmful to individual employees and to the organization. It is critical for the HR professional to identify when conflict is counterproductive. Destructive conflict must be addressed as soon as possible and with all parties involved. HR professionals must also know when to escalate matters to executive leadership. Depending on the type of conflict, it may also be appropriate to bring in a third party to investigate the conflict, mediate the issues, and work to a resolution. Regardless of the method used, it must be done quickly and effectively. Letting issues linger will only create more problems, which could include legal issues.

Negotiation

When extending an offer of employment to a candidate, it is important to have enough information available to ensure a complete discussion. A best practice is to have all information available that will be written into the final job offer or contract. Additionally, understanding which items can be negotiated is also important. This allows both parties an understanding of where flexibility is available in the offer. Suppose a particular item is not negotiable, such as when eligibility for health insurance starts. If the candidate asks about negotiating this item, the Human Resources professional can tell them there is no flexibility to negotiate it. This allows for a more efficient and productive conversation about the offer of employment. Extending a verbal offer with these details can allow for discussion and negotiation, resulting in a final and formal offer extension in the form of an offer letter or official contract.

An offer of employment should include the following items, if appropriate:

- Job title and summary of position
- Base salary and bonus potential
- Fair Labor Standards Act (FLSA) status and overtime eligibility, if applicable
- Benefits, including all insurance offered with eligibility and leave accruals
- Additional benefits, including relocation and signing bonus
- Miscellaneous allowances such as car, phone, and clothing
- Probation terms, if any
- Contingency terms such as medical screenings and background checks

- Supervisor and reporting relationships
- Start date, work schedule, and weekly hours
- Location, work environment such as dress code, and company culture
- Growth and professional development opportunities
- Acceptance terms including consideration time and a date to officially accept
- Direct contact for additional questions

If an employee is receiving an official employment contract, it may be necessary to include additional items. These could include non-compete clauses, confidentiality or non-disclosure agreements, severance terms, copyright and trademark ownership, and other specific terms negotiated between the organization and candidate. Additional items such as the annual calendar showing holidays and days off, company newsletters and articles, health insurance availability, and other information should be provided as well. It is also important to communicate **escalating benefits**, which increase over time based on length of employment. An example of this would be that a new employee accrues eight hours of paid time off for each month worked; once the employee reaches five years of service, this increases to twelve hours of paid time off.

Salary negotiation is the beginning of the employment relationship. There are generally four stages of negotiation:

- Preparation
- Exchanging information
- Bargaining
- Closing and commitment

Depending on the discussions, it may be necessary to navigate back to exchanging information after bargaining to ensure both parties on the same page throughout the process.

Four Stages of Negotiation

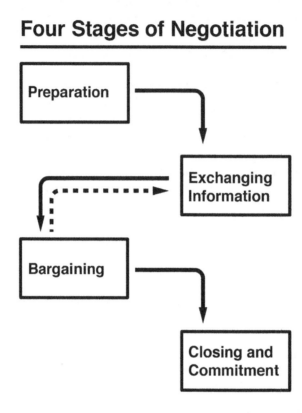

Items that may be appropriate to negotiate are base salary, bonus potential, leave accruals or receiving a balance of hours immediately upon hire, miscellaneous allowances, start date, work schedule, and potentially other items that a candidate requests to incorporate into the offer. It is important to understand which items are negotiable, along with the level of flexibility for each item. To expedite hiring, it may be appropriate during the verbal process to allow the individual extending the offer to agree to the candidate's counteroffer immediately. The organization may want a consolidated and complete list of the counteroffer to determine which, if any, items will be considered and potentially agreed upon.

Once there is a verbal agreement of the terms and conditions, a formal letter should be prepared to detail all the agreed upon items. It is important to note that some organizations may prefer to prepare an initial offer letter and then rescind and redraft a new, updated offer letter. This new offer letter would include the newly agreed upon terms and conditions after negotiation. Having thorough documentation of the employment terms at each step of the offer and negotiation process may be more appropriate based on the organization and the position. Offer letters or contracts should be signed by the organization's hiring authority. The offer letter or contract should also include a section indicating that the individual agrees to the terms and conditions of the offer with their signature and date.

A common and successful salary negotiation technique is summarized as the **five P's**: proper preparation prevents poor performance. This technique can be used by the hiring manager and recruiter as well as the candidate to assist with the negotiations process. Being properly prepared for the upcoming negotiations will result in successful outcomes for all parties. Prior to extending the offer of employment, it is important to be prepared with an understanding of why certain terms are being offered, especially the proposed salary amount. In general, most candidates are interested in this piece of information and will ask questions about how this amount was determined. Knowledge of the qualifications required for the position, the specific experience of the candidate, and growth opportunity within the position can be used to convey how the salary offer was calculated. Additionally, communicating the salary range can allow the candidate insight as to the growth opportunity within this position. This information can also assist the candidate when considering a counteroffer.

The goal in extending employment offers and negotiations is for all parties to be satisfied with the terms. The organization, hiring manager, recruiter, and candidate all have different needs and perspectives regarding what constitutes a successful offer negotiation. Depending on how the discussions progress, however, it may be appropriate to end negotiations and formally rescind the initial offer of employment if the candidate's requests are unreasonable or inappropriate. During these circumstances, understanding which items are negotiable and the flexibility for each can assist in making the decision to end the negotiation discussions. For example, if the candidate requests to negotiate a different job title and responsibilities or a salary outside of the range established for the position, it may be appropriate to end the negotiations. Once an offer of employment has been negotiated and agreed upon by both parties, documents have been updated and signed, and a formal agreement is in place, the organization's focus should shift to an onboarding mentality and bringing the new employee into the workplace culture and environment.

Upholding Professionalism During Negotiations

Negotiation is a process where two or more parties work toward achieving an agreeable outcome that is beneficial to both parties. A negotiation can be a formal and lengthy process taking up to several months, but it can also be informal and quick depending on the circumstances. Being proficient in negotiation requires education, experience, and specific skills that are developed and practiced frequently. Some of these skills include building relationships, communicating, being patient, actively listening, and establishing an open and honest environment for discussions. Formal negotiations generally include establishing a contract such as a bargaining agreement between an employer and employee's union.

In most formal negotiations, the parties set ground rules addressing issues such as press releases, meeting frequency, the length of time each party is allotted to bring new ideas and proposals to the table, and other important parameters required for each party to follow. Informal negotiations can take place daily and could include resolving a simple but urgent issue. A good example of this would be an employee requesting a change of work schedule to accommodate a childcare arrangement. The manager could work with the employee to negotiate a new schedule that addresses the individual need while also ensuring that the department and team needs continue to be met after making the change.

Being professional, courteous, and honest during negotiations is vital to achieving a successful outcome. It is important not to take anything personally. Negotiations can sometimes become tense, confrontational, or even volatile. When this happens, it is important to take a breath, work to remove the emotion from the dialogue, and remind everyone of the goal. Regardless of opposing positions, working toward the resolution should be everyone's focus. Additionally, it is important to come to the negotiations table prepared, educated, and aware of the current state of the organization. Preparing reports, reviewing survey information, and understanding the goals are the keystones to delivering a successful negotiation.

Understanding the Needs, Interests, and Issues in Bargaining

When planning for a successful negotiation, it is important to understand the needs, interests, concerns, and current state of the organization. If safety measures such as Personal Protective Equipment (PPE) are a concern to employees, it is important to address the issue while still giving priority to important obligations such as financial costs, training, and workforce needs.

HR professionals should also understand how the organization aligns with external agencies regarding compensation, benefits, safety protocols, policies, and other employee welfare matters. A knowledge of these standards will help ensure that the organization holds a similar position if the negotiations begin to move into an area that seems unreasonable or inappropriate. A good circumstantial example would be an employee requesting a wage increase of 7% when the market and competition is showing an increase of 3%. This could easily be regarded as excessive; however, providing information on current industry standards would support an appropriate and well-aligned response. Not only is it important to have information available from the market and competing agencies, but it is also important to have information from within the organization itself. Financial reports that provide operating positions, profit margins, and current costs that include operations and workforce are vital to providing a financial snapshot as to what the organization can afford when negotiating a new contract. Workforce reports that provide the number of full-time employees (FTEs), part-time employees (PTEs), contractors, and department budgets also provide insight when negotiating new terms.

Providing Appropriate Concessions to Achieve Agreement
When negotiating, it is important to remember that both parties will need to make concessions or adjustments to their initial proposals to allow for discussions to continue. It is unreasonable to enter negotiations with assumptions that changes and recommendations will not be met with counter proposals or different ideas to consider. Therefore, it is vital to have an overall goal defined prior to entering the negotiation process to ensure that all proposals—initial, revised, and final—align with this overall goal. Understanding that both parties will need to make concessions to reach an agreement will ensure that the negotiation process is fair and conducted in good faith. A good example of this would be relative to wage increases.

The union representation may start with a proposal of a 5% wage increase for each year of a three-year contract. The organization may start with a proposal of a 1% wage increase for each year of a two-year contract. After negotiating and discussing the financial impact of each proposal, along with reviewing the historical wage increases that employees have received in recent contracts, an appropriate compromise may be a 3% wage increase for each year of a three-year contract. This also assumes that the agreement meets the overall goals of both parties: an appropriate increase for employees while responsibly maintaining increased costs that align with projected revenues for the organization.

Practicing Applicable Laws and Regulations on Negotiation and Bargaining
Collective bargaining is a process required by law in some states to negotiate terms and conditions between parties in good faith. Good faith refers to both parties communicating and working together in complete honesty to come to an agreement. Both parties should be reasonable, appropriate, and fair as they work to arrive at an agreement that is unbiased and balanced on each side. Mandatory subjects of bargaining include wages, hours, benefits, health, safety, management rights, discipline, seniority, grievance procedures, arbitration, length of contract, and impact. An example of impact would be the layoff of employees due to an economic downturn.

While the decision of layoffs may be a management right, the impact to the affected employees must be considered. The impact could include severance, COBRA coverage, recall rights, or other items that would occur as a result of the decision to lay off employees. When negotiations break down and the parties are unable to compromise, mediators can be brought in to work with the parties and try to reach a resolution. When mediation does not result in an agreement, arbitration may be necessary. If either party refuses to negotiate in good faith, fails to respond to requests, or declines to meet, an unfair labor practice (ULP) claim could be filed with the state board that regulates collective bargaining and negotiation.

Evaluating Progress Toward an Agreement

During the negotiation process, it is important to communicate the negotiation's status and progress. Considering the confidentiality of all aspects of negotiation, particularly the discussions and proposals made, it is very crucial to provide an overview of the negotiation. This could include providing the number of meetings held, the number of proposals exchanged by each side, any future meetings scheduled, and the progress of the negotiations in reference to the goals set at the start of the process.

When planning formal negotiations, best practices include defining milestones and identifying timing requirements to track the progress. This is important when a contract is expiring on a certain date. Adhering to specific time frames allows the new contract to be finalized prior to expiration of the existing contract. This is especially important when implementing wage increases. If a new contract indicating a wage increase is effective on June 1, it is important to have the said contract in place prior to this date. This ensures that no retroactive payments need to be made. If the contract with an effectivity date of June 1 is not finalized until August 1, this could result in payroll having to calculate out two months of retroactive pay to all eligible employees, not to mention having to initiate the standard wage increase for future payroll.

Identifying an Ideal Solution

In most negotiation processes, the negotiation team meets with the leadership team, or other authorized individuals, to discuss the approved guiding parameters for the purpose of proposal conclusion and coming to an agreement. These parameters become the guiding focus for the final contract. They generally include total cost of compensation, total cost of contract, changes to working conditions, and other high-level changes that need to be implemented by the organization. While these parameters should be the final goal, it is equally important to allow for flexibility; therefore, all presented proposals should permit discussion and changes. Once the goal has been set, the negotiations team should frequently update the leadership on the progress. If there is information that should be shared as to why these goals are not met, it is vital to share this information ahead of time so that considerations can be made in making necessary changes.

If none of the changes get approved, it is up to the negotiation team to discuss flexible and creative proposals that will work to accomplish the goals. There may be occasions that the negotiation team is unable to reach an agreement due to the disparity between the goals of the negotiating parties. When this happens, it is important to try to achieve a resolution but also understand when an impasse has been reached. When an impasse is reached, it is appropriate to conclude negotiations in the interest of working through the next step, such as mediation or arbitration. However, it is still the most beneficial to both parties if an agreement can be reached by discussion, compromise, debate, and concession. Mediation and arbitration can be costly and time consuming, leaving employees in a state of uncertainty.

Communication

Communication happens formally and informally, in person and at a distance, verbally and without saying a word. With so many ways of communicating with others, it is critical for the communicator to understand their audience and ensure that the message and its means of delivery are appropriate. Regardless of the type of communication and method of delivery, all communications should be clear, concise, and deliberate while offering others the ability to request clarification and raise concerns. If there is confusion or misunderstanding, it is important to clarify so that all individuals are on the same page and the team can move forward with the same understanding.

Delivering Messages

Selecting the best way to communicate a message is essential to ensuring that the message arrives in a timely way and is understood accurately. Communication methods include email, website updates or blog posts, printed bulletins, in-person training, video messages, and newsletters. Some messages may require multiple styles of delivery to ensure that employees are fully aware of the information. Formal policies should be communicated via a memo to all employees as well as posted in an online portal for easy access. Additionally, formal policies should be provided to new hires in either a hard copy or a digital copy. State-of-the-business messages should be communicated in person or by video, so that employees can engage with the information.

Presenting Needed Information to Stakeholders

When presenting information to stakeholders or executive leadership, it is important to stay on message and provide details that are important to this level of management. Instead of focusing on tactical and day-to-day details and data, it is important to focus on the strategic and high-level priorities. This is the opportunity to engage the executive level of an organization. Therefore, it is important to stay at a level of detail that is appropriate for these individuals. The holistic overview and the overarching benefits, goals, and objectives are what key stakeholders in an organization will want to see.

Communicating with an Audience

In addition to presenting the appropriate information to the audience, it is also important to use the most suitable language. Each department or team typically has its own jargon: key words, phrases, or acronyms. An employee outside the group may not understand this jargon. It is important to recognize that one team may interpret a specific term differently than another team. Ensuring that every member of the audience understands the terms is vital to success. One example of this is the acronym "**RFP**." In most departments, this acronym stands for a **request for proposal**; however, in finance, this acronym stands for **request for payment**. A best practice is to have an in-person discussion to establish a standardized lexicon for terms and then follow up with a cheat sheet that defines these in writing for individuals as a reference.

Business Terms and Vocabulary

When creating a message, it is important to use the appropriate business terms to refer to the process, action items, resources, and employee titles. Prior to starting any communication, the HR professional should acquaint themselves with the appropriate terms currently used. In this way, not only can the author establish credibility, but they can also ensure that the audience will understand it and how it impacts the organization, department, and the individual. Often a draft communication from another agency will be used as a starting point so that an entire message does not have be reinvented. Each organization has its own language and when using this strategy to create messages, it is vital to review these materials and make update specific to your organization to avoid confusion or questions.

Receiving Communication

It is important to ensure that the individuals who received a message from HR understand it. Providing an opportunity to ask questions and engage in a dialogue can be a great way to ensure that there is clarity. Additionally, if many people have similar questions, this may indicate that the original message did not provide the information clearly enough. In that case, it may be a good idea to present a follow-up clarification. A frequently asked questions (FAQ) document is another great way to ensure clarity.

Crafting Clear Messages

Writing clear messages that are organized, effective, and accurate is an art. An HR professional should keep in mind that they are not the message's audience. When putting together a message, it is important to remember that audience will be encountering this information for the first time. The HR professional may have been working on this information for a while and may have a mindset that others already have this knowledge. It is vital to take a step back and ensure that the message is written for someone who may be less familiar with the topic. It is also important to use correct grammar and style in the communication. Presenting a professional message can also determine how engaged the reader will be with the information.

Creating Persuasive Arguments

In many cases, HR professionals may have to create a message that presents controversial information. In these instances, it can be beneficial to provide compelling information that provides the rationale as to why a particular decision was made. Sometimes, it is important to communicate that the decision has already been made, so that the message is not received as an invitation for critique or debate on the decision. Other times, HR may ask for feedback in order to include employees in the decision. Most decisions are based on data, information, and substantial discussion. Including some of this information in the communication can work to engage employees and obtain their buy-in.

Exchanging Organizational Information

A key function of the human resources department is exchanging information with other organizations. Completing salary and benefit information requests, providing policies and procedures, and establishing benchmarks are all key components of information that HR will need to provide. Ensuring that accurate and timely information is provided is necessary so that the requestors can complete their research. Additionally, this information will enable an HR professional to determine if the organization is a leader in their industry. With this information, the organization can make assessments and implement changes to keep the organization in the forefront of the industry. This fosters better recruitment and retention of employees.

Communicating HR Programs, Practices and Policies

When a new program, policy, or practice is implemented, generally HR is responsible for communicating this information to all employees. Depending on the organization, this includes employees in HR, finance, IT, engineering, operations, manufacturing, logistics, legal, and other departments. Each group of employees will have different needs; therefore, it is important to ensure that the communication addresses as many of these needs as possible while clearly conveying the new, updated, or revised policy. It is also important for the HR professional to ensure that the information is easily accessible and to make themselves available for questions and one-on-one meetings.

Communicating HR Issues

HR professionals are also tasked with assisting non-HR managers in communicating HR-related information with employees. A common communications strategy is a **top-down method** where the leader at the very top of an organization or department issues a communication to their direct reports. These direct reports then relay the message to the next layer of the organization, and the message continues to cascade downward through the organization until all employees receive it. From a guideline sheet with bullet points to a prepared PowerPoint® presentation, HR can provide tools and resources to ensure that a message is clearly communicated.

Voicing Support for HR

Being supportive of others is important in an organization. It increases morale, encourages engagement, and provides opportunities to work together better. HR professionals should support other HR professionals along with employees outside of the department. Employees look to HR to model appropriate behavior, and it is important to support each other. This behavior can have a substantial impact on day-to-day interactions between individuals, while fostering a positive and productive workforce. In addition to supporting individuals, it is important to support the organizational objectives and initiatives. Sometimes, certain employees may not fully support an objective or direction. In these cases, encouraging the individual to express these opinions while ultimately engaging them to work toward the goal is vital to the success of individuals and the organization.

Communicating with Senior HR Leaders

Senior HR leadership will need to understand where the HR department is in relation to the departmental objectives. Providing frequent and succinct updates will allow the leadership to know where the department is trending. It is also important to ensure that the HR leadership understands some of the tactical and day-to-day issues so that they can work to address these quickly. As the HR leadership sets objectives for the department, it is important to ensure that the leaders know how day-to-day tasks align with the overall objectives so that changes can be made as necessary.

Listening

Listening is more than just hearing the words that an individual says. Hearing is passive and does not require conscious effort. Listening is an active and engaged skill that requires a clear and conscious effort; this active listening may require practice. **Active listening** means being engaged with the individual who is speaking by giving them one's undivided attention, making frequent eye contact, and avoiding distractions such as ringing phones, pinging text messages, or other interruptions. Additionally, active listening includes demonstrating one's engagement physically, using facial expressions, posture, and bodily gesture. It is also important to provide feedback, ask questions, and repeat statements made by the speaker to ensure understanding.

Active Listening

HR professionals will frequently take statements from employees about grievances, problems, conflicts, or issues. In these situations, active listening is vital. Active listening includes showing empathy, which allows the employee to feel safe, respected, valued, and heard. This can be therapeutic, and it can enable a resolution to move forward. One method of expressing empathy is to paraphrase back to the speaker what was said and the emotions expressed. This lets the speaker know what the HR professional heard, and it allows an opportunity for clarification and discussion. By focusing on the speaker's emotions as well as the content of what was said, the HR professional can present differing points of view, clarifications, and recommendations to resolve the issue.

Competing Points of View

HR professionals are continually learning and growing in implementing new programs, policies, and laws. HR works with many different employees in different positions, all of whom have unique backgrounds and skill sets. Understanding these different points of view is a valued asset that HR can use to ensure that diverse programs and communications are implemented. Criticism is sometimes leveled at an HR professional. It is important for the HR professional to see any criticism as an opportunity for growth and learning. Most of an HR professional's day-to-day interactions are difficult, challenging, and emotionally charged. It is important to understand that sometimes HR can be a sounding board for other employees. Therefore, the HR professional should take criticism personally but use it as an opportunity to grow.

Seeking Further Information

An important element of active listening is asking questions and looking for more information to clarify specific details. Allowing an individual to speak fully and without interruption is necessary, but asking questions is just as important. An HR professional should ensure that the discussion is interactive and as much information as possible is gathered during the initial meeting. This will ensure that the HR professional has all the necessary information to proceed with an investigation, if needed. When there is vague or unclear information, or if certain elements remain unknown, the HR professional could be surprised by new information. This could cause the need for additional discussions with the first individual to gain clarity and insight, which could impact the level of trust.

Stakeholder Communications

When a message is received from a stakeholder or leader of the organization, it is vital to respond promptly with the specific information that is being requested. A key skill of all employees, including HR professionals, is to prioritize tasks and manage workload. This skill set is needed in both personal and professional settings. Knowledge of the key stakeholders and leaders is critical when prioritizing communications from these individuals. Responses to these communications should be concise, and they should answer all questions raised. Allowing for additional communication is also important if there are other questions or issues that come up later.

Understanding Received Communications

HR professionals have relationships with practically every employee and manager in an organization. These relationships benefit from an awareness of communication styles. When an employee sends an email asking for advice, clarification, specific requests, or guidance, it is important for the HR professional to be able to interpret the email's full meaning so that an accurate response can be prepared. Ensuring a clear, concise, and specific response is important so that the employee has the information needed. An additional positive outcome of providing the best communication is that it establishes credibility between the HR professional and employee. Credibility is earned through these one-on-one interactions.

Soliciting Feedback

The human resources department serves all other departments and employees; therefore, it is important to understand the needs of each department. Surveys, department meetings, and one-on-one meetings are all excellent ways to gather this information. Additionally, it is important to follow up about with the senior leadership regarding the implementation of the new ideas to ensure their success. As another level of follow-up, it is important to engage the department leaders in the effectiveness of the HR's functions and services. When HR is not effective, it is important to understand what is not working so that it can be corrected.

Global Mindset

When an HR professional values the different perspectives, backgrounds, experiences, and personalities of everyone they work with, they possess excellent global and cultural effectiveness. Diversity is incredibly important for an organization to be fully productive, efficient, innovative, and engaged. Bringing different ideas to the table is only one benefit of a diverse workforce. HR professionals foster relationships between employees who are diverse in thinking, background, and communication styles to facilitate creative thinking, brainstorm new ideas, and remain competitive in the industry. This diversity contributes to the overall organizational culture, which then cascades down to specific departmental and cultures.

Operating in a Diverse Workplace

Operating in a diverse workplace has both benefits and challenges. The primary benefits of working with a group of diverse employees are: 1) creativity and innovation; 2) recruitment and retention; and 3) personal and professional growth and development. The primary challenges of working with a group of diverse employees are: 1) cultural differences may impede engagement and discussion; 2) prejudice or stereotypes may slow connections within teams; and 3) professional etiquette and appropriate behavior may differ. HR professionals can work to break down these challenges by providing training and growth opportunities to move past these challenges and embrace the benefits and positive influences that a diverse workforce can provide.

Cultural Differences and Issues

HR professionals should have an understanding of diversity. **Diversity** includes differences in gender, race, ethnicity, religion, age, generation, marital status, physical abilities, education, geographic background, national origin, and experience. Understanding how each of these elements of diversity can enhance the workforce is a key function of HR professionals. Employees should be encouraged to engage positively with others to understand these differences and what can be gained from them. Some employees require additional growth opportunities to engage fully in accepting diversity, and these opportunities can be provided either internally or externally by a third party. Clear and robust diversity policies are also important to ensure that employees understand the expectations relative to diversity in the workplace.

Navigating Different Cultural Conditions, Situations, and People

Phases of denial, judgment, minimization, and acceptance must be worked through before an individual can adapt their behavior to navigate different cultural conditions, situations, and people. When an HR professional understands these phases and has first-hand knowledge of working through this process, the HR professional can better assist others in working through these phases to adapt behavior for specific situations.

Demonstrating Acceptance

The HR professional understands that the organization benefits from having diverse employees with different ideas, backgrounds, and experience. It is important for the HR professional to treat employees with fairness and respect. When employees feel safe about expressing their thoughts to the HR professional, they feel empowered.

Promoting a Diverse and Inclusive Workforce

Establishing a diversity and inclusion policy for an organization is the first step to promoting these characteristics in the workforce. Understanding the expectations of this policy is essential for each employee to ensure that these elements are incorporated into daily life. This policy should be practiced throughout the organization by encouraging employees to learn different strategies specific to diversity. These strategies include conflict resolution, negotiation, effective communication, creating inclusivity among teams, and respecting others regardless of level, position, or background. The primary benefit of incorporating these elements into the organization at all levels is a welcoming and inclusive environment that fosters productivity, encouragement, innovation, and satisfaction. Inclusion strategist Andres Tapia communicates the relationship between diversity and inclusion in a simple way: "Diversity is the mix. Inclusion is making the mix work."

Promoting Inclusion

Inclusion is when each employee has the same resources and opportunities as everyone else. Inclusion is a process, not a specific event. Inclusion happens when employees value diversity. HR professionals can encourage and promote inclusion by modeling behavior that respects others on a daily basis. Employees see each interaction that an HR professional has with individuals, groups, and teams. Formal and informal interactions are opportunities for the HR professional to engage in inclusive behavior. HR should be a role model by being respectful of others' concerns and needs. Inclusion enables individuals to feel valued for their contributions to the organization.

Cross-Cultural Differences

From the job posting and recruitment process to on-boarding and new hire orientation, HR should work to understand culture differences of job candidates and future employees. This includes identifying and eliminating any potential recruitment barriers that would create disinterest in joining a company based on the posting language and process. A best practice is to have all documents and information available in multiple languages. This encourages the inclusion of individuals who do not speak English well or as a first language. Additionally, maintaining a database of employees who are fluent in other languages is a best practice that will promote effective and accurate communications.

Operating in a Global Environment

Operating in a global environment requires awareness of different cultures, languages, laws, practices, and acceptable behaviors. Communication techniques, performance management tools, and resources require different methods to be successful. When HR professionals are aware of these differences, they can take action to minimize any potential barriers and ensure that the organization is successful. When an organization has employees from different countries, the HR professional can educate employees about these countries' differences to ensure positive working relationships. Having strong diversity and inclusion practices in the organization is vital to the accomplishment of a strong global organizational culture.

Understanding the Organization's Line of Business from a Global Perspective

The most successful HR professionals understand the organization's lines of business. Being a customer of the organization is an excellent way to have a key insight into its lines of business. Solutions can be prepared and recommended that will allow the business to be even more productive and engage employees at a high level. A global organization may have different lines of business for each country it's in. Spending time learning the organization's lines of business, using its products, and having conversations with employees enable HR professionals to best serve the employees and the organization.

Tailoring HR Initiatives

It is important to understand cultural differences to ensure that HR initiatives align with the standards relevant to various cultures. For example, an informal birthday party is thrown for an employee. In some cultures, this may not be seen as a positive event and could create an awkward or tense dynamic with a team. Additionally, an employee may be offended if a cultural practice is not adhered to. HR should ensure that any HR practice, either formal or informal, aligns with cultural norms and standard behaviors. When employees see an organization's commitment to being culturally sensitive in its initiatives and programs, employees are more likely to be engaged, motivated, and satisfied.

Differences in Rules, Laws, Regulations, and Accepted Business Operations

HR professionals should be educated on the laws and regulations specific to each country. This is also important when working within the United States, as each state may have variations. Knowledge of laws and regulations is even more important when working in other countries. From labor laws to safety standards, there may be differences from one country to another. There may even be situations where there is not a law, so a policy for the local employees may be misunderstood.

Global Trends

Global trends should drive the actions of HR professionals who are working to develop and maintain programs and policies. Understanding how the industry trends and benchmarks differ from country to country should influence how programs are delivered to the employees in each country. While the base programs should strive to be similar, variations may be needed to ensure compliance with laws and work to maximize efficiency and momentum in the current trends. HR professionals may need to spend substantial time learning about the organization in each country, which could include training sessions, surveys, networking, and other educational forums to develop this insight.

Operating with a Global Mindset

Having a holistic mindset is important when setting policies for each location. HR professionals should be sensitive to issues that local employees are facing but also ensure that there is alignment with the organization's overall global objectives and goals. All programs, policies, and objectives should be aligned with the local culture and laws as well as with the overall organizational objectives. Being strategic in this planning and involving the leaders at the local level is an excellent way to accomplish this difficult task.

Managing Paradoxical Practices

Today, many employees are moving to different countries to experience new career opportunities. With employees of many different nationalities and backgrounds working together, HR professionals need to understand these dynamics so that if there is conflict with employees due to contradictions in social customs, the HR professional can find solutions to ensure harmony. These could include sensitivity training, cultural education, or small coaching sessions with groups of employees. Working in a global organization is challenging, but it can be navigated by being thorough, educated, strategic, and thoughtful.

Advocating for a Culturally Diverse and Inclusive Workplace

A diverse and inclusive workplace has numerous benefits to an organization. When HR professionals implement strong policies, practice behaviors that support these policies and concepts, and ensure that all employees understand expectations, the organization will experience many benefits. A diverse and inclusive workplace does the following:

- Increases competitive recruitment and maintains higher retention rates
- Improves performance and engagement
- Increases innovation, creativity, and new ideas
- Improves customer satisfaction
- Enables a larger market of customers and partners
- Improves the brand, products, and marketing
- Increases profits, lowers costs, and ensures long-term success

One way of enjoying these benefits is to ensure strong and robust diversity and inclusion policies. Additionally, it is important for leadership to exhibit the behaviors that are expected from all employees so that every individual is supporting the common goals.

Diversity and Inclusion in the Organization

Diversity is defined as the similarities, differences, and opportunities inherent in the individual and organizational characteristics that form the workplace. **Inclusion** is defined as respecting and valuing diversity. Verna Myers provided the following description: "Diversity is being invited to the party; inclusion is being asked to dance." Diversity is integral to inclusion, but inclusion is the end goal.

Diversity and Inclusion Philosophy and Policies

Due to the many benefits of a strong diversity and inclusion policy, it is vital to encourage leadership to utilize these concepts when making business decisions, creating policies, or changing practices. HR professionals should also use these concepts when designing and implementing HR programs and policies. Being respectful to all employees, acting with integrity in all tasks, and behaving ethically and responsibly are three basic yet extremely important concepts of inclusion that should be incorporated into all elements of policy and decisions. Inclusion is not simply about being in the same location/office or working for the same company. Inclusion is intentionally engaging all employees in the achievement of objectives that are aligned with the overall success of an organization.

Designing Programs

HR professionals should use diversity and inclusion when designing and implementing HR programs and policies. HR should also frequently audit the current policies and practices to ensure that they continue to be successful in achieving a diverse and inclusive workforce. Surveying employees to get direct feedback regarding respect, integrity, ethics, and professionalism in the workplace is an excellent way to engage the workforce and understand the reality of the workplace. Anonymous surveys empower employees to be honest in their feedback.

Ensuring Consistent Policies

All employees should be treated fairly, equitably, and consistently. By training managers in the policies, programs, and practices while providing coaching when specific issues occur, HR can assist others to ensure that consistency is practiced among all employees. HR should audit departmental actions regarding coaching, counseling, discipline, and other measures that should always be applied consistently. If there are inconsistencies, training should be initiated to communicate the concerns and resolve any misunderstandings or provide rationale for the difference in treatment. HR should also use this opportunity to address concerns that managers may have regarding the policies and if their specific needs for the employees are being met with the current process.

Business

Business Acumen

Business acumen is often referred to as business savvy or business sense. Business acumen is the ability to identify, understand, and resolve situations that will result in a positive outcome. While business acumen has been previously seen as a tool to be used at the highest levels of an organization, its benefits are substantial for all areas. Strong business acumen can lead to stronger performance and increased efficiencies in finance, information technology, human resources, operations, logistics, and any other department that uses this information. When using business acumen, HR can see positive outcomes in strategic planning, performance management, leadership development, employee engagement, organizational culture, and retention.

Business and Competitive Awareness

Education in the organization's business and industry includes knowledge of the competition. The **Awareness Triangle** is a representation of how to process information and develop a level of intelligence surrounding the competition. The three sides, or steps, of the triangle are: 1) aware; 2) analyze; 3) action. These steps should be followed in this order to ensure success. Previous models maintained the same linear process, but the greatest focus was on the action step. Now the greatest focus is on awareness, to ensure that the best actions can be recommended and implemented. Becoming aware of available data is vital for full awareness of the competition. Using this data and awareness then allows the organization to analyze the information fully and completely. Once the data has been thoroughly analyzed, actions can then be taken to achieve better business practices and ultimately higher profitability.

Awareness Triangle

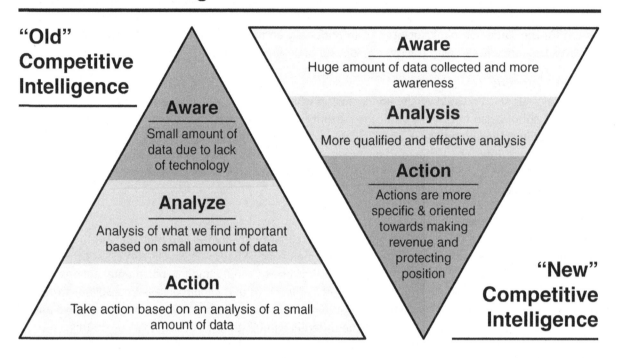

Business Operations

HR professionals have a wide array of resources available for learning about the organization's operations, functions, products, services, customers, and employees. These resources are available in four major areas: physical, financial, human, and organizational. **Physical resources** include the brick-and-mortar locations that the organization operates. This could include manufacturing facilities, call centers, customer service centers, administrative offices, or retail stores. **Financial resources** include reports that provide a financial overview of the organization. Annual reports, cash flow and revenue statements, and other compliance reports are excellent tools to use to learn about the financial position of an organization. **Human resources** include the employees of an organization at every level. Individual contributors, supervisors, department managers, and executive leadership are all resources that HR professionals can have one-on-one discussions with to learn about the organization. **Organizational resources**, including policies, processes, programs, practices, workforce skills and abilities, all lend a level of information vital to understanding an organization.

PESTLE Trends

Many variables influence the decisions that organizations make. Six trends that should be considered are represented by the acronym **PESTLE**, which stand for political, economic, social, technological, legal, and environmental. Using organizational resources enables an HR professional to gain insight into each of these areas. PESTLE can occur both internally and externally, and in some cases, external resources may be needed in order to fully appreciate the current circumstances. These could include networking with other HR professionals, initiating or reviewing surveys, and reading blogs or news reports. As the saying goes, "knowledge is power." The more data available, the more informed business leaders can be in making decisions that will have an impact on the organization and employees. HR professionals can use this information when creating, managing, reviewing, and updating policies and procedures.

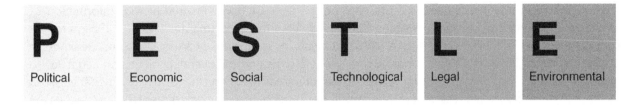

Knowledge of Operations

Having an understanding, even a general one, of the organization's business operations, functions, products, and services allows an HR professional to provide the best customer service to departments. This is especially true when recruiting new employees. This enables HR professionals to screen, interview, and approve applicants that will best support the organization based on their experience and previous responsibilities. HR can also engage in effective communications with potential hires and new employees about the current climate of the organization. When HR does not have this information, they can make decisions that may be shortsighted and do not support the overall objectives of the departments or organization. Understanding the organization's products and services will enable an HR professional to represent the organization in the best possible way to candidates.

Applying Knowledge to Implement HR Solutions

Similar to applying internal knowledge to HR initiatives, applying external knowledge gained through analyzing the PESTLE trends can enable HR to deliver a high level of customer service. Knowing how the industry compensates employees in wages and benefits will enable the organization to ensure industry competitiveness and encourage retention of existing employees. This information can also allow HR professionals to corroborate current compensation levels. These exercises are instrumental in negotiations and annual reviews, and they enable business leaders to make the best decisions possible.

Business Analysis

Business analysis is a strategic practice that focuses on an organization's functions, processes, methods, procedures, and performance in an effort to identify issues, create and implement solutions, and monitor the results of these actions. Business analysis is a continual process that empowers a positive culture. Business analysis typically works to identify and solve complicated problems that span multiple functions; however, this strategic practice and its tools can be used for even the smallest issues. Regardless of the size of the issue, business analysis strives to deliver positive changes throughout the organization. Business analysis takes time, effort, resources, and thought. When employees are brought together to work through this process, it is important to ensure that every concern is valued, considered, and discussed. This will ensure that employees are engaged in the process and motivated to participate at a high level.

Cost-Benefit Analysis, Organizational Metrics, and Key Performance Indicators

Multiple tools can be used when performing a business analysis. Depending on the issue, selected tools should provide the most appropriate data. Cost-benefit analysis, key performance indicators (KPIs), and SWOT are samples of tools that can be used to provide further information that can be used when making decisions and changes. A **cost-benefit analysis** reviews all the costs and benefits and then determines if the benefits are greater than the costs. Any cost that an organization takes on should be outweighed by the benefits that are gained; however, sometimes, this may not be the case, and the expense is simply a cost of doing business.

Analyzing this information allows the organization to understand this relationship and make the best decisions. **KPIs** are pieces of data that can be used to analyze how the organization is performing and if change should be made. From revenue, expenses, net profit, and staffing costs to headcount, attrition, days to fill a recruitment, and training costs, each department will have KPIs that provide information about the efficiency and productivity of the operations. All of the departmental KPIs should align to support the organization's overall KPIs. A **SWOT analysis** looks at four key areas: strengths, weaknesses, opportunities, and threats. These four areas are vital to discovering the overall positive and negative attributes of a project or organization. Each of these four areas focus on the positive and negative, as well as the internal and external factors that can contribute to the success, or lack thereof, of a project or the organization as a whole. These tools should be used on both an individual and group level, and employees should be comfortable with these techniques so that efficiency and productivity are continuously being improved.

Business Analysis Tools

When HR professionals analyze the effectiveness of HR policies, programs, and practices, it is important to apply the same business analysis tools discussed earlier to ensure a full and holistic review. If the review does not include these elements, then the results could be skewed and not fully embrace all aspects of the information available. HR affects every employee, department, manager, function, and objective. Because of this, it is important not to work in a vacuum and incorporate every piece of information available to ensure robust and effective policies and programs. The most effective human resources departments incorporate business analysis and strategic planning into the objectives of the department. Business analysis and strategic planning provide a positive working environment for all individuals and enable effective job performance.

HRIS and Business Technology

Human resources information systems (HRIS) are unique to each organization and HR department. As each agency has its own specific needs when it comes to reporting and the information to be tracked, HRIS platforms can be uniquely tailored to meet these needs. HRIS reports and data should be used to address issues and solve problems when appropriate. HR should use the data available to review trends, analyze performance evaluation information, and assess recruitment effectiveness. Using this data can provide insights, which can then be used to modify the departmental objectives. It is important to understand that the reports are only as good as the data entered. If incorrect data is entered into the system, then the reports created from the system will not provide accurate details. Trends and resolutions that are created from inaccurate information will lead to bigger issues instead of resolving the issues that the data was intended to fix. A robust HRIS has multiple benefits for the organization, including faster processing and time savings, improved planning and organization, recruitment status and details, and a more accurate level of performance.

Strategic Alignment

Strategic alignment is defined as the process of connecting an organization's resources, capital, tools, and workforce to achieve its goals. This process enables the maximum levels of efficiency and productivity by minimizing waste and ensuring that employees are working toward the same goals. Aligning an individual's goals with departmental goals is imperative. Similarly, aligning the departmental goals to the organization's is yet another level of strategic planning and alignment that will ensure an organization meets its goals. This planning will ensure that all effort is focused in the same direction: on the goals. Without this strategy, resources could be wasted, and time could be spent focusing on initiatives that conflict with the overall objectives. Additionally, when employees understand how their roles are aligned with the organization's overall initiatives, employees are more motivated and productive. Understanding how one piece of the puzzle fits into the larger picture to make it complete is vital to maximizing employee engagement.

Relationship Between Effective HR and Effective Core Business Functions

HR professionals should strive to understand the relationship between HR and the core business. Having this understanding will enable HR to provide more effective services. This is especially important when recruiting for open positions. If an HR professional does not fully understand the core business of the department and the specific position being recruited, there is a higher likelihood that the applicant pool will reflect this. While it is not necessary for HR to be subject matter experts in every position in the organization, it is important to understand the core business. This will ensure that the job descriptions accurately reflect the hiring needs while addressing the specific roles and responsibilities that will be performed. When this knowledge is conveyed through the interview and hiring process, the organization can make the best decision when hiring new employees.

Aligning Decisions with HR

HR professionals should follow four steps to align HR policies and practices with the organization's goals:

- Understand the business strategy, goals, objectives, vision, and mission.
- Identify the workforce requirements required to achieve the goals.
- Create and update policies and practices that allow employees to be productive.
- Develop specific HR dashboards and metrics to communicate success.

Employees are responsible for the success of an organization. Leadership can set structure, provide guidance, create a mission and culture, and establish the overall path for the organization; however, employees are the individuals who are performing the tasks, duties, and responsibilities that ultimately flow upward to achieve the ultimate successes. Without the talent and skills necessary to perform these tasks, it will be nearly impossible to be successful. HR professionals should continually assess the workforce and determine if there are skill gaps in any area. If skill gaps exist, HR should work to provide training opportunities immediately to ensure that the workforce is fully knowledgeable in the work that needs to be completed. There should also be practices that foster employees' innovation, creativity, effectiveness, and productivity. Finally, HR should be able to measure and communicate success in these areas through specific metrics and dashboards. Being able to communicate clearly how HR is assisting employees in achieving their goals and aligning them with the organization's goals will enable a holistic view and assist in pinpointing areas that need more focus.

Making the Business Case for HR Initiatives

HR has a major impact on an organization's success. Sometimes it is important to demonstrate HR's importance to the rest of the organization. Accurate data can showcase the return on investment (ROI) that HR provides. While there are numerous data points that will communicate this, some of the most common are absenteeism, attrition, and human capital. **Absenteeism** calculates how many employees are absent from work. Whether on vacation or sick leave, when employees are absent from work, there is a cost. Knowing this cost can be beneficial for staffing and workforce budgeting. Attrition is the rate at which employees are leaving an organization. Knowing the turnover rate is important, but knowing why employees are leaving the organization is even more important. If the turnover rate is low, it is important to know why employees are choosing to stay; simultaneously, if the turnover rate is high, it is important to know why employees are leaving.

Understanding the reasons for both scenarios is critical to ensure that HR initiatives are appropriate and addressing potential issues. Finally, knowing how the costs of the employee workforce compare to the revenues of the organization is necessary to ensure an appropriate balance between revenue and expenses. The ROI is determined by dividing the organization's net revenue (gross revenue minus operating expenses) by the total cost of salaries and benefits. Understanding this data point will allow HR to be able to assess whether additional workforce is required to meet the demands of the organization or whether there is not enough work and revenue to justify the current workforce.

Consultation

Consultation is a process in which discussions take place to address issues. In consultation, questions can be asked and answered, solutions can be proposed, and different perspectives can be considered. There are numerous types of consultation that are specific to various fields, such as legal, financial, marketing, operational, and human resources. In some cases, it may be beneficial to hire an outside party to engage in a consultation; however, the process of consultation can occur internally with a group of employees at any level. Consultation can be an informal or formal process. Regardless of the formality, consultation is intended to engage others, solicit feedback, and achieve improved efficiency, transparency, engagement, and productivity.

Evaluating Business Challenges

HR professionals can be an excellent resource to assist leadership in understanding challenges that are internal to the organization. From low employee engagement and motivation to minimal innovation and productivity, HR professionals can engage leadership from a different angle to understand the best ways to address challenges. One challenge that many HR professionals face is recruitment and identifying the most qualified individual to hire for an essential position. This process can take time, which can present numerous issues to the organization and the team. Every day that goes by with this role unfilled creates more workload for the team and may cause missed opportunities. While HR can prioritize recruitment and work to reduce the time it takes to complete a recruitment process, the organization is also dependent on the current climate in the job market and the quality of candidates applying for the open position. Having open communication with hiring managers and leadership is important to ensure that everyone is aware of the steps being taken to hire the most qualified candidate in a timely manner. It is equally important to discuss the challenges when milestones in the recruitment process are not met or the timeframe needs to be extended.

Current and Future HR Challenges
An organization's dynamics continually change as employees leave either to retire or take another opportunity. Additionally, new employees join the organization and change the makeup of the team, bringing different skill sets to the table. A workforce is never stagnant, and HR professionals should work to understand the dynamics of the current and future workforce. If many employees are due to retire soon, the HR professional should ensure that vital knowledge is retained. It is important to understand that these positions will need to be filled, and the labor force may not be substantial enough to provide qualified candidates. Understanding current employee demographics can enable HR to plan for the future.

HR-Related Threats and Liabilities
HR professionals need to be aware of issues that could create a liability for the organization. HR should work to establish appropriate processes that ensure compliance with internal policies as well as state and federal laws and regulations. The organization could face extensive fines, audits, or even lawsuits if there are violations in areas such as the following:

- Payment of wages and overtime

- Leaves of absence, such as the Family Medical Leave Act (FMLA)
- Accommodation requests related to the Americans with Disabilities Act (ADA)
- Harassment, discrimination, or retaliation
- Safety and occupational needs, such as personal protective equipment
- Sexual harassment or gender harassment

This list is not exhaustive, but it gives an idea of the various issues that HR should be reviewing to ensure fair treatment of all employees. If HR identifies any liability, they must correct the issue immediately by making any necessary revisions (specifically related to wage and overtime issues) and initiating training for all relevant employees. All employees involved should understand the issue while working to correct the concerns and eliminate them moving forward.

HR Policies for Business Success
When an issue does arise, HR professionals should not only work to remedy the issue and ensure that it does not occur again, but also work to address any policy, program, or practice that may have inadvertently contributed to the issue. A lack of policies can also be a problem. If something is not addressed in a policy, employees may have to rely on their own or others' assumptions to make decisions. This is remedied by having a policy addressing expectations for behavior. Employees will understand what to do when faced with particular situations and can act appropriately. Training in these situations is also important to ensure that all employees understand the message and apply the information in the same manner.

Designing HR Solutions
When designing an HR solution, a thoughtful process should be worked through to ensure that the solution aligns with policies and procedures, contributes to a positive working environment, encourages employee engagement, and supports the goals of individuals, departments, and the organization. HR solutions are typically implemented as a response to a behavior, issue, or need; however, these solutions should still be based on the overall needs of the organization and not specifically for one employee.

Design thinking is a strategic process that HR professionals can use to navigate a new solution or process. Design thinking involves five steps:

1. **Empathize:** understanding the situation and ensuring that others know the commitment of all employees is vital to the success of any program or initiative

2. **Define:** establishing the issue both broadly and specifically

3. **Ideate:** brainstorming, which will enable innovation and creativity, as well as engagement and motivation

4. **Prototype:** finalizing a proposed recommendation to implement along with a timeframe to review, update, and modify

5. **Test:** implementing and evaluating the recommendations either in a pilot program or organization-wide

Design Thinking

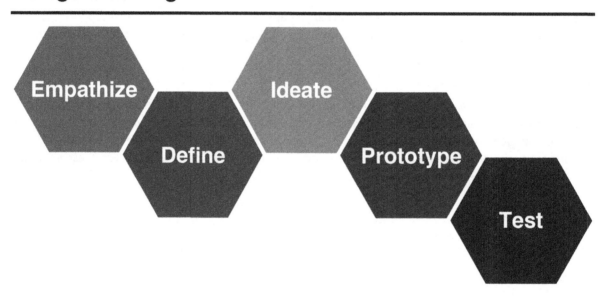

It is essential to ensure that employees understand that they are encouraged to provide feedback to increase the program's success.

Partnership with Stakeholders
Design thinking should be based on the philosophy of partnership with others to understand an issue and create a solution that resolves the issue while meeting the needs of the department and organization. Involving employees throughout the organization will encourage involvement and ultimately lead to a level of ownership for the new practice, allowing for a more successful implementation. When individuals feel heard, they are more likely to support the efforts and work to ensure success. Their enthusiasm gradually spreads throughout the organization as other employees also work to make the practices successful.

Providing Guidance to Non-HR Managers
In most cases, HR professionals provide guidance to managers who are outside of HR. Supervisors and managers throughout the organization often need guidance, advice, and training on HR-related matters such as payroll, timekeeping, safety practices, compliance, laws, ethics, and behavior. Additionally, it is imperative that HR train all supervisors and managers on the behavior and performance expected from all employees, as well as from the supervisors. HR should train supervisors in how to coach and counsel employees regarding performance, attendance, or other minor issues. When more complex issues arise or formal complaints are initiated, it is vital that supervisors understand when to involve HR in the matter so that it can be handled expeditiously per the policies and laws specific to that issue. An example of this would be a formal complaint of sexual harassment. Sexual harassment complaints should immediately be communicated to HR for investigation.

Using Clear Goals and Outcomes
Prior to initiating any HR solution, it is important to define what goals will be tracked to indicate success. This is important to know because it will allow HR professionals to confidently communicate the success of a program. Furthermore, if there are measurable items that can be identified with specific targets that indicate success, HR can use this data to show the accomplishment and importance of the HR initiatives. If the goals are not created prior to the solution being implemented, it will be harder to communicate the true effectiveness of the initiative.

Implementing and Supporting HR Solutions
When a new HR solution is introduced to the organization, it is important for all HR employees to support the new initiative and ensure that they are serving as role models to others. This behavior will help to create an environment in which other employees feel secure in voicing their support of the program or expressing concerns about it. Open and honest dialogue is one of the most important things that an HR professional can facilitate. This type of engagement is a direct response to the support shown by HR of any new programs or initiatives.

Implementing HR-Related Solutions
As indicated earlier, HR professionals often provide guidance to managers who are outside of the HR department. In many cases, this is the HR professional's sole responsibility. This is true for compliance and policy matters as well as HR initiatives that are implemented throughout the organization. A best practice is regular training on the initiatives so that managers learn directly from HR how the initiatives work, where to find information, and who to go to regarding questions. When training managers on initiatives, it is important to find common ground in how the initiatives can have a positive impact on their department and its goals. When managers understand how an initiative is aligned with their goals, they are more inclined to support the initiative and encourage their employees to do so as well.

Overcoming Obstacles with Partners
It is important for HR to understand the needs of each department and their unique challenges. When obstacles arise in relation to an HR initiative, discussions between the department and HR can be productive. HR does not have all the answers, and partnering with department managers and others gives HR access to department-specific knowledge while working through additional solutions to resolve specific needs. It is important to ensure that there is consistency and equity in an HR solution; however, there will be a need for flexibility to allow all employees to benefit from the solution.

Providing Follow-up
Once an initiative is implemented in an organization, it is important that HR follow up to respond to issues or questions, request feedback on possible changes, and continue to support the program. Annual

surveys are excellent tools that can be implemented to request feedback from employees on programs, initiatives, and new practices. Surveys can be anonymous to ensure that employees feel safe in providing feedback. When feedback is received, it is extremely important to let employees know that it was received and will be considered. When employees do not see at least a confirmation that the feedback was received, they will be less likely to provide feedback in the future. While some recommendations may not be implemented, it is still important to communicate with employees to ensure that they know their feedback was appreciated.

Ensuring Implementation of HR Solutions

As discussed earlier, **strategic alignment** is a philosophy that should be applied at all levels of the organization to ensure that every program, policy, practice, initiative, and solution aligns with the overall goals of the organization. HR solutions are intended to support employee performance, which ultimately supports the overall goals of the organization. When creating, implementing, and reviewing a solution, understanding this relationship is vital, as it will increase support from key stakeholders, leadership, and department managers from the very beginning. Additionally, when communicating about the status of an HR solution, it is important to convey how the solution is supporting the organization's goals. This will increase support of the solutions and may convince skeptical employees to become supporters.

Change Management

Change management is a complex and multi-step process that involves communication, innovation, engagement, creativity, planning, analysis, leadership support, and numerous resources and tools. The process of change management follows steps to ensure that any change is fully vetted and supported by the entire organization, including leadership at the top and the employees who will be responsible for implementing the changes on a daily basis. There are many ways to initiate change management, with some processes including numerous steps and approvals; however, a basic change management process consists of the following steps:

- 1. Identify the need for change.
- 2. Define the change and prepare for it.
- 3. Create, implement, and manage the change.
- 4. Evaluate, sustain, and reinforce the change.

These four steps have specific tasks and milestones that must be accomplished before moving on to the next step. Initiating a thoughtful change management process, one that encourages employee involvement during and after the process, will most likely result in a successful change to the organization.

Improving HR Policies

HR professionals should continually monitor programs, practices, and policies to ensure that they are appropriate and up to date, address organizational needs, protect employees, and provide guidance. Legislation is regularly updated, so it is important to ensure that all policies and practices strictly adhere to the current legislation. Not doing so can cause liability for the organization. Additionally, it is important to review practices on a regular basis to ensure that they still meet the need that they were created to address. Just like people, the workplace evolves. Therefore, policies and practices also need to evolve to stay relevant. For example, it would be completely inappropriate, and in some cases illegal, to have the same safety standards in place today as many years ago. Standards change and so should an organization's practices and policies to ensure the health, safety, and wellbeing of employees.

Promoting Buy-In

Before engaging in a process of change management, it is vital to solicit the buy-in of executive leadership, key stakeholders, and other key leadership. Without a top-down support of a program, practice, or behavior, employees will be less likely to support the concepts that are being initiated. If new communication techniques are implemented throughout the organization to increase efficiency and productivity, but the executive leaders' behaviors are not aligned with the new methods, the staff will be less motivated to engage in the practices. If there is a protocol about meeting time arrival, and yet those in leadership continually arrive late and leave early, employees will most likely not adhere to the protocol. A natural human tendency is to mimic the behaviors of those who are more established in the workplace. If leadership is not following the established protocols, then it is unreasonable to expect employees at lower levels of the organization to follow them.

Building Buy-In Among Staff

In addition to securing the buy-in from executive leadership for changes, it is equally important to secure the same level of buy-in from employees. From the employees who will be assisting with the change management process to the employees who will be expected to adhere to the new changes, garnering support will ensure success of the program. Furthermore, if the organization has union affiliations, consideration should be given to not only negotiate the required terms and conditions, but to also ensure union support of the new programs as well. Staff support can make the difference between a successful or unsuccessful new initiative.

Aligning HR Programs

Just as individuals' objectives should be strategically aligned with the organization's, HR programs should be strategically aligned with any initiative that is implemented. Working toward the same objectives should always be the goal. HR should also assess whether new policies should be implemented so that all initiatives have a level of support to be successful. This level of involvement, support, engagement, and understanding will promote a positive working environment and culture, lending to the success of individuals, teams, departments, and the organization as a whole.

Service Excellence

Customer interaction is the communication between an individual or organization and the party that is receiving a service from that individual or organization. Typically, the word "customer," is associated with a buyer, shopper, or consumer; however, the term is much broader. Citizens are the customers of a city mayor, children are customers of a school system, and employees and managers are customers of HR. In order to properly interact with a customer, it is necessary to first identify who the customer is and which service should be provided. Customers can be internal or external to the organization. Positive customer interactions rely on the relationship that is built and maintained in each point of contact.

Identifying Customer Needs

Understanding a customer's unique needs and providing the best customer service possible should always be the goal of the HR professional. The HR professional should treat each department manager and individual employee as a customer and work to resolve their issues. Frequent conversations with customers enable an HR professional to clearly understand their needs or morale issues. Additionally, it is a good practice to simply engage in conversation to establish a relationship of trust, openness, and honesty. The HR professional should also understand how the customers view the service. Tools such as 360-degree feedback surveys are an excellent way to collect this data.

Responding to Customer Requests

When a customer requests assistance, responding quickly and accurately should be a high priority. Sometimes the request may need to be researched or insight may need to be solicited from others, such as legal advice. If this is the case, HR professionals should respond immediately, saying that the request was received and that further review is required. Communication is the basis of a relationship with a customer and should be prioritized.

Meeting Customer Needs

Customer needs can be complicated, and they take up time and resources. When this happens, it is important to assess any risks or concerns early on to avoid a bigger issue in the future. Engaging with customers, understanding their current needs, and anticipating potential future needs result in a customer service relationship that supports the entire organization as well as individual employees. Being reactive when necessary and proactive when possible is an excellent philosophy to apply to customer service.

Managing Interactions with Vendors and Suppliers

External customers also require attention and communication to foster strong relationships. The HR professional may use vendors to provide such services as legal advice, recruitment tools, assessment tests, marketing materials, investigations, and training. Having strong working relationships with each external customer takes time and effort, but this will give the organization a strong reputation with the vendor and in the market. An organization's reputation should always be protected, nurtured, and enhanced with all external customers and internal customers. HR professionals should strive to maintain this reputation in the work done internally and externally.

Analytical Aptitude

Critical evaluation is the process of reviewing a process with an unbiased mindset. The process of critical evaluation leads to awareness of a problem, identification of resolutions, and evaluation of the proposed resolutions. One way to do critical evaluation is to ask broad questions that foster brainstorming. Asking the questions "Who?, What?, Where?, When?, Why?, and How?" will enable employees' discussions to take a deep dive into the issues that need to be addressed. Evaluating programs, policies, practices, initiatives, and solutions in this manner will lead to a more successful assessment, which will yield the best recommendations and solutions.

Data Advocate

Advocating for specific data to be used when making decisions is an important role, especially when the decisions concern employees. Changes that affect employees can have a major impact on an organization, positively or negatively. Understanding which data illuminates a situation enables the best decision to be made. Collecting and presenting this data should be an early part of the critical evaluation process as it will enable stakeholders to understand the issues that need to be addressed.

Using Data to Inform Business Decisions

HR professionals should work to provide accurate and up-to-date data to support changes and recommendations to policies, practices, and initiatives. As organizations continue to evolve, so should their practices. Data enables HR to provide an unbiased view of the issues that need to be discussed. If possible, quantitative data, or data that is measurable, should be used; however, often when working in HR and with people, qualitative data is more readily available. Any data that is being used to support the implementation of an initiative should be frequently updated to determine whether a re-assessment is necessary to realign the program.

Evidence-Based Decision-Making

In order for HR to stress the importance of data-driven decision making, HR must also address the challenges of working with data. The biggest challenges HR faces with gathering data that will drive decisions are that data can often be mixed or flawed, dependent on a platform or system, difficult to retrieve, or not the most recent information. When appropriate, HR should work with data that is accurate and easy to access.

Validating Policies

Validation of policies, programs, and practices should be the final step of critical evaluation. This should also be done in the planning phase to ensure that validation is understood and what the expectations are. Initially, the validation may need to occur on a frequent basis, such as quarterly, to ensure that needed milestones and targets are met. Later on, when stakeholders are confident in the success of the program, validation may be done bi-annually or annually. HR should also engage in random audits and validation of programs and policies to ensure they are still meeting the needs of the organization based on the data that is reviewed. HR will often do this as a response to reviewing performance measures or when a data dashboard indicates a need for change.

Identifying Decision Points

Whenever possible, HR should use data and evidence to make informed decisions. The decision may be about changes to the onboarding process due to a higher number of new employees leaving the organization within a year. If the employees leaving are in mid-career, HR may recommend an increase in training opportunities and internal promotions. The more evidence and supporting information that HR has to back up a recommendation, while also showing how this decision will affect the organization, the better the stakeholders will understand the decision and support the change.

Data Gathering

Data Gathering is the process of collecting and assembling information. This information can be used to support a current program, provide a recommendation for change, or identify a risk that needs to be addressed. It is important to note that accuracy and timeliness are the two most important factors during data gathering. Information that is flawed or out-of-date can provide support to the wrong recommendation, resulting in financial loss or worse. There are many methods of gathering data, but the four most common methods of data collection include:

- Observation
- Interview
- Surveys
- Database query

Observation involves watching and learning based on day-to-day operations and work performed. Time studies, performance standards, and standard operating procedures are developed from observation and can be instrumental tools in developing an efficient and effective workforce. The **interview** process involves a one-on-one discussion while asking a set of prescribed questions to gain insight into various subjects. Exit interviews, promotional hiring opportunities, and complaint procedures all utilize the interview process to gain specific and detailed information. **Surveys** offer employees an opportunity to provide feedback on either specific or broad issues. Employment satisfaction, workplace improvement, and benefits analysis can all be assessed through surveying employees' satisfaction or dissatisfaction. **Database Queries** are reports that are generated through a system that will provide data points at a certain time. The information stored in the database should be accessible through reporting within the database. Regardless of which data gathering method is used, it is important to ensure accuracy and timeliness.

Gathering employee engagement data through a survey is an excellent best practice to implement within an organization; however, it is just as important to ensure that the results are communicated and action is taken. The survey alone is not sufficient to implement positive change; communication and action are also necessary.

The first step to initiate an employee engagement survey is to plan the survey. Planning the survey involves determining the data that should be collected, how the data will be collected, setting up the method to analyze the information gathered, writing the questions, and setting up the survey. Once the survey is initiated, it cannot be changed. It is important to ensure that the survey is appropriate during the planning phase and will yield the necessary information.

The second step is to establish a communications plan. The communications plan should include who will be responsible for each message, what will be communicated, timeframes, and directions. The communications should be written for the employees who will be taking the survey. Ensuring that all messages are clear, concise, and specific is vital for all communications and will lead to better participation rates and responses. Additionally, employees should fully understand how the survey was planned and prepared, how the data will be analyzed and used, and that all responses will be kept confidential. While it may be necessary for employees to identify the department and area they work in, employees should be confident that their responses will not be used inappropriately.

The third step is to run the survey and allow employees adequate time to complete and turn in the survey. Employees should know how and where to ask for assistance, when and where surveys are to be submitted, and how to complete the survey. Surveys may be available online or in paper format, and employees should understand how to complete either format based on their comfort level with each. While the survey is being conducted, it is important to continue communicating with employees by sending reminders and requests to complete the survey.

Once the survey has been completed, the fourth step is to analyze the results. Computing a response rate is one of the first measurements that should be calculated, as this will show how effective the survey was in receiving feedback from employees. The response rate may even be a standard benchmark metric for the department to use to track success in the future. After calculating and analyzing the results, recommendations should be proposed to address key areas of improvement. It is also important to recognize areas that are successful. Focusing on the areas that are done well is just as important as focusing on the areas that need improvement.

Once the recommendations have been approved for implementation, it is vitally important to communicate the results and the action plans to employees. Employees need to know how the information will be used and what they can expect in the future. If there is ultimately no action or change implemented, employees will be less engaged in the future to participate and provide feedback. Conducting surveys frequently is a great way to determine if employees are responding to new programs. If an organization is taking proactive steps to communicate, implement change, and keep employees engaged and motivated, momentum and innovation will continue to grow and become part of the culture of the overall organization.

Data Collection, Research Methods, Benchmarks and HR Metrics

HR professionals should ensure that they are familiar with all types of data, collection methods, and sources. Each organization has unique needs and challenges, and it is important to understand how data can and should be used to address them. Data collection can be formal or informal depending on the data's intended purpose. If an organization is conducting an external compensation analysis to determine competitive wages, it is important to use a formal and structured data set. Companies often sell formal reports of this data. This ensures that the data was gathered using the same methodology so that comparisons can be made. If an organization is working to create a new telecommuting policy and wants to engage other organizations within the same market, an informal survey may provide the necessary information for this purpose.

Asking a series of questions to similar organizations would provide the data needed to make a recommendation. Regardless of the method, it is important to ensure that the data being used is accurate, timely, and appropriate. Each set of data may have a list of variables behind the number. Therefore, it is important to understand these variables so that appropriate and accurate comparisons can be made. An example of this would be a review of compensation to determine the competence of a current wage structure in the current market. Some organizations may report their total compensation, including company-paid benefits such as retirement plans, insurance benefits, or paid leave. It is important to have this knowledge so that the comparisons and subsequent recommendations can be made on an apples-to-apples basis, and to ensure that the information is valid.

Identifying Sources of the Most Relevant Data

Each organization has its own unique challenges, problems, and issues. HR professionals should work with the staff and management to identify the best solutions to solve problems. There is a plethora of information available on various platforms like books, seminars, webinars, presentations, social media, online forums, and more. Each platform presents unique ways of identifying issues and solutions. It is important to have a good understanding of each platform and the resource it can provide. Organizations in the state of California are now required to provide all employees with sexual harassment and ethics training. There are specific training requirements for employees at all levels, including elected officials within the government organizations.

Organizations must provide the same information and training to hundreds of employees on varying schedules and in different locations. Many organizations resort to online training platforms to provide web-based training to ensure that information is consistent and timely. HR professionals in these organizations are required to research the options available for this training, including the materials, training professionals, cost, and recurring availability for continuous training every other year. As the organization changes in needs or in technological capacity, HR professionals conduct this level of research on a continual basis. As HR professionals have an in-depth understanding of the organization and the employees, they can make recommendations of new technologies that will provide the best solutions for the needs and challenges specific to the organization.

Gathering Data Using Appropriate Methods to Inform and Monitor Organizational Solutions

As previously discussed, there are several methods to gather data. These methods include observation, interview, surveys, and database queries. Each method has its own pros and cons. It is important to evaluate them and determine which method to use in data gathering. Observation is an excellent method of data collection in determining how work is done and how efficient employees perform. Observation is neither opinion nor interpretation. It is a specific study based on the actual work. Interviews are excellent methods of data collection when investigating a complaint or conducting an exit interview. Interviews involve a structured and defined list of questions and are most often used in the recruitment process to determine the most qualified candidates for a position. Interviews do not usually have room for much variation in the discussion; they mostly stay on point with the prescribed questions. Surveys are an excellent method of data collection in getting an employee pulse regarding certain topics like leadership, communication, salary, benefits, training, and others. Conveniently, surveys can be conducted anonymously.

Many employees appreciate this element of anonymity as they can be honest without fear of repercussion. However, due to anonymity, it can be difficult to pinpoint specific concerns and address them. Database queries are excellent methods of data collection when the information required is simple data such salary, dates of hire, or job title. Database queries are static reports based on a point in time. They leave no room for variables such as opinions, culture, group dynamics, or supervisor relationships. If HR would like to learn more about employee needs in benefits and training, the survey method would be the best approach in collecting this information. With surveys, the anonymity of respondents and the urgency of responses are advantageous. Interviews can take a significant amount of time, so it is best to use a survey in this case.

Scanning External Sources for Relevant Data
Organizations will always source internal data to review the current status of projects, finances, and other metrics important to their overall success. However, it is also important to source external data to ensure that a holistic view of the organization is considered. External data is vital in measuring success against competitors. Furthermore, external data can provide new insights and fresh perspectives. However, it can sometimes be difficult to understand as it is collected, assembled, and reviewed by other parties who have different perspectives and insights. These individuals may simply collect the data and present it in a format for others to review and assess. It is important to know more about the external source of the data in order to assess the relevance of the information to the organization. Since many external sources charge a fee for access to information, it is important to have this understanding prior to purchasing the information. Some examples of this type of data are compensation data and total rewards information. Several organizations collect data from organizations across manifold industries for various positions. The information is then sorted several ways, broken down into different items, and presented in a binder or electronic file.

While having such information as this can be excellent for benchmarking, it is important to realize that there is no guarantee that similar industries or positions will be presented in the report. Additionally, if an organization has specific questions or needs, the answers may not be found in a report like this because data is usually presented without open-ended commentary. There is a large amount of data that can be mined through methods like searching online, reviewing publications and journals, and surveying other agencies. The internet has become one of the largest resources available to organizations. Many private companies and government agencies have a dedicated website that communicates information about the products and services available, as well as their goals as an organization. Some include financial reports, achievements, corporate responsibility efforts, and more. It is important to understand that any information sourced online should be thoroughly vetted to ensure accuracy. Professional organizations often have a subscription membership connected to their online websites. While the information should still be scrutinized and reviewed prior to being used for analysis, there is generally a higher level of accuracy in the information gained through these paid websites.

Benchmarking HR Initiatives and Outcomes Against Relevant Comparison Groups
Each organization has specific and measured metrics and initiatives that relate to Human Resources. It can be complicated to compare this data against other organizations as each agency calculates metrics differently, has unique and specific initiatives, and in some cases, may not report this information. Public

agencies often find this information more easily accessible as state laws require most data to be transparent and reported on public websites. The most common HR metrics are:

- Attrition rates or turnover
- Training rates
- Productivity
- Workforce demographics
- Engagement
- Recruitment, including days to hire

Each metric is important to review and understand so that appropriate measures and initiatives can be implemented to affect improvement. If an organization is experiencing high turnover, it is important to understand why. Is the workforce naturally leaving the organization due to retirement? Are employees leaving for promotions or higher wages somewhere else? Implementing a robust exit interview process will help an organization find out why employees are leaving and identify changes that can be made to retain the workforce. Many organizations adhere to a diversity and inclusion policy that includes the recruitment of diverse employees. Analyzing the workforce demographics will enable HR professionals to determine if additional measures need to be taken regarding recruitment and attracting a diverse, qualified candidate pool for positions within the organization.

Data Analysis

Data Analysis is the process of collecting, reviewing, analyzing, and presenting information for the purposes of meaningful discussion and proposed recommendations. In most circumstances, there is a problem or question that needs to be addressed. When this happens, decision makers want to look at data to determine what should be done. Once the problem has been identified, the next step is to determine the data that should be collected and how. Once the data has been gathered, it is important to review the pieces of information so that questions can be asked about outliers or anomalies that appear in the data.

Cleaning, or scrubbing, the data is important to ensure that the analysis is accurate. Once the data has been verified to be thoroughly accurate, analyzing the information includes looking for trends, themes, or concerns that present themselves in the data. Assembling the information and presenting the details is the final step of data analysis. A common way to present data is to tell a story, first starting with the problem, then describing the current state that the data presents. Finally, the data should naturally suggest a future state and recommendations that are supported by the information. Recommendations that are derived based on data and information are more likely to be approved and implemented.

Maintaining Working Knowledge of Statistics and Measurement Concepts
HR professionals should understand how to calculate metrics and data points such as average pay, median pay, percentage of degreed workforce, percentage of benefits to total wages, turnover rate, employee satisfaction, and other important statistics that measure HR performance. More importantly, HR professionals should have a full understanding of how this information affects the organization whether positively or negatively. Microsoft Excel is an excellent tool to calculate metrics such as averages, medians, and percentages. It is important to remember that the measurements calculated are only as good as the data that is used. Bad data in equates to bad data out. Having a dashboard of statistics and data is excellent, but the narrative of what this information means is the most important piece.

This data drives decisions and recommendations to affect change and improve the organization. To achieve such improvement, it is important that the organization understand the importance of low median compensation over an actual raw number. Another example of this would be turnover rate calculation. Having a low or high turnover rate is simply a piece of data that needs to be supported by the information behind that turnover rate. Sometimes, a low turnover rate may not necessarily reflect positively on the organization, just as a high turnover rate may not reflect negatively on them. It is important to know what is behind the actual number and be prepared to address the reason for the data.

The **scientific method** is a formal method of primary research that can be used to solve HR problems. The steps in the scientific method, along with a corresponding example, are listed below.

1. Problem analysis → Turnover is too high.

2. Hypothesis formulation → The turnover rate is higher with employees who have been at the company for less than one year.

3. Experimental design → HR can use a correlation analysis of length of employment and turnover data to determine if the hypothesis is confirmed.

4. Data collection → HR will review employee files and exit interview notes to correlate the hire and exit dates of employees.

5. Data analysis → HR will say if the correlation analysis verifies the hypothesis. The analysis will prove or disprove the hypothesis. HR personnel may also uncover other issues that contributed to the problem during the process detailed above, which can be helpful to the company moving forward.

Quantitative analysis is based on statistics and facts. The following are three measures of central tendency often used in data analysis.

- **Mean**: The mean is calculated by taking the sum of the values in a data set and dividing that total by the number of values in the set. The mean for the set of numbers below is $60 \div 8 = 7.5$.

- **Median**: The median is calculated by placing the values in a data set in sequential order and selecting the value that falls directly in the middle. If there is an even number of data points (which means that no value falls directly in the middle), the median is found by taking the average of the two numbers that fall in the middle. The median for the set of numbers below is $(6 + 9) \div 2 = 7.5$.

- **Mode**: The mode is determined by finding the number that occurs the most frequently in a data set. The mode for the set of numbers below is 9.

Number Set: {1,3,6,9,12,15,9,5}

Identifying Potentially Misleading or Flawed Data
Before making conclusions such as trends, concerns, or achievements based on a data, it is important to ensure that the data used is accurate, complete, and appropriately used. Bad data can lead to bad decisions. Similarly, misleading data can also lead to bad decisions. Misleading data can be done on purpose or accidently. Either way, data should be transparent, clear, accurate, and timely when used in making decisions. Sometimes, data is incorrect simply due to a technology-related issue. Other times, data is incorrect due to an outlying piece of information that skews the conclusions. When calculating percentages, averages, or other high-level data point, HR should strive to identify these outliers so that they can be addressed, or even removed from the data set if necessary. It is also important to remember

that there should be a narrative that accompanies any manual changes to the data to ensure transparency and open lines of communication.

Conducting Analyses to Identify Best Practices
Evidence-Based Practice (EBP) is the objective, fair, balanced, and responsible use of current data and information to propose changes to policy, practices, and initiatives that will improve the organization at all levels. HR should implement EBP in all aspects of the HR function. HR is typically responsible for numerous programs, policies, and initiatives for employees. It is critical that HR audits and reviews these programs to ensure effectivity and provide employees with the necessary resources. Applying the EBP method to analyze and evaluate these initiatives will provide valid and unbiased results relating to the initiative's success. There are five basic steps when utilizing the EBP process:

1. Determining the problem or question
2. Determining the best data or information to use in answering the problem
3. Reviewing and evaluating the data and information
4. Applying the data to the problem to determine possible solutions
5. Evaluating and applying the best solution to resolve the problem

Utilizing this method provides an opportunity to be unbiased. It allows the data to provide a path to determine the necessary solutions and changes to address identified and unidentified challenges within an organization.

Maintaining Objectivity When Interpreting Data
When reviewing and analyzing data, it is critically important to ensure that there is no bias. Sometimes this bias can occur unintentionally based on background, historical knowledge, or assumptions. There are steps that can be taken to maintain objectivity and remove intentional or unintentional bias from this process. First, engage a team to review the data. Having multiple perspectives to analyze the information can help eliminate assumptions and provide various views. Second, conduct discussions with relevant individuals and ask their perspectives of the results. Third, verify the information by looking at available data sources. Fourth, address any outliers in the data, and provide explanations for these specific data pieces. Finally, review the results with the team and conduct a discussion about the results. By following these steps, HR professionals can eliminate bias and assumptions in reviewing data.

Evidence-Based Decision-Making
Once data have been collected and analyzed, the results should be used to inform policies, procedures, and decisions for maximum effectiveness. HR professionals should be able to communicate findings from data analysis to other leaders in the organization and discuss their implications or the strategic direction and goals of the HR department and company at large.

Reporting Key Findings
An excellent way to keep senior leadership involved in the current state of HR and the employees is to provide performance measures and data on a regular basis. In addition to providing the raw data, HR professionals should also analyze trends and changes in the data, while indicating potential reasons for the variance. Communicating this information could then lead to additional conversations to address possible underlying issues. The evidence-based decision-making process would then be initiated to analyze the data, assess the cause for the changes, and provide recommendations to address the issues before a larger and potentially more complex issue arises.

Using Research to Evaluate Different Courses of Action

Before making a final decision on a recommended course of action, the HR professional should identify the various options for addressing the issue. Each option should be fully vetted with an assessment of possible outcomes, including unintended consequences, positive results, and challenges. Having an understanding at this level will enable the decision maker to select the option that will cause the least amount of disruption or negative consequences to the organization. An excellent way to assess this information is to look at other programs or practices that mirror the current recommendations and view the outcomes of these changes. Understanding how employees have reacted to similar changes in the past will be an excellent indicator of possible future reactions.

Applying Data-Driven Knowledge

Some data may be applicable to multiple situations. Even if data points were gathered and analyzed for one initiative, it may be appropriate to reuse them as the foundation for another. Recycling data to support numerous projects is an element of good business, and it should be a goal to minimize workload and save time and effort. When a strategic process is used to define an issue and then gather, analyze, and apply evidence needed for the decision, it is in the organization's best interest to try to use this same evidence, when appropriate, to support other decisions. Not only does this make sense from a resource standpoint, but decisions will then be aligned with each other.

Ensuring HR Policies Reflect Findings and Best Practices

HR professionals should work to incorporate data from both internal and external sources. This ensures that an organization's decisions appear competitive and equitable to outside agencies and the marketplace. This will have many benefits, such as increased employee retention and higher morale and satisfaction. Decisions should be based on the data, information, research, and analysis conducted while also working to support the organization's overarching goals. Strategic alignment should always be the goal of any change or decision. Evidence-based decision-making works to accomplish this goal by examining data in a clear and unbiased way to initiate change that resolves the issue.

Examining HR Policies in Light of Data

Auditing HR programs and policies should be a common practice to ensure that they are meeting the needs of the organization and employees. When the HR professional reviews data, particular programs and policies may stand out as needing to be audited outside of a standard timeframe. When this occurs, it is important to respond to the need immediately to eliminate any risks or liabilities to the organization and employees. While no changes may be necessary, reviewing the situation in light of the available information is important. This allows employees to see that HR takes matters seriously. Additionally, if there is a concern in the future that may relate to this specific policy or program, evidence can be furnished that an audit was conducted, and the corresponding results indicated no change was needed.

Practice Quiz

1. What process is defined as the ability to identify, understand, and resolve situations that will result in positive outcomes?
    a. Critical evaluation
    b. Situational awareness
    c. Customer interaction
    d. Business acumen

2. Ziad is working on developing a new wellness program to be rolled out to the organization by the end of the year. He is hopeful that the leadership team will approve the new program and wants to ensure that the presentation communicates the necessary and important details needed. He has included the cost of the program, employee feedback, timelines, and industry trends. What else should he ensure is included to maximize the likelihood of the program being approved?
    a. Screenshots of the website platform and draft forms provided
    b. More statements from employees indicating their personal feelings about the program
    c. Quantitative and measured data that show the return of investment in a cost-benefit analysis
    d. Drafts of policies, manuals, training programs, and employee communications

3. Evidence-based decision-making relies on the combination of three specific things. Which of the following is NOT one of these?
    a. Organizational demographics and needs
    b. Available resources
    c. Best available evidence
    d. Root cause of issue

4. What is the biggest strategic benefit of using the same evidence or data for multiple decisions?
    a. Decisions will align with each other while also supporting each other.
    b. It is easier and reduces the time to research and compile data.
    c. Data should never be recycled or reused, and new evidence should be found for each decision.
    d. Leadership is more likely to approve because they approved previous programs with this data.

5. Making decisions that ensure the organization is competitive and equitable to other agencies will have many positive impacts. Which of the following is one of those benefits?
    a. Higher employee attrition
    b. Higher employee retention
    c. Lower employee satisfaction
    d. Lower employee morale

Answer Explanations

1. D: Business acumen is the ability to identify, understand, and resolve situations that will result in positive outcomes. Business acumen is often referred to as business savvy or business sense. Choice *A* is incorrect because critical evaluation is the process that reviews, analyzes, and audits a program or initiative. Critical evaluation is conducted with a fair, balanced, and unbiased mindset. Choice *B* is incorrect because situational awareness is a concept that refers to having complete attentiveness to an individual's circumstances. Choice *C* is incorrect because customer interaction is the communication between an individual and a party that is receiving services.

2. C: Ziad should ensure that quantitative and measured data are included in his presentation to leadership. The leadership team should have knowledge of the return of investment in a cost-benefit analysis when deciding to approve a program and allocate funds to it. Choice *A* is incorrect because while screenshots of the sample platform may be nice to have, pictures of a website will not be the data that drives a decision. Choice *B* is incorrect because employee feedback has already been included, and this information is qualitative and based on personal feelings. Again, leadership will need more than emotional statements to approve a new program and funding. Choice *D* is incorrect because it is too early in the process to create drafts of documents such as policies and employee communications. The data and details such as costs and benefits need to be presented to ensure that the program is approved.

3. D: Evidence-based decision-making relies on three specific things, and the root cause of an issue is not one of them. The root cause of an issue may determine that a new decision should be considered and implemented, but it may not necessarily be appropriate information to use depending on the issue. Choices *A*, *B*, and *C* are incorrect because they are the three tenets that evidence-based decision-making relies upon. The organizational demographics and needs, available resources, and the best available evidence are required to make the best decisions.

4. A: The biggest strategic benefit of using the same evidence or data for multiple decisions is that these decisions will align with each other. These decisions will also support each other as they share the same foundation of data. Choice *B* is inaccurate because while it is true that reusing data is easier and takes less time, it is not necessarily a strategic benefit. Choice *C* is inaccurate as data should be recycled or reused as appropriate. Sometimes new evidence is not available, so as long as the data is appropriate, it should be used. Choice *D* is inaccurate because leadership will assess each program on its own merits, costs, benefits, and resources needed. Leadership will not just give a stamp of approval because the same data was used for a previously approved project.

5. B: Higher employee retention is a positive benefit that is seen when an organization makes decisions that maintain a competitive and equitable edge with other agencies. Employees staying longer with the organization and not leaving for a better opportunity defines higher employee retention. Choice *A* is not correct because higher employee attrition means that more employees are leaving, which is not a positive impact. Choice *C* is not correct because employees will actually have a higher satisfaction rate with the organization. Choice *D* is not correct because employees will have a higher morale due to the good decisions that are being made.

Functional Areas

People Knowledge

HR Strategy

A company's strategic planning process is comprised of the following four steps:

1. **Strategy Formulation:** During this first step of the strategic planning process, a company focuses on the business it is in and develops its vision statement, mission statement, and values accordingly. Plans are also made for how best to communicate the company's mission and when it may be necessary to change the company's mission or adjust its strategy. This first step can be summed up by identifying where a company currently is and defining where it wants to be in the future and how it can arrive at that place.

2. **Strategy Development:** Environmental scanning and a SWOT (Strengths, Weaknesses, Opportunities, Threats) analysis are performed during this step of the strategic planning process (both of which will be described in greater detail). Additionally, long-range plans are established that will set the company's direction for the next three to five years. This second step can be summed up by collecting information that is both internal and external to the company, along with developing alternative strategies.

3. **Strategy Implementation:** During this step of the strategic planning process, short-range plans are created that will set the company's direction for the next six to twelve months. Additionally, there is a focus on motivating employees by developing action plans and allocating the necessary resources in order to achieve objectives (e.g., human, financial, and technological). This step can be summed up by implementing a plan for the strategy that is chosen.

4. **Strategy Evaluation:** During this last step of the strategic planning process, a company agrees to continue reviewing an implemented strategy at specific intervals by performing a SWOT analysis and taking note of any changes. In the event of changes, corrective action may be necessary. This step can be summed up by evaluating the success of the implemented strategy while continuing to monitor it and make any necessary tweaks.

Using Systems Thinking to Understand How the Organization Operates

Peter Senge was the founder of the Society of Organizational Learning and continues to serve as a senior lecturer at the MIT Sloan School of Management. He is a proponent of **systems thinking**, where managers spend more time focusing on the big picture than on individual actions, since actions and consequences are correlated. In this same manner, Peter Senge believes organizations should seek out and embrace change versus waiting and responding to changes in crisis mode.

Informing Business Decisions

Strategic planning is dependent on the knowledge and awareness of the goals and objectives for both the organization and the HR department. Ensuring alignment between the organization and HR is vital to being successful at every level within an organization. Strategic alignment of goals and objectives sets up success for individual employees, teams, departments, and the organization. This strategy also allows for better decision making for the business, which includes policy changes, practice updates, and possible reevaluation and redesign of the current state. Business decisions that are strategically implemented using this information will have a higher likelihood of being successful.

Developing and Implementing an Action Plan

In order for the HR department—or any department—to be successful in accomplishing their goals, objectives, and projects, HR leadership must develop an action plan. Action plans can be simple and high-level or complex and detailed. Regardless of the depth of detail included in an action plan, the items identified in the plan should be aligned with the SMART methodology to ensure that success can be accurately defined and described. The **SMART** methodology requires that all objectives be specific, measurable, achievable, realistic, and time-targeted. Without these elements, it is more difficult to know when an objective has been successfully achieved.

Additionally, it is more difficult to determine where improvements or course corrections are needed if the objective is not on track. Action plans are excellent tools that should be implemented at both the departmental and individual levels. Department action plans outline the course and path that will be taken by the entire department and all employees to achieve specific items. Individual action plans outline the course and path that will be taken by a single employee to achieve the specific items identified in the department action plan. Individual action plans can also be used to chart out an employee's growth, development, and potential career path for the future by identifying skills, gaps, and opportunities.

Using Benchmarks, Metrics, and Trends to Understand the Organization's Market Position

Achieving a competitive advantage can be done by identifying and analyzing factors that will allow an organization to distinguish their product or service from the competition. Human Resources should engage in this process regarding the employment experience and workforce planning in order to differentiate the organization from the competition. Strategically defining and maintaining the organization as an employer of choice allows for attracting and recruiting the best candidates, retaining top talent, and ensuring the success of the organization through the workforce. When assessing the competition from an HR perspective, it is important to have a holistic understanding of the organization. From the products and services offered to the total rewards provided, including compensation and benefits, HR should assess the competition and work to make enhancements as necessary to attract and maintain an exceptional workforce. This may include providing employees with a better retirement system, increasing compensation, or allowing for telecommuting and alternate work schedules. Each employee will value something different. Human Resources can truly make an impact by being aware of and understanding what motivates employees. In doing so, the organization will be seen as a leader in the market.

Informing HR Leadership of Opportunities to Align HR's Strategy with the Organization's

Organizations often employ practices to solicit feedback and ideas from employees. Being engaged with the workforce, while allowing opportunities to provide insight into new programs or practices, is vital to the evolution of the organization. From suggestion boxes to employee surveys, the Human Resources department is in a unique position to have insights into what employees want, need, or value. When new ideas for programs or practices are discovered, it is important to communicate them to leadership for further discussion, if necessary, and the idea should be fully investigated for possible implementation. This same philosophy should apply to previously considered ideas or even ideas that were previously implemented but found to be unsuccessful. Timing is vital to the success of a new initiative, as is leadership commitment and communication. It is important to communicate effectively when presenting these new ideas to leadership for consideration. Effective communication can be accomplished by following the 7 C's:

- Clear
- Concise
- Correct
- Complete
- Considerate
- Concrete
- Courteous

Communications are most effective when they are simple, specific, accurate, thorough, thoughtful, tangible, and respectful. When new ideas are presented to leadership with these elements in mind, there is a much higher likelihood of approval than when information is incomplete or vague.

Providing HR Leadership Information

Timeliness and accuracy are two of the most important factors when presenting information that will be used for making decisions. Data that is outdated and inaccurate can result in decisions that are not the best or most appropriate given the reality of the current circumstances. Decisions could be made that do not adequately resolve issues or may even create more issues. It is equally important to ensure that information is regularly updated when new insights are gained. This will allow for adjustments to projects or decisions that accurately reflect the new circumstances. Wyatt Earp, a deputy marshal in the early 1900s, stated "fast is fine, but accuracy is everything." This quote holds true when HR professionals are delivering data and information to leadership when making decisions.

Talent Acquisition

Talent acquisition is the strategic process of hiring individuals with specific skills and abilities that will align with the organization's goals. It includes not only filling an open position but also taking a holistic view of the workforce needs, both current and future. Talent acquisition begins with identifying the need, specifically the vacant position and the skills needed within that department. Reviewing the position requirements, including the essential functions, is critical to ensure that the role and responsibilities are properly communicated to prospective employees. Next is the actual recruitment process that includes advertising the position on job boards, websites, career fairs, or hiring an external recruiter. **Recruitment** is the tactical process of filling a vacancy.

The recruitment step includes the sourcing of candidates that are interested in joining the organization and being considered for the particular position. After the recruitment process comes the selection phase in which resumes are screened, phone screens are scheduled, and on-site interviews take place. Once the most qualified candidate is identified and selected by the hiring managers, the offer is extended, any negotiations take place, and the background checks are completed. Finally, the new employee is onboarded by the Human Resources department and trained in the fundamentals of the organization. **Onboarding** includes all of the appropriate new hire paperwork, benefits orientations, policy distribution, and required training. Talent acquisition is the entire process from when a vacancy occurs to the hiring of a new employee. Talent acquisition then looks beyond the initial hiring to how the organization can benefit from the employees' skills in the future.

Understanding the Talent Needs of the Organization

The current market situation and the available talent pool are constantly evolving. Organizations must keep themselves informed about trends in several markets: industry, city, state, and country. Depending on the needs of the organization, it may be necessary to expand recruitment efforts into new markets. Market expansion assists by providing a larger applicant pool that is also more diverse. Locating qualified candidates is a common concern for any organization. HR professionals can assist with this issue by understanding the immediate surrounding market as well as other opportune markets.

Having knowledge of various educational programs, both collegiate and skilled trade, professional associations, and networking affiliations, allows recruiters to tap into the most appropriate areas to locate potential candidates. Establishing partnerships with these groups can allow for recruiters to have immediate insight into potential talent pipelines that can directly feed the organization's applicant pools. Another resource to take advantage of is talent pool reports provided by agencies such as LinkedIn. These reports show the supply and demand of the prospective employees an organization is looking for and the demographics of these individuals.

One current area of concern is the talent pools for fields related to science, technology, engineering, and math (STEM). Efforts have been made to increase the number of women studying STEM fields and to increase the opportunities for these women. From specific marketing to government funding, concerted efforts are being made to increase participation in these fields. The future result will be more qualified applicants to hire in related positions. Another area of concern is the talent pools for skilled trades such as carpentry, machinery, and maintenance related fields including construction, electrical, plumbing, and heating and cooling. The shortage of skilled trade workers across the country is becoming more demanding as current workers are moving closer to retirement. Many organizations hiring skilled trade professionals are offering apprenticeship programs to new employees who have little to no experience. By offering incentives such as in-house training, professional development, career paths, and competitive wages and benefits, many organizations are meeting their recruitment needs through these efforts.

Human Resources professionals can work with leadership to understand the organization's skill shortages and align those with the current labor surpluses. Using the same supply and demand principles as economics, organizations can work to fill the recruitment gaps and meet needs based on the current and potential available workforce. This is becoming harder to do in today's marketplace, but it is possible. The first step is to look at the incentives that encourage potential candidates to consider working in certain fields. Incentives such as free training to learn a specific trade, sign-on bonuses, career advancement within a certain time frame, or educational reimbursements may entice an individual to consider a particular career. In some cases, the more creative the offer, the more potential applicants will submit their credentials for consideration. By bringing in new employees with little to no experience, organizations can develop these individuals professionally then have experienced candidates in the pipeline to promote to new opportunities.

In order to fully understand prospective applicants and their needs, it is critical that Human Resources professionals and hiring managers be aware of generational differences in the talent pool. Many organizations have three to four generations working as employees at any given time, and each generation has different values, goals, motivators, and needs. Understanding this enables recruiters to gain a better understanding of how to incentivize individuals to consider some of the hard-to-fill positions as possible career choices.

In general, the generations have distinct values and objectives. Baby boomers—individuals born between 1946 and 1964—value dedication, one-on-one time, and working in teams, and they are focused on the health and wellness of their families. Generation Xers—those born between 1965 and 1980—value work/life balance, independence, flexibility, experiences, and a global perspective. Generation Yers, or millennials—individuals born between 1981 and 2000—value constant feedback, recognition, personal fulfillment, fun, happiness, advanced technology, and diversity. Generation Zers—those born after 2000—value equality, activism, collaboration, sustainability, and flexibility.

By looking at the needs of the organization and aligning them with the values of each generational dynamic, human resource professionals can create a plan to market and promote the available opportunities to each group of potential applicants. When marketing these opportunities, it is necessary to ensure multiple communication platforms. Generation Xers and Generation Zers will need different information. Organizations should adapt, using various communication methods to ensure that employees in each demographic receive the information they need. While a recruitment flyer posted to the corporate website may be the best way to communicate with a Generation X candidate, it may not be the best method for a Generation Z candidate. Posting information on social media platforms such as Twitter or Instagram may be a better method for Generation Z candidates.

The employment market will constantly evolve and change. While there is no way to know for sure how this will directly affect the talent pool, Human Resources professionals can stay informed about the changing market and attempt to update recruitment plans to address this. Some of these changes may not result in a marked improvement in sourcing candidates; however, it is beneficial to continue to evolve recruitment strategies so that organizations can stay informed and show a willingness to adapt. Social media is a great example; recruitment trends when using social media platforms have changed substantially in the past few years. Research has shown that in 2011, 56% of organizations used social media for recruiting; in 2015, this number increased to almost 90%. Organizations that evolve with current trends stay relevant with both passive and active job seekers and are more likely to be seen as potential employers. This is one way for an organization to maintain an active role in the talent pool from which they are sourcing candidates.

Using a Variety of Talent Sources and Recruiting Methods

Recruitment uses sourcing methods to generate a robust, qualified candidate pool. There are numerous ways to source candidates, and some methods may work better for particular positions or markets. Human Resources professionals should understand the positions they are recruiting for and how best to find candidates. Specialized positions in information technology may require postings on a niche IT-focused job board. Positions in maintenance and operations may need online postings in the local newspaper or on Craigslist.com. Each position should be reviewed before advertising so that an appropriate sourcing method can be established to ensure the best possible candidate pool. A sourcing method helps to limit costs and decrease the time needed to build a qualified candidate pool.

Job boards and social media are among the most common sourcing techniques. Candidates do not generally visit individual company websites to see if there is a hiring opportunity. There are job boards on many social media platforms, and many organizations use targeted advertising on particular sites to appeal to prospective candidates. From LinkedIn to Indeed, job boards can provide a large audience for job opportunities. Organizations also have corporate accounts on Twitter, Facebook, Instagram, and other social media platforms. Having an inviting corporate profile and a list of open job opportunities on a social media platform can increase the number of applicants.

Some organizations use an internal program for employee referrals. By entrusting the workforce with referring individuals for open positions, organizations let employees play a part in the hiring initiative. Many programs reward the referring employee with an initial bonus if their referred candidate is hired and then a secondary bonus if their referred candidate remains employed after a certain period of time. This encourages employees to engage with their network and assist in the recruitment process by being ambassadors and champions of the organization. Current employees who are working in the culture and climate of the organization can be the best recruiters.

Some positions are harder to fill than others, and in these cases, an executive recruiter may be the most appropriate sourcing option. Executive recruiters can specialize in certain fields, markets, or levels such as executive leadership. While contracting with a recruiter can be an increased cost, it can also serve to fill a position with the best, most qualified candidate, one who otherwise would not be sourced. Executive recruiters can tap into established networks and passive job seekers, sometimes yielding a candidate pool that an organization would otherwise not be aware of.

Regardless of the sourcing methods used, organizations must ensure that recruitment is fair and equitable, affording all qualified candidates the same opportunity to be considered for an open position. By initiating multiple sourcing methods to search for candidates, an organization can increase its candidate pool.

Using Technology to Recruit Employees

Applicant tracking systems (ATSs) are software applications that manage an organization's recruitment processes. These applications can track various components of the recruitment process, including hiring requests submitted, applications received, interviews scheduled, and offers extended. ATS applications also provide various reports specific to tracking recruitment information. Most organizations utilize an ATS to handle applications, resumes, and candidate data; however, some organizations may use a simple tool such as Microsoft Excel® or Access® to create a customized database. Some companies receive a large number of applications on a daily basis, and an ATS application can provide the capability to manage these applications efficiently. The ATS can perform initial screenings, separate qualified and unqualified candidates, and screen out candidates that do not have the required skill sets.

An ATS provides functionality in multiple areas such as applicant workflow, candidate communications, interview management, skills assessments and tests, background checks, and on-boarding. Human Resources professionals manage the ATS for the organization, and, through the ATS, provide information specific to the recruitment process. Reports can include information such as how long it takes to fill a position from the initial request to the date of hire, the number of applications received, and the number of qualified candidates for each position. This information can assist in making decisions for future recruitments.

While most ATS applications are customized, the basic structure should incorporate the following:

- Search engine optimization
- Job posting distribution and resume collection
- Advanced candidate search
- Employee referral management
- Integration capabilities
- Robust candidate relationship management
- Advanced reporting and analytics

The ATS application should provide an organization with the specific tools required for their recruitment needs. Most ATS applications can be integrated into an organization's existing website. An example of a widely used ATS that is integrated into corporate websites is Taleo. Taleo offers the ability for the organization to incorporate all recruitment elements into the branding and culture of the organization. Once an organization has determined a recruitment need, the request, often referred to as a **requisition**, is submitted by the hiring department. The requisition is approved and the job posting is created and managed directly within the ATS.

Job postings should include the complete description of work, including the scope, roles, responsibilities, examples of work, and supervisory duties. Additionally, the job posting should indicate required qualifications, preferred qualifications, educational requirements, and previous experience necessary to be considered for the position. Timeframes should be clearly communicated on the job description so that candidates understand when the posting will close. The ATS will publish the job description to the corporate website, job boards and other organizations as structured within the ATS platform.

Organizations can also add supplemental questions for candidates to answer as part of the application process. Candidates who are interested in submitting an application are guided through a structured, customized, electronic process in which they can attach additional documentation or other information to be considered. After applications have been submitted, the ATS can be programmed to send out standard communications, such as receipt of the application and next steps. Once the application window has been closed, the ATS can then screen the applications to determine which candidates meet the qualifications and which do not. Their status can then be updated in the ATS, and, again, standard communications can be sent to candidates indicating the status of their application. Throughout all the steps of the interview process, the ATS can facilitate screening and communication.

Organizations should implement an ATS that maximizes the recruitment process for the hiring managers, leadership, recruiters, and candidates. ATS applications that provide robust and expansive services offer benefits on a financial, operational, strategic, and technical level.

Financial benefits can include increases in productivity, elimination of manual processes, and freeing up more time to focus on projects that improve profitability and achieving goals. Additionally, positions can typically be filled in less time, which can improve employee morale, customer service, and overall satisfaction. Organizations can see substantial costs when recruiting for and filling an open position. Costs, such as overtime to fill the opening, can add up to much more than anticipated. An effective ATS can assist in decreasing these costs by streamlining the process and reducing the time needed to fill an open position.

Operational benefits can include having a standardized and automated recruitment process, providing advanced reports and statistics, and identifying continuous improvement opportunities. By having a standardized process, organizations implement the same hiring practices across all positions. This is highly recommended by the Equal Employment Opportunity Commission (EEOC) and can dramatically reduce the risk of discrimination in hiring.

Strategic benefits can include improved compliance with regulations, having access to larger, more diverse, and better qualified candidate pools, which results in highly qualified new hires. This, in turn, provides an excellent candidate recruitment experience and increases the employment brand with prospective employees.

Technical benefits can include minimizing information technology support when using a web-based system, as well as affording unlimited data storage to maintain the records. Additionally, by maximizing the technical capabilities of the ATS application, organizations may see opportunities to re-purpose resources that are now available.

An effective ATS can also enhance the candidate experience throughout the recruitment process, potentially resulting in an immediate effect on the new employee and a commitment to the organization. **Candidate experience** refers to the feelings, behaviors, and attitudes a job candidate faces when they interact with a hiring manager and organization during the recruitment process. Candidate experience begins with the organization's webpage, job description, and initial information available to prospective employees.

Studies show that candidate experience is vital to an organization's recruitment efforts. Over 90% of candidates are more likely to apply for future positions if they have a positive candidate experience. Almost 100% of candidates who had a positive recruitment experience would refer others to apply for employment. Almost 90% of candidates with a positive recruitment experience would purchase the products manufactured or sold by the organization. Over 50% of candidates with a positive experience would communicate with their social networks about the experience. Even seasoned marketing professionals with a targeted advertising campaign could not have this kind of reach. With potential talent pool shortages and hiring challenges, organizations cannot afford to lose highly qualified applicants due to a bad candidate experience that is announced over a social media platform.

Using the EVP for Sourcing and Recruiting Applicants

Employee value proposition (EVP) refers to the overall brand that an organization provides to its workforce, both current and future. The EVP answers the question "what's in it for me?" and allows candidates and employees to have a full understanding of the total rewards that are available as an employee of the organization. Five primary components make up the EVP:

1. Compensation
2. Benefits
3. Career
4. Work Environment
5. Culture

Compensation includes not only the current salary paid, but also future salary opportunities such as merit increases, bonuses, and promotions. Compensation should be managed with accuracy, timeliness, and fairness, and it should align with performance. **Benefits** include retirement programs and insurance such as medical, dental, vision, and life; however, benefits also includes paid time off, holidays, flexible work schedules, telecommuting options, educational reimbursement, and training opportunities. The **career** component refers to the ability for employees to move within the organization while progressing within their career. Career also includes stability, training, education, coaching, evaluation, and feedback. Employees should know where they stand with their supervisor and within the organization. Encouraging new opportunities to grow and develop, as well as to promote, is vital to supporting the EVP for employees. **Work environment** within the EVP includes recognizing and rewarding outstanding performance, balancing work life and home life, providing challenging and rewarding assignments, and encouraging engagement and involvement at all levels within the organization. Finally, the **culture** component of EVP encourages an understanding throughout the entire organization of the overarching goals and objectives. Culture includes the practice of values such as trust, support, teamwork, collaboration, and social responsibility.

A robust EVP will lead to a higher retention rate of current employees as well as maintain a higher employee satisfaction rate. Employees will trust the organization and its leadership while working hard to accomplish the goals established. A strong EVP will also attract highly talented candidates wanting to join the organization. This will lead to a higher number of qualified job applicants, increased candidate referrals from current employees, improved survey ratings that report the best places to work, fewer vacancies to fill, lower absenteeism rates, and ultimately, a lower cost per hire.

Using Appropriate Hiring Methods

The talent acquisition lifecycle is a multi-step process that begins with a hiring need—usually a job opening—and ends with the hiring and onboarding of an employee. This process should be objective and standardized, ensuring that it is free from discrimination or other unethical and illegal practices.

As mentioned, the first step in the recruitment lifecycle is to determine the need of the department. If an organization has an opening due to a resignation, promotion, or transfer, the recruitment need must be evaluated. Once the need has been assessed, a job posting should be created that communicates the job description, information about the company and employee benefits, and anything else that a prospective employee would need to determine whether to apply.

The second step in the process is to source candidates and assess the candidate pool. By utilizing various sourcing methods, such as social media platforms, niche job boards, and other appropriate methods, a robust candidate pool can be gathered for the initial screening review. The initial screening review should group candidates into two basic initial categories: meeting required qualifications and not meeting required qualifications. The third step in the process is to further screen the candidates who have the required qualifications. These candidates should be further screened into such groups as "most qualified" and "least qualified." Then candidates should be selected for invitation to interview for the position. Candidates should be selected based on criteria such as education, years of experience, accomplishments in previous positions, and leadership experience.

The fourth step in the process is to assess the most qualified candidates via assessment tests or interviews. Assessment tests should be conducted to determine the validity and strength of the candidates' skills. When candidates are invited to interview with the organization, the interviews should be conducted by individuals who are familiar with conducting interviews. Interviewers should be able to assess responses to score and rank the candidates for the hiring manager to review. Once the initial interviews have been completed, finalists should be selected. Hiring managers should then conduct final interviews with the most qualified candidates to make a final selection.

The fifth step in the process consists of the employment offer and orientation. The employment offer should include not only the job title and salary, but also the name of the hiring manager, potential start date, necessary background checks or screening required prior to starting, and any pertinent employee benefit information. Benefit information often makes or breaks an offer, so employment offers should include information regarding vacation time, sick leave time, holiday schedules, medical insurance, (including when coverage starts and whether the organization assists with premiums), and any other pertinent information. If the prospective employee has other needs and wishes to negotiate the terms of the offer, it is appropriate at this point to engage in these conversations. Relocation expenses, deferred compensation, additional vacation time, or signing bonuses are all potential benefits that a prospective employee could negotiate.

Once the offer has officially been accepted; and the background, references, or medical screening has been conducted; and the individual has been cleared to start employment, then an official hire date should be established. Once the new employee has begun working for the organization, it is important to immediately orient the individual to the company culture and procedures such as benefits enrollment, payroll, safety, work-related injuries, union participation, policies and procedures, and any other important information for a new employee to be exposed to.

Conducting Appropriate Pre-Employment Screening

Because there are various elements to recruitment, it is important to outline and describe each step so that everyone involved understands the overall process, timing, and responsibilities. The recruitment process includes advertising the position, screening the applicants, setting up interviews, developing the interview questions, selecting the most qualified candidate, and negotiating an offer, as well as completing the background and medical screening, reference checks, and onboarding process. It is important to note that internal recruitments can be substantially different from external recruitments and may require less time to select, hire, and onboard the successful candidate; however, the recruitment should still be outlined thoroughly to ensure complete understanding.

Implementing Effective On-Boarding and Orientation Programs

New employee orientation (NEO) is the first formal experience that an individual has as an employee with an organization. An NEO is part of the overall onboarding process that is initiated when an employee joins an organization. The NEO can range from a few hours to several days. In addition to showing employees their new workspace, restrooms, exits, and the breakroom or lunch area, the NEO should cover several main areas of focus:

- Organization overview
- Human resources basics
- Health and safety
- Policies and procedures

The organization overview should discuss the corporate mission and vision, company history, executive management, and organizational structure. Employees should gain an understanding of where their position is located in the overall hierarchy of the organization. Additionally, separate locations should be identified and a complete directory provided.

Human resources basics should also be provided to new employees immediately upon hire. These basics include a complete tour of the corporate intranet. The **corporate intranet** is the internal website provided only to employees; it includes an employee portal for access to information such as medical information and summary plan descriptions, change forms for personal contact information and beneficiaries, policies and procedures, and important information. Some organizations incorporate the payroll portal into the corporate intranet; other organizations maintain a separate payroll portal.

During the NEO, employees should receive a full tutorial of the payroll system. This tutorial should provide training in how to submit a timecard, request leave time, and, if the employee is a supervisor, how to approve timecards and leave requests. Employees should receive an overview of the paycheck to explain compensation, deductions, and other information provided on the paystub. Employees should also know how to access leave accruals and request time off.

Employees should also receive all paperwork necessary to enroll in benefits such as health insurance, life insurance, deferred compensation and retirement programs, and union membership, if needed. Employees should have a full understanding of the deadlines for returning these documents to ensure enrollments can be completed. Other items such as signing up for direct deposit, finalizing new hire paperwork such as the I-9, and taking a formal picture for the corporate directory should be conducted during the NEO.

Health and safety also constitute an area of focus that should be discussed at length to ensure that new employees are aware of and understand the organization's policies and procedures. Health and safety items such as the workers' compensation program, workplace injuries, personal medical leaves, and safety policies should be reviewed in depth. Procedures such as reporting a workplace injury, applying for a personal medical leave, understanding the safety protocols specific to the organization and the position, and knowing evacuation plans for the location are important pieces of information that all new employees should be made aware of. Policies and procedures should be thoroughly reviewed, and a copy of the employee handbook should be provided. Many organizations request that employees complete and sign an acknowledgement form to indicate that the handbook has been received, read, and understood. Policies and procedures such as sexual harassment, workplace violence, harassment, performance management, and other significant policies should be discussed at length during the NEO.

If the new employee is a supervisor or manager, additional time should be spent orienting the employee to this specific role. New supervisors should receive an informational report about the employees who they will be directly supervising. Standard information such as job title and duties, salary, and seniority can be provided as well. Approving timecards, leave requests, and running reports are standard job responsibilities for supervisors. Performance evaluations are also standard job responsibilities for new supervisors, as are providing an overview of the documents used, timeframes necessary for providing the evaluations, and resources available for performance management.

A new employee needs a lot of information. Therefore, an NEO best practice is to break up the information into blocks or sessions. This allows the employee to absorb the information in a more complete way and ensures a higher retention rate. The four main areas discussed above may be broken down into separate blocks, offered on multiple days or provided in one long session. Additionally, new employees should receive a tour of the workplace, including other locations if appropriate, introductions to the team and other employees, and a list of local resources such as local restaurants, coffee shops, post office, banks, gyms, and other amenities. If local businesses offer discounts, specials, or incentives to employees, this information should also be provided.

Some organizations provide a mentor or buddy to new employees during the NEO. The mentor is responsible for going to lunch with the new employee, meeting informally to discuss the organization and answer questions, and being a general resource and friendly face to the new employee. Depending on the working relationship between the new employee and mentor, it may be appropriate for the mentor to bring the new employee along to meetings or other events that would be helpful and informational. Depending on the size of the organization and resources available, multiple mentors may be assigned to allow for various viewpoints. Assigning a mentor from different departments such as payroll, information technology, human resources, customer service, and the hiring department can provide insight to the internal operations, lending to a more informed employee.

Finally, it is a best practice for human resources to schedule frequent NEO follow-up discussions with the new employee. Some organizations schedule these discussions for 30 days, 60 days, and 90 days following the start date. These discussions allow for specific questions that a new employee may realize were not addressed during the original NEO. New employees should be aware of the resources available through HR and the mentor assigned during NEO. If an employee has a specific question due to a certain life event or for other information, HR should be available to meet on an as-needed basis to ensure that employees have the necessary information at the time it is needed.

Designing Job Descriptions

Every position should have a job description that reflects the minimum qualifications, specifically the experience and education required for being able to do the job. The salary range should align with these minimum qualifications in that more experienced candidates could earn more within the salary range than less experienced candidates. If the information from the job analysis does not align with the job description, the Human Resources professional should first work to update the job description with the accurate description of the work being done.

Employee Engagement and Retention

Knowledge retention is one of the most important components of learning. If knowledge is not retained for future use, then the training is not successful. Retention is increased when information is processed and practiced at many levels. Repetition is also key to improving the retention of information learned in a training session. In order to determine the appropriate retention concepts to apply to a training, it is important to understand how individuals retain knowledge based on certain teaching methods.

There are two primary teaching styles: passive and participatory. **Passive teaching** includes giving lectures, reading to an audience or having participants read materials, watching videos, and providing demonstrations. Retention rates of knowledge achieved during a passive teaching method are relatively low, though. The average retention rates for passive teaching methods are: lectures: 5%; reading: 10%; audio-visual: 20%; and demonstration: 30%. These retention rates are extremely low, and a training program that contains only these elements could prove to be unsuccessful.

Participatory teaching includes engaging groups in discussion, providing practice opportunities, and teaching others. Retention rates of knowledge achieved during a participatory teaching method are relatively high. The average retention rates for participatory teaching methods are: group discussion: 50%; practice: 75%; and teaching others: 90%. These retention rates are much higher than those seen with passive teaching methods. A training program that contains only these elements could be seen as moderately to extremely successful. It is important to note that these retention rates are averages. This means that individual retention rates could be higher or lower than the reported average.

Average Retention Rates

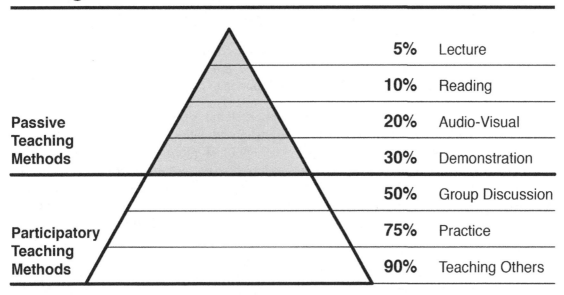

Including various teaching methods can increase the retention rates of participants and maximize the learning opportunity. While some content should be taught with a passive teaching method, trainers should also incorporate participatory teaching methods to increase the knowledge retention. A training program may begin with a lecture on the subject matter, followed with a video, and then close with a practice exercise that results in a group discussion. By incorporating multiple teaching methods from both categories, participant retention can be maximized, which will result in a successful training program.

Incorporating the above methods in training programs can increase participants' retention of the information as well as ensure a successful program. While it is important to ensure that the actual training program is robust and incorporates multiple teaching methods, it is also important to implement strategies after the training program. Data has shown that after participating in a training program, individuals lose knowledge and information at a relatively quick pace unless the knowledge is immediately applied. Some research indicates that professionals could lose up to 80% of the training material learned within three to six months after the training is delivered. In order to maximize, enhance, and maintain knowledge retention, it is important to implement specific strategies before, during, and after the delivery of a training program. By having robust strategies in place, an organization can ensure that the information in maintained.

Before training is delivered, the program should be previewed to ensure that the training is complete, appropriate, and responding to a need. It is also appropriate to understand what the needs will be after the training program is delivered so that a plan can be put in place to address knowledge retention. Questions should be asked before the training is delivered to ensure that any concerns and issues can be resolved before the training is conducted. The program should then be communicated to all levels of the organization as appropriate. This communication should include the topic and subject matter, the goals and expectations of the training, and the learning objectives. This ensures buy-in at all levels of the organization, including supervisory support.

During the training, it is important that managers and leadership are visible and participating. Employees will be more likely to respect and accept training when they can see commitment from the leadership. If employees see leadership practicing principles of integrity, work ethic, honesty, and respect, they are generally more willing to exhibit these principles individually. This also is true for behaviors in the workplace. If employees see that management and leadership are not respectful of time, always arriving late to meetings or not being considerate of other's time and commitment, this will be reciprocated. Minimizing disruptions to a training is also important as it shows a clear commitment to the program and the importance of the subject matter, as well as the participation of individuals.

To reduce disruptions, have participants turn off their phones. If this is not possible, then phones should be muted and only checked during breaks or other specific opportunities. Having a room of 25 participants all checking their phones for messages, emails, or other information can severely diminish the focus of the group. This is another example of how leadership can project an important message—if individuals see leadership focused on their phones, they will mirror this behavior and receive the message that the training is not that important. Individual commitment to a training program should not be taken lightly. It is only with the support of all levels of an organization that a training program can truly be successful.

After delivering a training program, it is important to communicate the expectations and commit to a follow-up plan. Participants should understand what is expected of them following a training program in both the short term and the long term. Participants should commit to a follow up plan to ensure that the information and knowledge learned in the training program is retained and utilized in the course of their work. Additionally, it is important to ensure that the follow up plan include new resources, additional sessions, or other items as appropriate to continue engaging individuals in learning and growing.

One of the most vital components to ensuring the success of a training program is to have the support and commitment of upper management and leadership. A training program can have the great resources, insightful information, engaging trainers, and amazing tools, but without support and commitment from the top of the organization, the program will not be nearly successful as it could be.

Designing and Interpreting Surveys of Employee Attitudes
Employee surveys are an efficient and effective method to measure employee attitudes, opinions, and overall satisfaction. Surveys can provide perspectives at various levels of the organization, including the satisfaction of individuals with their specific position, supervisor, executive leadership, and the entire organization and company culture. Surveys allow an organization to monitor trends in specific areas, assess impacts of policy changes, compare employee satisfaction with other organizations and competitors, and provide insight on the areas of improvement that are important to employees. Additionally, surveys can offer the opportunity to review employee perspectives regarding compensation, benefits, time off, recognition, training opportunities, communication, culture, leadership, and any other area that may need to be assessed. The survey results can then be used to determine and support necessary actions to implement for improvement.

Surveys evaluate attitudes and satisfaction in various categories. It is important to survey employees periodically to gain insight on how the culture is changing, for better or for worse. It is also important to involve and engage employees in the survey early on in the process. When employees are involved in the planning, coordination, and implementation of any program, including surveys, the organization usually sees increased participation, fair and honest feedback, and increased motivation to participate in the actions that result from the survey. It is extremely important to note that it is vital that an organization communicate with employees before, during, and after the survey. Post-survey communication should include the results, actions, and goals that will be implemented from the information received. If an organization does not intend to act based on the survey results, then a survey should not be conducted. In cases where organizations do not communicate or take action from employee surveys, employees generally become disengaged, lose motivation, and are less likely to participate in future surveys.

Surveys can take various forms. Organizations may want an overall, holistic view of employee satisfaction and opinions to fully delve into changing culture and process as necessary. Organizations also may want to conduct a short and specific survey that provides an opportunity for employees to respond to one focused topic. Regardless of the depth or topics of a survey, it is important to follow best practices:

- Conduct a survey only when a committed leadership team is supporting the entire process.
- If appropriate and feasible, partner with an expert who will conduct the actual survey and provide the results; if this is not an option, ensure that the Human Resources professional conducting the survey is educated and trained on conducting employee surveys.
- Establish a strong and thorough communication plan.
- Establish a task team to review the results and determine an action plan; identify champions for specific topics.
- Share data consistently at all levels of the organization.
- Keep the survey simple and execute the process flawlessly.
- Identify resources to implement the survey and the resulting action plan.
- Plan for a follow-up opportunity to provide additional and new information based on the action plan for leadership to adjust a course of action, if necessary.
- Do not commit to another survey for a minimum of eighteen to twenty-four months.
- Invest in post survey results and action plan, including time, budget, training, and other resources.

When creating the survey, an organization may want to provide a voluntary opportunity for employees to identify demographic information. Demographic information such as department, age, years of service, gender, and supervisory responsibilities can serve to provide the organization with specific concerns and areas of focus within certain departments or for certain segments of the employee population. An example of this would be a survey question regarding safe working conditions. An overall satisfaction rate may yield a satisfactory score; however, if the data are broken down further by department, a lower satisfaction rate may be seen for particular departments, which could indicate there is an issue that should be reviewed and resolved. Without having the ability to sort and separate the data, concerns may be missed as the overall satisfaction rates are an average of all responses. An employee concern, however, when paired with identifying information, provides the chance for consideration and rectification.

Confidentiality is an important component to surveys, and employees should feel comfortable providing honest feedback without fear of repercussions. This is one positive aspect of using a third-party provider to conduct the survey, as the external vendor can compute the information provided on the survey, including the demographic information, and then produce requested reports to show the results.

Conducting employee surveys is driven by the desire to understand the organization and implement change that will positively impact the culture, engagement, motivation, and progress on an individual level as well as an organizational level. If surveys are conducted professionally, results are communicated clearly, and action plans are implemented with full commitment from executive leadership, organizations will see positive changes. These positive changes can include loyalty and higher retention rates, satisfaction and motivation, innovation and creativity, and ultimately, higher customer satisfaction. Satisfied employees provide excellent customer service, resulting in satisfied customers.

Administering Programs to Improve Employee Attitudes

Numerous HR and organizational programs work to improve and enhance employee attitudes and the workplace culture. HR professionals should strive to understand the motivations of the workforce as each organization and department will have unique needs. An excellent way to source this information is through employee surveys. Instead of trying to guess what will engage and motivate employees, or affect a cultural change, simply asking questions that are geared toward providing this information can allow HR professionals to provide solutions that will be utilized and effective.

By providing options that are based on the direct feedback from employees, not only will employees feel engaged and a part of the process, but they will also be more likely to be further engaged in the day-to-day operations and affect change on a larger scale, such as workplace culture. Examples of unique programs that may engage employees are wellness programs, training and learning opportunities, recognition and achievement programs, company events such as picnics or holiday parties, telecommuting options, alternate work schedules, or vacation buy-back options. Each organization and its employees are unique and have unique needs and wants. The programs established should address these unique needs and wants, and HR should strive to meet them.

Identifying Opportunities to Create Engaging Jobs

Employees want to be encouraged, engaged, and motivated in their work. By providing meaningful opportunities for training, growth, and learning, an organization can work to provide new skills and resources to employees. These new skills and resources can enhance their current performance as well as provide for new future opportunities such as promotions, special assignments, or career growth. There are several types of redesign that can be implemented within a position that will allow for growth while remaining in the current position. Job design, job enlargement, job enrichment, and job rotation are all effective tools that can be used to encourage individual employee growth. **Job design** is creating a new position that is a different composition of roles and responsibilities than currently found within the organization.

Job design may be an important tool for employees with unique skill sets and backgrounds that will encourage the use of their skills in relation to a specific objective. **Job enlargement** is adding new tasks that are related to the current job roles and responsibilities. While these tasks are in addition to the current workload, they are aligned with and related to the current tasks being performed. **Job enrichment** is adding brand new, unrelated tasks that may not be aligned with current tasks. **Job rotation** is a form of job enlargement that allows for employees to trade positions or rotate duties. Job rotation is also referred to as **cross training** and allows for an organization to have a more prepared workforce with a deep bench strength of multiple skill sets. When appropriate, each of these programs can be initiated to provide employees with new opportunities while increasing their skills, experience, and ultimately, future opportunities.

Monitoring Retention Metrics

A dashboard that clearly communicates metrics is an excellent tool to show the effectiveness of a staffing program. Additionally, it is important to convey how the staffing program is aligned with the overall human resources program. Basic information can be incorporated into the dashboard, such as total salary, average salary, average age, average years of service, total headcount, turnover rate, absenteeism rate, new hires, and the number of employees who left the organization. These are all important pieces of information that tell the story of the organization. Dashboards are typically updated on a quarterly basis. Configuring each dashboard to show particular periods of time then enables an organization to display informational trends to indicate success or opportunities. Each HR program can also have a separate dashboard for their metrics.

Multiple metrics can be used to measure staffing effectiveness. Organizations should select metrics that are appropriate and effective for their specific needs. Metrics should also be selected for which the data can be obtained without a substantial undertaking or extensive resources. There are four primary areas that metrics should focus on: cost, timeliness, outcomes, and reactions.

Metrics should focus on each of these areas to convey the effectiveness of staffing elements such as the overall staffing system, recruiting, selection, final match, and retention. Any metric implemented should be measured against specific targets so that success against the target can be determined.

Staffing systems can be evaluated for effectiveness by incorporating the aforementioned metrics:

> 1. Cost: staffing budget including actual expenditures, staffing-to-employee ratios, and staffing expenses for full-time hires
> 2. Timeliness: amount of time to respond to requests
> 3. Outcomes: evaluation of employee readiness for achieving objectives
> 4. Reactions: communication and satisfaction with services

Recruiting can be evaluated for effectiveness by incorporating the same four metrics in a recruiting capacity:

> 1. Cost: advertising budget including actual expenditures and cost per applicant
> 2. Timeliness: recruits per week, month, or quarter based on actual hiring needs
> 3. Outcomes: number of recruits
> 4. Reactions: quality of applicants

Selection can be evaluated for effectiveness by incorporating the metrics in the following ways:

> 1. Cost: test costs per candidate, interview expenses, and total cost per candidate
> 2. Timeliness: time to hire and days to fill
> 3. Outcomes: competence and workforce diversity
> 4. Reactions: candidate quality and satisfaction with tests

Final match can be evaluated for effectiveness by incorporating the four metrics as well:

> 1. Cost: training costs per hire and cost per hire
> 2. Timeliness: number of days to start and time-to-perform
> 3. Outcomes: number of positions filled and job performance after 30 days, 90 days, 6 months, and one year
> 4. Reactions: new employee satisfaction

The four metrics can also be used to evaluate retention:

> 1. Cost: exit interview expenses and replacement costs
> 2.Timeliness: length of time to respond to external offers
> 3. Outcomes: voluntary separation rate, involuntary separation rate, and overall attrition rate

79

4. Reactions: employee job satisfaction

An organization should select the metrics appropriate to the story being told about the program. Some staffing dashboards call out specific items that are important to the organization and dive into more detail for others. A **recruitment funnel** is a specific metric that shows the number of overall applicants who progress to each step of the recruitment process, beginning with the application, progressing to the phone screen and then the on-site interview, and then finalizing the offer and eventual hire.

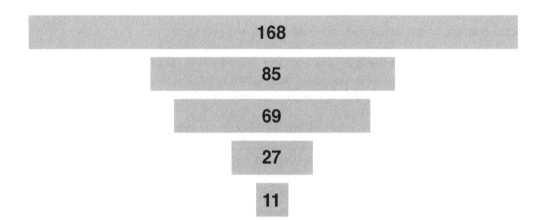

Three other specific metrics that some organizations choose to include in the staffing dashboard are the application sources, the decline reasons, and the pipeline efficiency of hiring. The **application sources** metric provides the main areas where applicants locate a job posting and then apply for the open position. This metric also shows the number of applicants hired from these sources, which allows the organization to pinpoint the most effective sources and dedicate additional resources to source more qualified candidates. The **decline reasons** metric provides the main reasons that applicants are disqualified or declined from consideration. This metric allows the organization to pinpoint areas that could be improved or clarified to ensure qualified candidates are applying for the open positions.

Changing the language in a job description may be the solution needed to ensure that candidates are receiving the most accurate information about the position and its qualifications. The **pipeline efficiency of hiring** metric shows the average number of days taken for each stage in the process as well as the overall process. Each step of the recruitment process is broken down in this metric to show where the process is slowing down and taking more time. Screening applications, conducting phone screens, initiating in-person interviews, interviewing with the hiring manager, extending the offer, and hiring the new employee are all steps in the process that can be viewed as separate timeframes as well as one larger overall timeframe. This metric shows the organization where efficiencies can be gained within the process.

Organizations review staffing data from an organization-wide viewpoint to show the effectiveness of the entire program. Many organizations also present staffing data from a department-wide perspective to communicate with department directors and managers specific to their hiring needs. Having departmental breakdowns of this information also allows human resources to identify areas that need additional focus or change in direction to meet the specific staffing needs of each area. The Finance department may meet all their staffing needs through advertising with a specific website; however, the Maintenance department may meet all their staffing needs through career centers and jobs events.

Each department and position may require a different recruitment plan to reach and attract qualified candidates for the open positions. By reviewing this data, HR is able to pinpoint areas that can be improved or areas that are effective. Understanding the status and results of implemented recruitment programs is the primary reason to track this information. Without an understanding of where the issue actually lies, it is impossible to accurately determine the best course of action to recommend. By using data to locate issues and make decisions, HR professionals can implement solutions to increase the effectiveness of the program. Using data allows Human Resources professionals to provide solutions to actual issues rather than guessing and hoping a solution works. Implementing effective solutions that result in meeting the needs of the hiring department and the organization is the ultimate goal of HR. Dashboards are an important and highly useful tool that can result in effective solutions.

Coaching Supervisors on Creating Positive Working Relationships

The **employee lifecycle** is the roadmap that an organization uses to create a collaborative and engaged workforce. It consists of various stages that include attracting qualified applicants; recruiting the best and brightest candidates; onboarding new employees; developing and managing employees, their careers, and professional growth; retaining employees; and transitioning employees out of the organization when the time is appropriate. Human Resources professionals are responsible for ensuring that each stage of the employee lifecycle is robust, appropriate, and meets the needs of both the organization and the employee. When opportunities to enhance a lifecycle stage are identified, recommendations should be made and changes implemented. The employee lifecycle should encourage and deliver a strong employee experience throughout an entire career or working experience with an organization.

The employee lifecycle can be assessed for effectiveness based on the level of employee engagement at each lifecycle stage. Additionally, each stage should be adaptable, relevant, sustainable, and executable. The first stage of the lifecycle is attracting qualified applicants. Employees should take an active role in representing the organization. Engaged employees can serve as ambassadors to the organization and attract applicants to apply for open positions. The second stage of the lifecycle is recruiting the best and brightest candidates to work for the organization. Engaged employees who like the job, team, coworkers, and organization are more likely to recommend friends and professionals to apply for open positions. The third stage of the lifecycle is onboarding new employees. Engaged employees are excited about joining a new organization and are generally more likely to help others transition into the new organization and role. The fourth stage of the lifecycle is developing and managing employees, their careers, and professional growth.

Engaged employees seek out and request learning opportunities to increase their knowledge and skill sets to enhance their productivity in their current role and to increase their future opportunities for promotion. Organizations that encourage employees to be innovative and creative allow for an even more engaged workforce that quickly translates to efficiency and productivity. The fifth stage of the lifecycle is retaining employees. Retention can be encouraged through recognition and acknowledgement as well as ensuring appropriate and necessary compensation and benefits. The sixth and final stage of the lifecycle is transitioning employees out of the organization. While this can occur voluntarily or involuntarily, employees must be separated from the organization in an appropriate and respectful manner. If an employee is retiring, the organization should ensure that knowledge is retained and as much information can be transferred to new employees or the existing team to ensure continuity. Engaged employees who leave an organization in good standing, whether through retirement or resignation, will generally stay in contact with their coworkers.

Each stage is vital to the overall employee experience. While the development and retention stages will last the longest in terms of time, every stage is necessary and dependent on the other stages. Assessing the effectiveness of each can be determined by establishing key metrics that measure the success of programs within each stage. Additionally, initiating employee surveys to provide direct feedback in each of these areas is an excellent best practice. This feedback should be considered when determining to continue programs or establish new ones to revitalize an initiative.

Training Stakeholders on Using Performance Management Systems

Performance management is the strategic process that creates a work environment where employees are enabled and engaged to perform to the best of their abilities and achieve their goals. The performance management process includes setting goals, gathering information on performance, reviewing and evaluating performance against the goals, providing feedback to employees, and offering learning opportunities. This process allows employees to have clarity regarding roles, responsibilities, and expectations, while offering opportunities to discuss achievements and accomplishments.

There are two primary purposes of performance management: strategic and administrative. The strategic purpose of a performance management process is to align employee performance and actions with the overarching organizational goals. Employees should understand how these achievements and accomplishments tie into the broader organizational strategy and objectives, and the discussions within the performance management process provide these opportunities. The administrative purpose of a performance management process is to identify strong-performing and high-producing employees. Identifying the strong performers within an organization allows for better decision making regarding administrative decisions such position changes, salary increases, and future special assignments and opportunities.

There are four phases known as the "four D's" of performance management: define, document, discuss, and develop. The **define phase** refers to the step in which managers define what should be achieved and accomplished through the performance review. Defining these goals allows for specific metrics to be developed that can measure performance.

The **document phase** refers to the step in which managers evaluate individual performance and maintain a record to provide specific feedback to employees during the performance review. By keeping an ongoing record of performance, information will be readily available when preparing formal review documents. Performance can then be more accurately measured and assessed.

The **discuss phase** refers to the step in which managers have a regularly scheduled conversation with employees to openly discuss performance over a specific period of time. Many organizations require annual performance reviews, with additional reviews added based on probation periods, poor performance, or other factors. It is a best practice for managers to meet more frequently than once a year to discuss performance. This allows employees to quickly identify when performance is not meeting expectations and take corrective actions instead of waiting for an annual review.

The **develop phase** refers to the step in which managers take the information available through the performance review process and provide learning opportunities to employees. Employees who are not meeting expectations or are struggling in their position should be offered learning opportunities to improve their performance. Likewise, employees who are meeting and exceeding expectations should be offered learning opportunities to expand their knowledge base and further professional growth.

Helping Stakeholders Understand Employee Performance

Human Resources professionals are responsible for ensuring that the performance management system, process, methods, tools, and forms are designed to accurately reflect an employee's performance in a fair and objective manner. Managers should be trained in how to use the tools and forms as well as how to deliver the review. Human Resources professionals are also responsible for tracking the performance reviews that are completed and providing managers with updates and reminders when reviews are due. Additionally, the performance reviews should be maintained in the employee's individual personnel file. If a negative review is warranted, managers should work with HR to ensure that training opportunities or corrective actions are identified and deployed. If more frequent reviews are necessary, a schedule should be developed to ensure that the employee is given all of the necessary information and tools.

Managers are responsible for evaluating the performance of the employees who directly report to them. Managers should complete the forms as accurately as possible and provide as many details as possible to ensure that employees have a full understanding of their performance and achievements. Likewise, if an employee is not performing to the standards required, specific details should be provided to ensure a full understanding of the concerns and issues as well as the plan moving forward to address these concerns. Managers should deliver performance reviews face-to-face and provide employees with the opportunity to read and comment on the review. Employees should also be provided the opportunity to comment on, and provide responses to, the information within the performance review.

Implementing Processes that Measure Effectiveness of Performance Management Systems

It is important to understand that the performance management process is only as good as the information provided by managers and supervisors within the process. If an organization has a "check the box" culture regarding performance reviews, then employees are most likely not getting good information regarding their performance. Organizations should institute a culture of learning, achievement, recognition, and promotion. Managers and employees should feel valued and integral to the success of the organization. When performance management is done well, the process can lend to a strong culture that supports employees and ultimately succeeds in meeting the organizational achievements. Tools should be created to support these efforts and allow for a robust dialogue with employees regarding performance; however, even the best tools will not change a culture that does not value recognizing employee performance and achievements.

Learning and Development

Evaluating Data on Gaps in Competencies

HR departments can contribute to succession planning discussions by providing relevant and meaningful data to management. Before even determining what data should be used, it is vital to establish criteria to identify which positions will be reviewed in succession planning. High-ranking positions in the organization—chief executive officer, chief financial officer, and information technology director, for example—are not necessarily the only positions to consider. Identifying the hard-to-fill positions, the positions with the highest turnover, and the positions that have the largest scope and impact on the organization are also important to review for succession planning.

Tracking sheets created for each position can also be a helpful tool for those reviewing this information. The tracking sheets can include such information as position title; compensation; minimum requirements, including education and experience; primary roles and responsibilities such as supervisory and budgetary duties; and other important information. Potential candidates and their current status can be listed on this tracking sheet as well. Then, by assessing the tracking sheets, HR professionals can help determine whether the organization has viable internal candidates for the position and when those candidates will be ready. Some candidates may be ready for the position immediately; other candidates may need two to three years to transition. This is important to assess during the succession planning process so that the organization can provide training and mentoring to ensure that candidates are ready for future opportunities.

A vital piece of information that should be reviewed when determining which positions to include in succession planning is attrition. **Attrition** is the percentage of employees who leave the organization. Voluntary attrition occurs when employees leave of their own accord for reasons such as retirement, resignation for a new position, or relocation. Involuntary attrition occurs when employees are terminated or laid off. Attrition should be calculated on an annual basis and broken down into such categories as voluntary and involuntary, department, job classification, and rank. Analyzing this data enables a holistic view of the organization to determine which positions should be considered in the succession planning process. This data can also be used in the succession planning process to visualize gaps in the organization, such as gaps related to promotions, career paths, and other opportunities.

Organizational charts, job descriptions, and total rewards are also important pieces of data that should be incorporated in succession planning discussions. Organizational charts can show clear career paths for employees as well as positions that are significant to the organization. Job descriptions can provide an even clearer picture when aligned with the organizational charts regarding roles, responsibilities, education, and experience for each position. Total rewards can provide the information that would attract potential candidates—internal and external—to the position during a recruitment process. The total rewards information can also be aligned with the attrition data to show an area that needs additional focus. If certain positions have higher than usual turnover, it may be appropriate for human resources to conduct a total rewards review to ensure competitiveness and eliminate any potential concerns for future recruitment and retention.

Creating Individual Development Plans (IDPs)
Individual Development Plans (IDPs) are a great way to engage employees directly in their career growth. IDPs enable employees to work with their supervisor and HR to discuss their current position and learning opportunities to increase their knowledge and skills specific to their current role. IDPs also enable employees to discuss future opportunities and the skills needed to achieve those opportunities and be successful. These assessments are known as **skills gap assessments**; they review the requirements for future positions and the skills and knowledge the employee lacks. These gaps can then be filled with training and learning opportunities, provided either in-house or outside.

Developing Learning and Development Activities
Many organizations understand that offering career enhancement through training programs is beneficial to their overall success. Training opportunities that enable growth and development in current and future roles can enhance an employee's employment experience and dedication. It is important to understand that while many training programs are voluntary and based on the needs of the organization, all employees should be offered training program opportunities and not be discriminated against when seeking them out. Organizations must ensure fair and equitable learning and development opportunities for all employees. The training programs themselves should also be discrimination free in their materials and presentation to employees. Requesting feedback on the training content and instructors after each session is a best practice that can help an organization determine if changes need to be made.

Additionally, it is important to understand when employees should be compensated for training opportunities. The Fair Labor Standards Act (FLSA) provides specific details regarding when training programs should be compensated for. In general, if a training program 1) is considered to be directly related to an employee's current job and 2) is conducted during regular working hours, then employees must be compensated at their regular rate of pay. If a training program is not considered mandatory but meets the two terms indicated above, employees must be compensated for the time to attend the training program. Human Resources professionals should ensure that they have a complete awareness and understanding of compensation requirements.

The Occupational Safety and Health Act (OSHA) is a federal regulation that requires training in various safety and health areas. Organizations are required to ensure that all employees are trained in the emergency plan. Each facility should have a specific plan that is regularly communicated and delivered to employees via a training plan. Providing practice drills along with classroom training enables employees not only to read the emergency plan's materials and maps but also to physically familiarize themselves with such details as escape routes, meeting points, and signage. Many organizations require this training on an annual basis for all employees and provide additional opportunities throughout the year for newly hired and transferred employees. Emergency plans should also include information specific to natural disasters, based on the location. While all facilities should have plans for fires and other events, they should also have plans for location-specific natural disasters. Depending on the location, possible natural disasters include earthquakes, tsunamis, floods, hurricanes, and tornadoes. Employees should never have to guess about safety protocols in the case of an emergency.

OSHA also requires employees to be fully trained in all areas related to safety for their specific job. Every employee should be made aware of all safety procedures and protocols before beginning their work. Specific trainings related to safety procedures include but are not limited to the following: machinery and equipment, fire hazards, chemicals and other hazards, hearing protection, personal protective equipment (PPE), and Automated External Defibrillator (AED) equipment. Employees should be fully trained on every piece of equipment they use to do their job. Each position should have a specific training schedule depending on the equipment being used. Organizations may even provide a separate training program for PPE alone. Some positions require multiple pieces of PPE, and training should include not only how to use the PPE in the scope of the work being performed, but also how to clean, prepare, and request new PPE. From coveralls and safety glasses to Kevlar vests and handguns, organizations are responsible for delivering the training programs that ensure employees are completely aware of and understand how to accurately use the PPE.

Many organizations require that an employee complete and sign a written notification that training has been provided and the employee understands all aspects of performing their job safely. This document can be important if an employee refuses to abide by the protocols and needs to be disciplined. Additionally, refresher training should be provided to ensure that employees are aware of updates to regulations and procedures. The goal should be to ensure that employees leave work at the end of the day in the same physical condition in which they arrived. Providing consistent, frequent, and thorough safety training will decrease on-the-job injuries and accidents. Many organizations reward employees for adhering to safety practices and procedures. Another common practice is to communicate how many days have elapsed without a safety incident or accident.

The Supreme Court has ruled that organizations can be held liable for sexual harassment if there is not reasonable effort made to prevent and correct inappropriate workplace behavior. Even if the organization is unaware of the behavior, it may still be liable for an employee's inappropriate behavior. Therefore, organizations must take every action necessary to provide training about sexual harassment. This training should include definitions and examples of sexual harassment, appropriate examples of lawsuits and case law, legal standards, the workplace policy, and the process for reporting sexual harassment. Additionally, training should include prevention techniques, employee responsibilities, and how sexual harassment investigations are conducted.

Sexual harassment training should occur frequently to ensure that employees understand the organization's policies and procedures as well as the legal ramifications for individuals and for the organization. Some states have passed legislation mandating sexual harassment training, and they conduct audits to ensure compliance. For example, in the state of California, Assembly Bill 1825 requires that all employers with 50 or more employees have their supervisors attend a two-hour class on sexual harassment at least once every two years. Additionally, all new supervisory employees must attend this training within six months of their hire or promotion to the supervisory role. Organizations must keep accurate records of when these trainings are offered, employees in attendance, and the content delivered.

Some organizations may choose to include diversity training in the scope of sexual harassment training. This inclusion can ensure that employees understand that, although these are separate topics, they intertwine with each other on many levels. Diversity training enables employees to be exposed to information regarding individuals with differences working together, providing different perspectives, and allowing for a more robust dialogue. Employees should understand an organization's policies regarding diversity and how each individual plays a part in creating the culture of the organization. Valuing each other's differences and treating each other with respect is vital to the success of the team, department, and organization.

Using Resources to Develop and Deliver Effective Learning Programs

Career development and training programs can take many different formats, and HR professionals are responsible for understanding which programs are best for the organization and the employees. Individuals learn in different ways, so it is important to have multiple training methods to ensure that all employees can learn and grow in a way that works for their learning style. While the variety of training methods may be limited by budget and resources, it is important that human resources regularly evaluate programs to update them by incorporating new ways of learning.

Organizations can incorporate mentoring and job shadowing to enhance an employee's opportunities. An employee may express a desire to hold a position at certain level in the future. Human Resources can implement programs and policies to identify mentors for such employees. Similarly, job shadowing can enable employees to see the day-to-day workings of a position and take this information into account when determining their own career path and goals.

In addition to planning and implementing training programs for individuals, HR professionals also need to incorporate specific training programs for supervisors and managers. Training in how to be a successful supervisor and manager is vital to having strong teams. There may even be an opportunity to align this training with IDPs and offer individuals the opportunity to attend a training program for supervisors *before* becoming a supervisor. The benefit of doing so is a clear understanding of the roles and responsibilities that are expected at the supervisory level.

Human Resources professionals can structure specific training programs for each position with a pre-defined career path. Another option is to enable flexibility in designing training programs and career paths for the needs expressed by employees and departments. Both are legitimate and both enable career development and growth. Training employees at an individual level as well as at a group level is also an important component to training programs. Understanding how each individual contributes to the organization's priorities and objectives is vital to overall success. Additionally, having an understanding of how each team and group can contribute to success is an important piece of the puzzle to ensure success at an individual level and an organization-wide level.

Creating Internal Social Networks

Before creating a training program, it is important to understand the organization's goals and needs. Training programs should be relevant and appropriate for both the organization and employees. A needs analysis can provide insight as to the training needed instead of trying to guess. The following are resources that can be used to determine training needs:

- Organization goals
- Departmental goals
- Results
- Performance measures
- Attrition
- Job descriptions
- Safety logs and performance
- Complaints
- Legal requirements and compliance needs

Additionally, interviewing or surveying employees may also provide important information. Sometimes training programs overlook speaking to and hearing from employees about the skills and training that would help them be more productive. An organization may think it knows what employees need, but unless it seeks confirmation from the employees themselves, the organization may end up providing unnecessary training. Such training can be costly, wasting time, money, resources, and energy while also undermining future training opportunities. When employees are included in the conversation about training, they are most often supportive of the training program.

Once training needs are determined, Human Resources professionals then need to decide which employees need to be trained and how often. Many training programs are necessary or even required for all employees and should be conducted on a frequent basis. Some training programs are specific to certain departments or employees at different levels of the organization.

All employees should be trained in communication, teamwork, company policies, and applicable safety, but only management employees may need training in team development and strategic planning. Knowing which employees need the training also enables insight into how the training should be developed and presented. If a software update training is being proposed for all information technology employees, understanding how these employees learn is necessary in delivering a successful training program. Allowing individuals at computer stations to practice and follow along with the instructor may ensure maximum learning for a particular group of employees. Additionally, logistics such as location, workload, schedules and coverage, work group dynamics, and cost should be taken into account when developing and delivering a training program.

Individuals learn in different ways; therefore, it is important to incorporate multiple ways of learning into each training course. Planning flexibility into the course is important because each session will be different, based on the individuals in attendance. Each participant brings unique experiences, examples, and questions that the instructor needs to integrate into that specific training session. Group dynamics also change from session to session. Experienced instructors include these exchanges in future sessions to enhance learning for all employees. A best practice is to keep a list of ideas, questions, and suggestions. At the end of the program, the instructor can then compile this information and send it to all participants so that learning can continue after the course.

Training sessions should be as interactive as possible, encouraging conversation and engagement. Keeping participants involved and attentive can be challenging. A great way to start the session is by reviewing the course objectives. Each course should have a complete list of objectives that individuals are meant to learn by the end. This is also a great opportunity to begin engaging with the participants about their own individual objectives. Questions like "why are you here?" and "what do you want to know by the end of this class?" are great ways to start a dialogue. Breaking up a training session to include various learning methods can keep a steady flow going. Incorporating quizzes, case studies and breakout discussions, role-playing and demonstrations, and debate opportunities can also keep participants engaged. Employees tend to sit near the people they know. These are the day-to-day, naturally occurring working groups. Breaking up these groups and having employees sit with unfamiliar colleagues can facilitate new conversations and ideas.

Not every training topic is exciting. Some sessions are mandatory. Some training material is difficult to grasp or even uncomfortable to listen to. Regardless, the challenge is getting individuals to participate and be engaged in the training. By incorporating various methods of learning and discussion opportunities, an instructor can usually get maximum participation. In fact, several studies show that a training session incorporating multiple learning methods is more effective, takes less time, and results in individuals retaining the information longer. Using PowerPoint® slides and handouts, asking questions and involving participants, acting out situations with different outcomes, and having fun when appropriate can all support a robust and successful training program.

Training must be supported by executive management in order to be accepted and fully integrated into the organization. Employees must see the commitment from all levels of the organization, especially executive management. If possible, having a member of upper management present in every training session will assist in showing the organization's commitment to the training programs. If a training is required for all employees, dispersing the executive team among various sessions is a great way to include different levels of thinking in every session. It is also helpful in providing an opportunity for executive management to interact directly with employees at various levels in the organization. It is important to note, though, that this strategy may not work for all organizations, depending on the personalities and culture. Having an executive manager present may stifle conversation, and employees may be less vocal than usual, for fear of retribution. It is incumbent on the Human Resources professional to assess whether this could be a concern and develop an appropriate and effective training plan.

Administering Programs to Support Knowledge Transfer

Organizational development (OD) is defined as a series of methods and techniques that are used to facilitate long-term changes in an organization. OD is a strategic, planned, interactive, and ongoing approach to improve employee and organizational effectiveness. Any OD method or process can be broken down into the following components: diagnose a situation; introduce solutions; monitor the progress. Throughout the process, it is important to provide feedback. This feedback may start the cycle over again to ensure that any changes include the feedback received.

Basic Organization Development Model

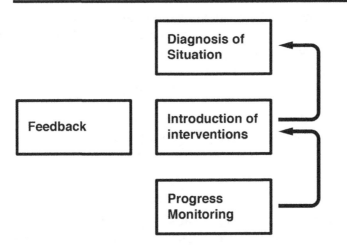

The model can be expanded to add more steps, but the core steps are always the same. A more expansive, more detailed model could include the following steps:

1. Determine the needs of the organization as they are aligned with the mission, vision, and values
2. Understand the current state of the programs and process being reviewed
3. Propose and adopt a future state of the programs
4. Design updates and changes while reviewing current resources
5. Implement changes after thorough communication to ensure understanding
6. Evaluate the changes and impacts, making adjustments if necessary

Even with these additional steps, the same three-step process is still the core of the OD process.

Throughout an OD process, it is important to involve employees and bring them along in the conversation, as this will increase their motivation and engagement throughout the entire process. Ensuring they are a part of the conversation can also help ensure that any new program or process implemented is successful.

OD methods focus on changing the organizational culture while engaging in continued and constant communication. Throughout this model, OD techniques can be incorporated to engage employees and determine the changes that need to be encouraged and implemented. OD techniques include survey feedback, process consultation, team building, sensitivity training, and workgroup growth. These techniques all lend to a more effective interpersonal working environment with deeper relationships and understanding between coworkers.

Positive by-products of working through an OD model to increase efficiency and productivity among employees include the creation and maintenance of motivation in the workforce. When employees feel as if they are being heard and are part of a process to implement change, their satisfaction and continual motivation in the future can be substantially increased. This motivation occurs because the organization is creating an environment that values empowerment, individual growth and development, and high morale.

Within the OD process, there are three main techniques that can be used to motivate employees:

1. Facilitate development
2. Align goals
3. Communicate

By facilitating individual learning and growth, an organization creates opportunity for employees to be invested in the process and the change. When an employee is invested at this level, increased motivation can be seen. This increased motivation lends to a smoother implementation of changes and increases comfort level for individuals to come forward with additional suggestions and concerns. Ultimately, this can substantially increase productivity and efficiency while seeing higher employee retention levels.

When individual goals and objectives are aligned with the organizational goals and objectives, employees understand how their daily work supports the organization's overall work. Even if employees do not have a direct impact on meeting certain organizational goals, ensuring there is understanding of the goals enables employees to support these goals.

Frequent communication within an organization—both upward and downward—establishes transparency. Communication can establish trust in the changes that will be implemented. By ensuring that messages are clear, concise, applicable, and honest, an organization can motivate employees to be engaged in the process of change and implement the change successfully. Messages should be direct and, in the case of delivering negative information, messages should also inform employees of the potential positive aspects of the challenges presented. This type of communication can also lead to employees being more open to sharing ideas and issues that may not otherwise be discovered.

A key component of OD methods is problem solving. There are various structured techniques that can be applied when solving a problem, and each technique comes down to the same basic core steps: (1) define and analyze a problem; (2) identify and choose a solution; (3) plan and implement the solution.

Problem Solving Steps

Analyze Problem

Define Problem

Identify Solutions

Implement

Choose Solutions

Plan of Action

Various structured techniques have been created to assist in the process of solving a problem. Below are three specific techniques and the corresponding steps that can be followed to solve a problem:

- P.D.C.A.: Plan. Do. Check. Act.

- D.M.A.I.C.: Define. Measure. Analyze. Improve. Control.

- A3: Clarify the problem. Break down the problem. Set a goal. Determine the root cause. Develop an action plan. Implement the action plan. Evaluate and review the results. Adjust if necessary and standardize the process.

Many organizations will adopt one technique to apply to all situations. Regardless of the technique selected, the goal is always the same: solve the problem. When applying a problem-solving technique, it is important to encourage teamwork and group participation.

Having many individuals work through a problem allows for different perspectives to be brought to bear and can enable a deeper understanding of the problem. This can be extremely important when determining the root cause of an issue. If the root cause is not fully determined, then a solution could be implemented that will not affect the issue, or it may even cause other issues. When determining the root cause of a problem, a common practice employed is the "**Five Whys**" technique. This Six Sigma method is an excellent tool that can be used without needing data or other information. Asking the question "Why?" five times can assist in getting to the bottom of why a certain issue is occurring, or the root cause. Once the true root cause is determined, then real solutions can be discussed to solve the initial problem. Without understanding and addressing the root cause, solutions will not truly address the issue or affect the change needed. When this occurs, it can have a negative impact as employees could become discouraged, and their engagement and motivation could suffer. There may be a future impact to engagement as well.

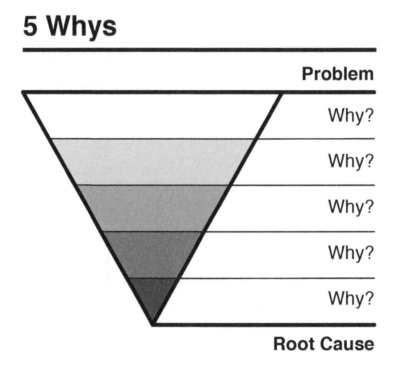

The ADDIE Model

Instructional design is a multi-step process to create and deliver an effective training program. While there are many different structures available to work through, a frequently used design model is the "**ADDIE**" model. This model is a generic instructional design model that can be used for various subject matters in multiple fields. Each step builds on the previous one; because of the simplicity, this model can eliminate wasted time, money, and work. This model is generally seen as the foundation for other instructional design models and is easily adaptable to most training program needs. The ADDIE model follows these steps in the design of a training program:

- Analyze
- Design
- Develop
- Implement
- Evaluate

Each step is vital to the success of a training program and should be conducted thoroughly before moving to the next step. The ADDIE process is linear, meaning that before moving to step 2, step 1 must be completed. If changes occur in the timetable, content, or organizational need during step 3, the process must be started over again at step 1.

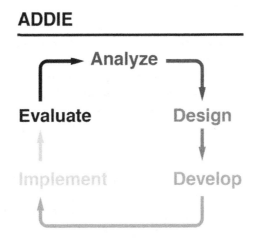

Analysis is the first step; it focuses on what is needed. A needs assessment should be conducted to determine the needs of the organization, departments, teams, and individuals before designing or delivering any training program. The analysis step determines the organization's needs and skills gaps. Having an understanding of who will be in the training is important. Defining the "audience" will help structure the training program in later steps. Additionally, understanding the goal and objectives of the training is vital to having a relevant and respected training program. Aligning training with an organization's overall goals will help employees understand their purpose in the larger organization and how their contributions affect the company.

Design is the second step; it focuses on what should be included. This step also focuses on the audience—who this training program will be delivered to and who will be learning—as well as the instructor who will be delivering this program. Design is the sketched-out plan for the program. Understanding the characteristics of the audience and instructor can help to define how the materials and course should be structured, the learning techniques applied, and how issues such as resistance to training should be addressed. During this step, course content is identified, lessons are structured, tools are selected, and assessment options are reviewed. Storyboards are a great way to visually show the training program to ensure that the flow is steady and maintainable.

Development is the third step; it focuses on the actual content and materials. Development consists of the actual deliverable training program that will be implemented, including the visual tools such as PowerPoint® presentations, handouts, lecture notes, tests and quizzes, resource material, and assessments such as discussion questions and group exercises. This step uses the information gathered in the analysis and design steps to create the actual program. Development can also include running trial sessions to determine if there are issues to resolve before delivering the training to participants.

Implementation is the fourth step; it focuses on delivery of the training program. Conducting the training session is the culmination of the first three steps. Preparing the environment, delivering the course, engaging the participants, and closing out the course are all important components to the implementation step. This step is "where the rubber meets the road," and as soon as the participants enter the training room, they should be engaged with each other and the instructor. The instructor should be prepared to handle the unexpected and answer far-afield questions. The instructor is responsible for keeping the training program on track and the participants engaged.

Evaluation is the final step of the model; it focuses on two components: evaluating the effectiveness of the course and validating it for the future. Evaluation forms should be provided to all participants to gauge the overall response of those receiving the training. The evaluation forms should include rating areas such as instructor effectiveness and knowledge, content and material, if the course was helpful and will be used in the scope of work, the best and least liked parts of the training, and suggestions for opportunities to improve. Additionally, an individual may be assigned to sit in during the course to evaluate the responses received from the participants. Because the instructor will be busy delivering content and focusing on the time, agenda, participant engagement, material, and other items, an assigned evaluator for the course can observe the reactions of participants and other interactions that the instructor may miss.

The assigned evaluator can then give constructive feedback on how to enhance the training. Validating a training program is reviewing how participants take and use the information and knowledge back to their work. Frequent follow-ups and check-ins with those that attended a training to keep the material and information fresh can help retention. Taking this information into account is vital to validating a training program. Follow-up surveys can also assist in gaining information and insight related to how a training program is continuing to impact an employee and their work. Once data is compiled, trends can be potentially seen and reviewed to suggest recommendations for the training program.

Although the ADDIE model is easy to follow when creating a training program, it does have a few drawbacks. The steps are linear and build on each other, which may not work well in certain situations. Additionally, if there are multiple changes and continual evolution happening, this model may not work well. Repeatedly going back to previous steps due to the model's linear nature may waste time and resources or cause setbacks and delays if training is needed by a particular time. There are positive and negative aspects to all techniques, and it is important to consider them to ensure that the applied model or technique is the best and most appropriate method for the particular situation.

Total Rewards

Total rewards refer to the entire package that an employee receives when joining an organization. This package includes compensation, benefits, work-life programs, learning and development opportunities, and performance and recognition. Each of these components is extensive, unique, and important to the entire package. **Compensation**, or pay, indicates the salary that is paid for the work being performed. Compensation also includes merit increases, bonuses, cost of living adjustments, and promotion increases. Benefits include retirement programs such as deferred compensation plans known as 401(k) plans and defined contribution pension plans; insurance coverage including medical, dental, vision, and life; paid time off including vacation leave, sick leave, holiday leave, and other types of leave such as maternity, paternity, and bereavement.

Work-life programs include items such as telecommuting options, alternate work schedules such as a 4x10 or 9x80 schedule, and wellness or employee assistance programs. Learning and development opportunities include internal training courses and educational reimbursement programs. Performance and recognition programs include service awards, contribution awards, and formal or informal recognition of achievements. Each of these components lends to the overall total rewards package that is offered to new employees. HR professionals should be fully aware of each of the elements and ensure that new employees have this information when offered a position.

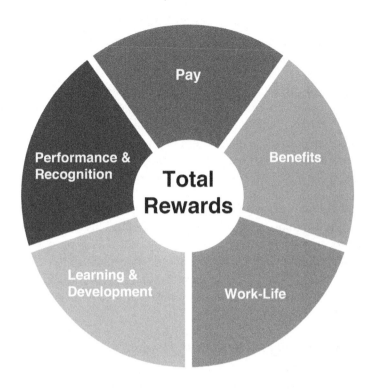

Collecting and Interpreting Compensation and Benefits Data

Human Resources professionals are responsible for understanding the needs of the organization and its employees. This includes having a robust knowledge of the best options in the areas of health insurance, retirement programs, employee assistance programs, life insurance, disability insurance, worker's compensation programs, flexible spending accounts, and voluntary insurance programs such as short-term and long-term disability programs.

It might be beneficial to conduct surveys with other agencies that provide similar services to ensure that an organization's offerings are appropriate for the employee population. It could also be beneficial to survey the current employees to determine which elements of the benefit package are meeting their needs and which elements should be reviewed or added.

Frequent review of costs and services should also be conducted to ensure that the return on investment of these programs is appropriate. It may be time to conduct an analysis to determine if another program or vendor would be suitable to provide better services at a lower cost.

Organizations can offer multiple choices to employees for health insurance coverage, including both preferred provider organization (PPO) and health maintenance organization (HMO) options, and sometimes, many choices of each type of plan to ensure the needs of employees can be met. Dental insurance, vision insurance, and prescription coverage are also options that employers can offer to employees to ensure that employees protect their health on all levels.

Employee assistance programs usually offer services related to a wide array of personal and professional counseling, including legal, financial, change management, stress management, marriage, divorce, and parental counseling, and on many other topics that individuals deal with in their personal and professional lives.

Communication of these plans is extremely important so that employees understand their options and can make informed choices. Often, organizations conduct a health fair or benefits exposition with vendors from all their benefit providers to allow employees direct access.

Many organizations also allow a cafeteria style plan, which is a type of benefit plan dictated by Section 125 of the Internal Revenue Code. This type of plan allows employees to choose from two or more benefits consisting of cash or a qualified benefit plan. A Section 125 plan would identify a certain dollar amount that an employee is eligible for to assist them in paying for their benefits. If there are dollars remaining after their selections have been made, the employee can opt to take those dollars in another way. Employees could also "opt out" and receive the dollars provided as compensation.

Usually, an organization will structure their Section 125 plan so that the "opt out" amount is substantially less than the total amount given to assist with paying for benefits. This has become a huge matter in the State of California with a recent settled lawsuit *Flores v. City of San Gabriel*, in which the dollars received from the insurance "opt out" should have been considered when calculating overtime and other premium pay. As a general reminder, it is important for Human Resources professionals to know as much as possible regarding federal and state laws—as well as current case law—as they might change the way an organization needs to implement benefit programs.

Implementing Appropriate Pay and Benefit Packages

Regardless of the programs offered concerning total rewards, each program must be federally compliant with all laws. It is important to remember that some states have their own individual laws and versions of compliance. In some cases, the state law does not align with the federal law. In these situations, it is important to remember that, in general, the law that is the most generous to the employee is the law that should be followed. From the Fair Labor Standards Act (FLSA), the Family and Medical Leave Act (FMLA), Americans with Disabilities Act (ADA), Affordable Care Act (ACA), and other state leave programs providing benefits such as paid family leave, additional leave rights, disability, and worker's compensation, Human Resources professionals must ensure that every benefit and program aligns with the most generous level of benefit provided.

An organization's policies should ensure that employees receive compensation and benefits in alignment with these federal laws. Policies should clearly communicate to employees their rights as well as the responsibilities of the employer and employee. While an employer may offer FMLA because the company employs more than fifty employees, it should be clearly communicated that employees must be employed for twelve months and have worked at least 1,250 hours in that twelve-month time period to be eligible under the FMLA law. The policy should also clearly communicate the procedure for applying for this benefit, what the benefit is (including how compensation is handled), and what is expected of both parties throughout the process. In the same manner, employees should know the process for working with their employer if they have a disability under the ADA. This process should be clearly outlined in the policy and include the rights and responsibilities of the employer and employee, the complete process, including how to request reasonable accommodations and work restrictions, and how independent medical evaluations will be handled.

Additionally, it is important to understand the Equal Pay Act (EPA) of 1963. Gender equality in pay is a major topic of discussion today, and organizations must ensure that their practices regarding compensation and benefits are compliant with these laws. The EPA amended the FLSA law relative to gender inequality to ensure that men and women are paid the same wage for the same work. The Equal Pay Act of 2010 was passed to help correct the disparity faced by many women regarding their pay when doing jobs similar to those of their male counterparts. This law helped to ensure that a woman's contract terms for a position were the same as a man's contract terms. Continued legislation has been seen to correct these disparities as well. Recently, the state of California passed a law stating that an organization cannot request historical salary information from a candidate to use in preparing an offer of employment. The reasoning for this is that if a woman has experienced discrimination in her job history relative to pay, and that information is used to determine her new salary, the disparity of pay will most likely continue and never be corrected.

Complying Compensation and Benefits Laws and Best Practices

The Department of Labor (DOL) administers and enforces over 180 federal laws, many of which govern the areas of Wages and Hours, Workplace Safety and Health, Workers' Compensation, Employee Benefit Safety, Unions and Their Members, and Garnishment of Wages. While all federal laws and regulations are important and must be incorporated into an organization's policies and practices, the focus of this section is on the following: the Fair Labor Standards Act (FLSA) and the Family and Medical Leave Act (FMLA). These two laws focus on the total rewards components of compensation and leave related to illness or injury.

The FLSA federal statute was passed to ensure that workers are protected from abuses related to compensation. The FLSA ensures that workers are paid a living wage and mandates how workers are paid for overtime work. Often referred to as the "wage and hour law," the FLSA controls minimum wage, overtime, equal pay, recordkeeping, and child labor. Private sector and public sector employers are subject to following the FLSA and understanding which guidelines apply. In addition to the above list of compensation-related items, government agencies must also be familiar with other labor laws such as the Davis-Bacon Act, which requires the agency to pay a prevailing wage rate and fringe benefits to certain contractors for certain work.

The overtime rule under the FLSA requires that employees be paid an annual salary of $23,660 or more in order to qualify as an exempt employee. This salary threshold is in addition to a duties test that would qualify a position as exempt or nonexempt. In general, executive, administrative, professional, outside sales, and certain computer-related employees are exempt from the FLSA. There are other exemptions; each position should be evaluated to ensure its specific FLSA status based on the most recent law and current duties of the position.

An **exempt employee** is not subject to the FLSA requirements, and as such is not eligible for overtime. Exempt employees are paid a fixed salary regardless of the total number of hours they work. They are paid for a body of work regardless of how long it takes to complete the work. Per the FLSA, there is no limit on the number of hours an exempt employee may work. A **nonexempt employee** is an employee who is subject to the FLSA requirements and is eligible for overtime. Nonexempt employees are considered hourly employees and are to be paid at least the minimum wage of the state as well as all overtime due. Overtime must be paid at time-and-a-half for all hours worked over forty hours in any one week. Some agencies have practices put in place to pay daily overtime for all hours worked over eight hours in any one day. However, it is up to the Human Resources and Payroll professionals to ensure that all criteria are met based on the state requirements for paying overtime and the policies, procedures, and practices that align.

The Family and Medical Leave Act (FMLA) of 1993 requires covered employers to provide employees with job protection and unpaid leave for qualifying medical and family reasons.

FMLA entitles eligible employees to take up to twelve weeks of unpaid, job-protected leave each year for the following reasons:

- The birth or care of a child
- The placement of a child for adoption or foster care
- The care of a child, spouse, or parent with a serious health condition
- The employee's own serious health condition

Additionally, covered servicemembers with a serious injury or illness may take up to twenty-six weeks of FMLA leave. Organizations must be covered under the FMLA law to be able to offer their employees FMLA—this requires employing more than fifty employees for at least 20 weeks of the calendar year. Employees must have been employed with this employer at least twelve months and have worked a minimum of 1,250 hours within that time period to be eligible for FMLA.

While FMLA is unpaid, employees can take their accrued leave to cover this time and ensure they remain in a paid status while on FMLA. Depending on the organization's policies, employees most generally can take sick leave, vacation leave, personal leave, and other forms of leave to receive a paycheck during the time being on FMLA. Many states such as California have programs such as disability insurance and paid family leave for which employees can apply to assist with compensation while out on FMLA. Organizations can then coordinate benefits with these state programs so that employees receive the maximum amount of benefits while on FMLA. Human Resources and Payroll will work with the employee and the state agencies to provide accurate compensation and leave information to coordinate benefits and determine how to best assist the employee during their leave. In many cases, depending on the salary, leave balances and state benefits, an employee may be able to collect one hundred percent of their salary between all the available benefits during their FMLA leave.

It is also important to understand that certain states may have their own regulations allowing additional unpaid leave relating to specific qualifying events. For example, in the state of California, the California Family Rights Act (CFRA) allows for eligible employees to take additional unpaid time off for qualified leave requests. These additional state laws require a robust partnership between Human Resources and Payroll to ensure that employees receive the maximum benefits allowable under federal and state laws. Understanding how each regulation works and how they interconnect or differ from each other is vital to ensuring that policies are written to reflect all benefits afforded to employees. These policies should be reviewed periodically to ensure that they comply with the current regulations. As lawmakers frequently pass new bills to add, change, or update benefits, it is vital to ensure that the organization complies with managing an employee's FMLA and other leave benefits. And as previously mentioned, if there are differences between the federal and state laws, the law that is the most generous to the employee is the law that should be followed.

Government-Mandated, Government-Provided, and Voluntary Benefits

The federal government, as well as many state governments, mandate that certain benefits are made available to employees. The Affordable Care Act (ACA) requires health care coverage be provided and defines eligibility and program requirements. While the insurance plan or plans made available can be determined by the organization, the government mandated requirements must be met with the plans offered. The Family Medical Leave Act (FMLA) allows for eligible employees to receive twelve weeks of protected leave to care for a family member or for the birth of a child. FMLA is a government mandated program; however, how the employee uses their paid time off in coordination with the FMLA leave is a policy decision made by the organization.

Organizations must provide the government mandated benefits like the two examples provided—ACA and FMLA. Organizations can also provide additional benefits to ensure that a robust total rewards package is available and that employees have options. An example of a voluntary benefit would be legal protection coverage or long-term care insurance that is provided through an approved vendor, but at the entire cost of the employee. Regardless of a benefit being government mandated or voluntary, clear communication is required along with easy-to-read, understandable, and fillable forms. Contact information should also be made available for every vendor that provides a benefit or service to employees, including government agencies or local vendors.

Performing Job Evaluations to Determine Compensation

Human Resources professionals are responsible for managing information regarding compensation appropriately, responsibly, and accurately. Ensuring that employees are paid a fair, equitable, and appropriate wage for the work being performed is at the core of compensation-related work. There are numerous tools and resources available to ensure that compensation is being managed appropriately for an organization. Best practices and benchmarking can also be used to align an organization with standards that are practiced across a particular field or industry, business market, state, and beyond.

It is important to have robust practices relative to employee information that assure employees of the confidentiality and security of their information. With the ongoing threat of security breaches and identity theft, it is necessary to safeguard personal employee information, including compensation-related information. Data such as home addresses, dates of birth, social security numbers, direct deposit routing and account numbers, and other highly sensitive pieces of information should be held under lock and key, and when necessary and possible, encrypted.

Human Resources professionals are also responsible for assisting Payroll staff in resolving issues related to inaccuracies in payroll such as salary information, overtime calculations, hours to be paid, and retroactive changes including both overpayments and underpayments. Attention to detail in this area is vitally important as not only can this impact employees personally and financially, but noncompliance with federal and state regulations can cause fines, audits, and further scrutiny into an organization's policies and practices.

Another component that HR is responsible for is understanding and determining the Fair Labor Standards Act (FLSA) status of a position—whether the position is exempt or nonexempt in relation to overtime. Often referred to as "the wage and hour law," the FLSA law will determine if a position is eligible for overtime. Regular audits of this status for every position in an organization should be conducted to ensure compliance with this important law. Understanding that a position's roles and responsibilities evolve with time, it is important that positions are reviewed often to ensure that job descriptions are accurate.

Job descriptions are the foundation of determining the FLSA status; if they are outdated or an inaccurate representation of the actual work being performed, the FLSA status could be inaccurate. The FLSA status for a position is an extremely important component to total compensation and how payroll will calculate an employee's salary. Without a robust knowledge of FLSA and how each position is impacted, Payroll could very well be compensating employees inaccurately. If an audit is conducted and errors and inconsistencies are discovered, an organization could face extreme penalties, fees, and retroactive payments to employees. This could have a huge negative impact to the business and the bottom line.

Human Resources is instrumental in ensuring that compensation is managed appropriately and conveyed to Payroll accurately. A strong working relationship that includes direct lines of communication and understanding of the roles and expectations between these two functions will only benefit an organization and the employees. Some organizations align Payroll within the Human Resources functions, while others place Payroll within the Finance functions. Regardless of where these two functions lie within an organizational reporting structure, Human Resources and Payroll are integral components to each other's success.

Organization Knowledge

Structure of the HR Function

All departments within an organization are structured to deliver services to the customers in the most effective manner possible. The same is true for Human Resources. The organizational structure of an HR department describes how the group is designed, how work is assigned, and how positions report to each other. Organization charts are excellent tools to present this information by showing the hierarchy of the department, the authority levels of each position, and the span of control for each position. Organization charts can be simple or detailed depending on how the department wants to communicate the roles and responsibilities of each team member. Below is an example of a high-level HR organization chart.

Many organizations provide in-depth and detailed organization charts so that they can be used as a tool to educate departments on who the appropriate contact is for specific topics. Below is an example of a more detailed and in-depth HR organization structure.

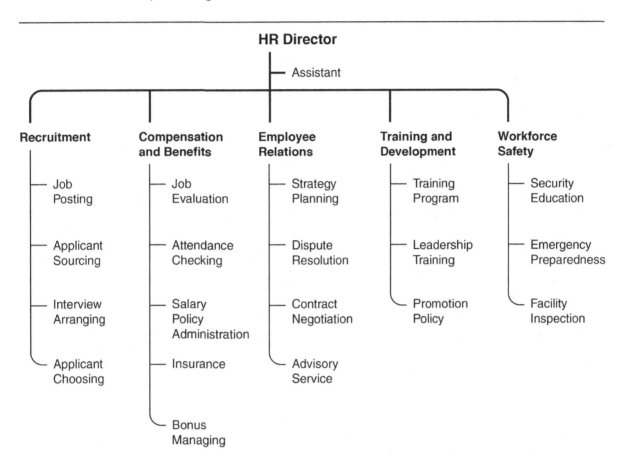

The HR department's structure should be aligned with the organization's needs for services. Some HR departments are **centralized**, meaning all HR services report to the HR leader and provide services to assigned customers. Some HR departments are **decentralized**, meaning certain HR services report to external department leaders and provide services within that department. Centralized and decentralized HR models both have positive and negative attributes. The models should be discussed and assessed prior to making changes to ensure that the departments, or the customers of HR, receive the services they need.

Adapting Work Style to Fit the Organization's

Shared service models are another form of organizational restructuring where a company's administrative staff positions in specific groups, such as HR or information technology, are consolidated across business groups so as not to be redundant. This allows for these types of overhead costs to be distributed across various geographic locations. For example, Bayer Group moved to an HR shared services model several years ago to allow their HRBPs to be more strategic in nature. By doing so, the HRBPs were able to focus on human capital development instead of on managing employee leaves of absence and administering tuition reimbursement. Benefits of an HR shared services model include the following:

- Internal resources placing focus on strategic tasks
- More efficient HR operations
- Greater continuity of HR operations
- Economies of scale gained from combining HR software and tasks
- Higher-quality HR services

Seeking Feedback from Stakeholders

Individuals who have an interest in what a company does or how well it performs are known as **stakeholders**. They are called stakeholders because they have something at stake, or at risk, in the company. Therefore, a company's activities can result in their loss or gain.

Companies have both internal and external stakeholders. Cross-functional stakeholders are simply internal stakeholders that are representative of different areas of the company, such as finance, information technology, legal, customer service, research and development (R&D), and manufacturing. It is important to note that internal stakeholders also have a direct claim on a company's resources.

HR personnel are focused on building strategic relationships with cross-functional stakeholders to contribute to the work they are doing and to make decisions to meet the company's goals. The strategic relationships are built over time as the character and actions of HR personnel increase their credibility with a company's employees, managers, top executives, and board of directors. For example, HR employees work alongside management on a daily basis performing the following labor-management tasks, which helps to form these strategic relationships:

- Adhering to federal, state, and local regulations and laws
- Creating new policies, procedures, and rules in the workplace
- Developing and revising job descriptions
- Establishing salary ranges and position grades
- Conducting a training needs analysis
- Retrieving data for a reduction in force (RIF) and preparing corresponding employee packets/severance packages
- Creating a succession plan

A company's internal stakeholders typically remain motivated to participate in company activities if they are rewarded (e.g., power, personal accomplishment, salary, bonuses, and stock options) in an amount greater than the value of their contributions (e.g., expertise, skills, and knowledge). If this is not the case, the support of internal stakeholders may be withdrawn, and they may even choose to exit the company.

Therefore, HR personnel should stress to cross-functional stakeholders the importance of collaboration leading to successful outcomes, from which they will ultimately benefit through meaningful contributions, and perhaps a bonus program. Cross-functional stakeholders working together toward a common company goal can help break down silos and allow the whole to be greater than the sum of the parts. This will also enable all staff within a company to contribute, thus enhancing the organization's level of inclusiveness.

Acting as HR Contact for Stakeholders

Many organizations utilize a **Single Point of Contact**, or **SPOC**, methodology when delivering customer service. SPOC simply means that a customer has one specific person who is contacted for all questions, concerns, or other matters. A SPOC methodology eliminates the need for a customer to search for the right person to call for a specific question. Rather, the customer contacts the SPOC and if the SPOC is unaware of the answer, they then work to find the answer from the appropriate subject matter expert.

Many HR departments structure the workforce in this type of model based on the organizational needs. For example, there may be one HR Specialist who is the SPOC for all employee leave matters; therefore, any questions related to the Family Medical Leave Act, Worker's Compensation, Disability Leaves, etc. would be directed to this SPOC. Another way of aligning the HR department with an SPOC methodology is to assign one HR Generalist to a specific department to act as that department's SPOC. This could include handling employee leave requests, discipline and coaching issues, training needs, and compensation concerns. Regardless of how the SPOC methodology is implemented, the basic premise is that customers have one single point of contact for all concerns.

Providing Consultation on HR Issues

Human Resources professionals are responsible for providing consultation to managers and employees on professional growth and development opportunities. In order to provide the best recommendations, it is important to understand individual, team, department, and organizational needs. Each level is vital to the overall success of an organization's holistic training program. While training programs should be provided to ensure that updated information is available, new skills and techniques are learned, and certifications are renewed, it is also important to understand individual needs for employees who may be struggling to perform their job. From individual development plans to all-employee focused training programs, Human Resources professionals are responsible for delivering a robust and holistic growth and development program. Additionally, training programs should be aligned with the organization's goals and priorities to ensure that employees are working toward the same goals and priorities in their specific position.

Robust training combines individual skill enhancement with overall training for the entire department. HR can deliver such robust training opportunities by working with department managers. Human Resources departments are responsible for delivering training opportunities with either internal staff or an outside third-party agency. Even if an organization employs individuals who can offer in-house training, it may be beneficial to have a third-party agency deliver certain types of training. Examples of topics that may require a third-party agency to deliver training include legal updates, compliance issues, health and safety matters, and state certifications. Examples of topics that could be provided by internal staff include written and verbal communications, developing relationships, writing emails and reports, and building effective teams.

All employees should be trained in how the organization's systems work and how they will need to use these systems in their position. From submitting timecards for payroll to approving requisitions and purchase orders, HR should ensure that there is a standard protocol for all employees to be trained on the important systems that will be used in their job. Providing opportunities to expand employee's knowledge of these systems can also open future career opportunities for them. Knowledge really is power, and understanding how to gain this knowledge through data and utilizing the systems and programs available can potentially increase the opportunities available to an employee.

Professional growth and development can also be facilitated through access to programs such as tuition reimbursement and job shadowing. Enabling employees to further their formal education by reimbursing their tuition is a great way to show employees that they are supported. Tuition reimbursement also benefits the organization by encouraging employees to use this knowledge to increase their productivity and effectiveness. Job shadowing provides an opportunity for employees to gain exposure to different areas of the organization and the work being done to support overall goals and objectives. Whether formal or informal, job shadowing enables an employee to watch or "shadow" another employee while they work to see what is being done on a daily basis. Job shadowing can be a great tool for employees to use in gaining an understanding of how their work fits in with other employees' work and in the organization as a whole.

Human Resources is instrumental in ensuring that an organization's training program is managed and delivered appropriately. When HR has a strong working relationship with managers and employees, a holistic training program can be developed.

Coordinating with Other HR Functions

An excellent customer service philosophy for HR departments to establish is an expectation regarding the timeframe in responding to customers along with a consistent delivery of information. Nothing is more frustrating than waiting a long time to have a question answered. Additionally, it is equally frustrating to ask the same question to two individuals and receive two different answers. HR should coordinate information, knowledge, and resources to ensure that customers receive accurate and updated information in an efficient manner. If a response is due to a customer within 24 hours and the HR representative needs additional time to research and provide the answer, it is an excellent practice to communicate this information and delayed response to the customer. Allowing for an open exchange and dialogue, along with establishing expectations, is vital to providing excellent service to HR customers.

Integrating Outsourced HR Activities

Many HR departments utilize automated processes and programs such as software that tracks HR information. Data such as personnel information, hiring statistics, recruitment processes, leave management, and timekeeping are often tracked using this type of software. In addition to software, many HR departments employ outside contractors to provide specific services to the organization and department. Specific skills or unique circumstances may require an outside party to provide services. These services could include negotiating a contract with a new bargaining unit or investigating a sexual harassment complaint. Regardless of the service being provided, it is vital for HR leadership to communicate the mission, values, goals, and objectives of the organization and department. By communicating these elements to the outside vendors, it will help to ensure that the services and products provided align with and support the strategic plans and goals of the organization.

Analyzing Key Performance Indicators

Training metrics are important for determining the effectiveness of a training department and all programs being delivered. Organizations should determine what is important to measure and how readily available information is to calculate these measurements. It may not be effective to track certain pieces of data due to a manual process or timely and potentially inaccurate data source. These metrics are often referred to as **key performance indicators**, or **KPIs.**

KPIs are measurements that show the achievement of a certain goal, or in some cases, the lack of achievement. KPIs add the following value:

- Clarity by showing a clear picture of the strategy being implemented
- Focus by showing what matters and what requires attention
- Improvement by showing the progress toward the goals and objectives

Below is a list of potential KPIs to evaluate a training department:

- Average training cost per employee
- Average training hours per employee
- Budget spent on training—by department and overall
- Internal training sessions offered and attended
- External training sessions offered and attended
- Return on investment

Each KPI is a valuable metric that illustrates data used to determine the effectiveness of a training department. KPIs should be clearly defined, and any calculation required should be clearly established, including where and when data will be sourced. When put together to tell the entire story of a training department, these metrics can show where successes are occurring, where opportunities are available, and if there are deficiencies to address. The primary purpose of any metric or KPI is the behavior or change that the measurement creates. When KPIs are established, a training program can be discussed honestly. These discussions then lead to focused training programs in areas that can actually make a difference.

Organizational Effectiveness and Development

According to Richard Beckhard, American organizational theorist and pioneer in the field, organizational development is a process that includes three factors: it is planned, it is implemented organization-wide, and it is managed from the top levels of leadership. **Organizational development** works to achieve an increase in effectiveness and health through planned changes and enhancements across the organization. **Organizational effectiveness** occurs when these specific actions are taken to address challenges and positively resolve issues such as process or skills gaps throughout the organization. HR has an integral role in organizational development through the entire lifecycle of an employee. Beginning with hiring and selection, working through career planning and training, and finally recognizing and promoting employees, HR is instrumental in creating and fostering the workplace culture. Having a positive, healthy, and rewarding culture will continue to motivate employees and develop their skills while enhancing the organizational effectiveness.

Ensuring that Documents and Systems Reflect Workforce Activities

Human Resources handles many key documents and paperwork that must be stored appropriately, securely, confidentially, and accurately. This documentation should also be readily accessible and easy to locate. Files should be handled in the same way to eliminate wasting time to locate specific documents. It is also important to have a centralized location for all files to ensure that all of the information is accessible and available when needed. HR professionals should not have to look in multiple places for documentation. A good example of this is personnel files. HR should be responsible for maintaining the master personnel file which includes all new hire paperwork, status change information, benefits selections, training records, disciplinary records, performance evaluations, and more. While many departments like to maintain a separate file of documentation for their employees for easier access, it is vital to ensure that HR has the master records on each employee so that there are no missing documents. This could be a cause for concern if the department is not maintaining a secure and confidential filing system or adhering to the strict retention laws about maintaining certain documents for required time periods.

Identifying Change Initiatives

Change Management

Organizational changes can come about as the result of internal forces (e.g., exit interviews revealing low job satisfaction, a rebranding initiative, or an effort to create a flatter organization by removing levels of management). Organizational changes may also be the result of findings from an environmental scan (e.g., regulatory and legal changes or discovering the need for a new service or product). **Change management** refers to an organization's ability to implement changes in a diligent and comprehensive manner. This concept of change is holistic and encompasses sweeping change of an organization.

Change agents are individuals who are charged with implementing organizational change effectively. These individuals tend to wear many hats. For example, they:

- Investigate. They need to understand the organization's dynamics as well as employees' attitudes and behaviors surrounding the change.

- Advocate. They must be persistent and continually supporting the change initiative when employees have forgotten about it and are busy with their full-time jobs.

- Encourage. They are skilled at listening to employees who are experiencing a wide range of emotions and may not feel comfortable taking risks or going outside of their comfort zones.

- Facilitate. They design and utilize processes, tools, and forms to assist employees when going through the change.

- Mediate. They manage conflict and help employees find common goals to assist them in collaborating to implement the change.

- Advise. They build credibility with employees through their knowledge and ability to assist them and point them in the right direction.

- Manage. They are conscientious and hold employees accountable to ensure they are on track to meet the due dates and goals for the project.

Executive sponsors, such as senior executives or the CEO, are also critical to the success of change initiatives, because they display commitment to the change at their level of the organization. By being enthusiastic about the change, executive sponsors inspire employees to commit to the implementation process.

Kurt Lewin's Change Model

Kurt Lewin was a social psychologist who presented a change management model back in 1947. His change process theory is a three-step organizational program that seeks to explain how entities change, the catalysts that precipitate change, and how change can be successfully accomplished. Fundamental to the theory is the notion that an entity will respond to the need for change when there is an external stimulus that compels it.

The first phase of the theory is **unfreezing**. The need for change is identified and communicated during this stage, which creates the motivation for change. During unfreezing, it is important to create a clear vision for the outcome that will follow the change while creating a sense of urgency for obtaining that new outcome. The second phase is **changing**. Communication is key during this phase as resistance to the change is managed and the organization comes into alignment with the change. Training on new processes may also take place during this phase. The final phase is **refreezing**. In this phase, the new adjustments are solidified and cemented into the functions of an entity (the change becomes the new norm). During the refreezing phase, evaluation of the outcome takes place, which may lead to some additional fine-tuning. Positive reinforcement is very important during this phase to ensure that employees will not backslide into behaviors they engaged in prior to the change.

Kurt Lewin Change Model

Unfreeze

Create the correct atmosphere for change

Change

Come into alignment with change

Refreeze

Solidify change

John Kotter's Change Model
John Kotter was a well-known change expert and professor at Harvard Business School who introduced an eight-step change model in 1955 that was built upon the previous model by Kurt Lewin. The steps in his model are described below:

- Create urgency. This step involves developing a strong business case around the need for change so employees will buy into the change.

- Form the change coalition. In this step, key stakeholders and true leaders in the organization who will be able to lead the change effort with their influence and authority are identified. The coalition should be made up of a mix of individuals from various levels and departments throughout the organization.

- Create a clear vision for the change. This step involves identifying the purpose for the change.

- Communicate the vision. Since it is important to keep the vision for the change in the forefront of employees' minds, in this step, a communication strategy is developed from the top down.

- Empower action. This step involves removing barriers to change and encouraging or rewarding employees who are thinking creatively and are willing to take risks.

- Create short-term wins. Instead of having a single, long-term goal, this step involves finding some short-term targets that can motivate employees as "wins" when they are achieved and celebrated.

- Build on the change. This step involves utilizing the short-term wins in step 6 to reinvigorate aspects of the change process that have stalled somewhat and to involve employees who have been resistant to the change effort thus far.

- Root the change. In an effort to make the change stick and replace old habits, in this step, discussions about the connections between the successes that have been experienced and the new behaviors continue.

Providing Recommendations for Eliminating Barriers to Organizational Effectiveness

When organizational development and effectiveness are not being realized, there could be multiple reasons for not achieving the desired results. These reasons, often referred to as **barriers**, could exist in various areas of the organization. HR can work with the departments and individual employees to determine the barriers that are prohibiting effectiveness and provide recommendations or resolutions. Some barriers could include a lack of communication, insufficient resources, ineffective technology, increased workload, mental fatigue, inadequate incentives, minimal engagement, low motivation, or lack of specific skills to accomplish required tasks. HR can work to determine what the barriers are and define a plan to address these barriers, if possible, so that the organization can realize its full potential.

Collecting and Analyzing Data on HR Initiatives

Human Resources data is typically organized in six key areas:

1. Workforce Planning, Recruiting, and Applicant Data
2. Employee Data and Job History
3. Performance Evaluation and Succession Planning
4. Training, Growth, and Development
5. Compensation and Benefits
6. Operational and Departmental Information

Each of these areas has specific, unique, and detailed information that allows Human Resources to provide key information and status snapshots to department managers and leadership. This information provides insight for budgeting, planning, forecasting, and modeling. Being aware of and understanding this information is vital; however, integrating this information to create a full overview of an organization's workforce is a tool that can provide exceptional value to the leadership. A holistic view of the workforce can assist with defining new goals and objectives, negotiating new labor contracts, providing succession planning for future growth, awarding performance, recognizing achievements, and more.

Workforce Management

Identifies Gaps in Workforce Competencies

Human Resources professionals need to be able to assess how their organization's current staffing meets the goals and needs of the organization. This includes not only ensuring that the organization has the correct number of personnel for the various roles and requisites of each department, but also that the levels and skillsets of the current personnel are appropriate and can meet the needs and intended functions of their designated roles. This involves a current working knowledge of the goals, tasks, and responsibilities of the various departments and the staff working within those departments.

Implements Approaches to Ensure Appropriate Staffing

Organizations must be strategic when assessing the workforce to ensure readiness and preparedness for both expected and unexpected staffing changes. Workforce assessments should be holistic, thorough, and broad in scope to ensure that planning is as effective as possible. While forecasting is basically a guess, if a robust process is defined and supported with data, these guesses can be useful and, in many cases, accurate in addressing the organizational needs. Workforce planning should include a series of steps to ensure that all available information is utilized in this process.

The first step in the workforce planning process is to understand the business objectives and goals and translate them into personnel needs. Every action taken or program implemented should be directly or indirectly aligned with the business objectives and goals. The work that employees complete is directly aligned with the organization's accomplishments. It is vital to understand how this work is being done and if opportunities are available to increase efficiency and productivity. An excellent tool for assessing personnel needs is a SWOT analysis: Strengths, Weaknesses, Opportunities, Threats. Strengths and weaknesses are usually internal factors, and opportunities and threats are usually external factors. Regardless, this information can be used to determine where resources are available, are needed, and should be deployed relative to personnel needs.

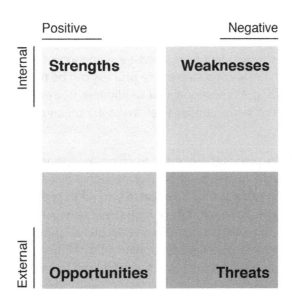

The second step in the workforce planning process is to analyze data. Gathering various pieces of information and analyzing the data will help to provide a complete and holistic view of the organization's personnel needs—both currently and in the near future. Employee demographics, staffing levels, skill mix, turnover trends, retirement opportunities, assumed growth, and available talent pools are all vital pieces of information that can be used to identify the risks and concerns to be addressed. If the majority of the employee population is eligible to retire within the next three years, it is vital that steps be taken immediately to ensure that there is an internal talent pool with the necessary training that would qualify them for promotion. Additionally, understanding the external talent pool is also vital to ensure that any recruitment needs not met by internal promotions can be met by external hires.

Engaging in partnerships with trade schools, universities, professional organizations, or other networks for internships, mentoring, or job training can assist an organization in preparing the external talent pool for future recruitment needs. It is important to note that employee demographics in the context of workforce planning should include more information than is available in a standard system report. While standard information such as years of service, current position and department, former positions and departments, and salary information is important, additional information should be gathered to understand the complete picture of employee demographics. This information should include the following:

- Highest degree received
- Special certifications
- Total years of experience
- Total years of supervisory experience

- Special skills
- Computer software and program proficiency
- Recognition and awards received
- Performance review history

By obtaining and reviewing this information, the HR department can conduct a robust assessment of the workforce, and HR will be able to better assess any skills gaps. This will then enable training and development programs to be implemented to provide the current workforce with growth opportunities or for a specific recruitment plan to be deployed to recruit candidates with the specific skills needed.

The third step in the workforce planning process is to assess the organization's current recruitment and retention practices. This step includes identifying short-term and long-term risks of recruitment and retention. The data gathered in the second step of the process can be further reviewed to ensure that hiring practices identify the strongest, most qualified candidates. Reviewing recruitment timeframes and the number of days that positions remain unfilled can assist the organization in determining new strategies and methods.

The fourth step in the workforce planning process is to recommend and implement programs to address any risks and concerns identified. Training programs, professional development opportunities, external candidate sourcing, and other programs may be necessary to address the current and future needs of the workforce. If an organization sees that a majority of high-level management will be eligible to retire in the next three years, it may be appropriate to work with an educational program to deliver an on-site degree program in management, leadership, or other appropriate fields. Understanding the program and the details such as cost, resources needed, interest, and time required to implement should be a part of the proposal for consideration.

The fifth and final step in the workforce planning process is to prioritize and adjust programs based on the actual results. Once the recommended programs have been implemented, metrics should be developed and reviewed on a reasonable basis to determine the success of each. Certain programs may take longer to see a level of success, and this should be considered when reviewing the data. If a program is not meeting the required milestones and delivering the results anticipated, discussions should determine whether it is necessary to implement an immediate change or course correction. It may be necessary to end a particular program if there are no reasonable results that justify the expenditure of resources.

Organizations that implement a strong workforce planning process are more likely to see the following benefits, which also yield benefits:

- Readily available talent pool
- Optimized employee investments
- Protected historical knowledge

Organizations that have an available talent pool of candidates have shorter recruitment periods, filling open positions faster. This talent pool can be formed by both internal and external candidates. By understanding the current employee dynamics, as addressed in the second step above, HR can regularly determine the talent pool of employees who have promotional or advancement opportunity. Organizations that optimize employee investments in areas such as training, growth, and development realize lower turnover and increased employee morale. Employees that feel valued and supported are more likely to remain with an organization. Organizations that protect the historical knowledge of their employees are more likely to be able to address the impact of employee retirements. Creating programs and tools that facilitate the transfer of knowledge are best practices that should be incorporated at all levels within an organization. All of these benefits provide costs savings to the organization, increase employee morale, and ensure that staffing needs are properly met.

Planning Short-Term Strategies to Develop Workforce Competencies

There are instances when short-term strategies need to be implemented to address issues that arise. These circumstances can include economic downturns, high turnover rate and low recruitment turnout, or an evolution of the business model to increase product sales. In most cases, these include developing a workforce plan that provides targeted recruitment efforts, enhanced training programs, job reassignment, or succession planning and promotion. Other examples of short-term strategies could include the following:

- Providing an employee with an opportunity for a new assignment due to another employee being on an extended leave of absence

- Coordinating a job shadowing program to allow employees to cross-train and learn new skills

- Creating a mentoring program that will encourage members of the leadership team to engage with employees who have communicated a desire to achieve the same accomplishments in their career

Regardless of the program implemented, HR should first communicate these efforts to employees. It may even be beneficial to conduct an employee survey to engage the workforce directly and gain feedback from directly involved individuals. As with all strategies and programs, HR should continue to monitor and assess the effectiveness so that if modifications need to be made, they can be implemented quickly. Short-term strategies should have specific check points to ensure that they are meeting the immediate need; adjustments should be made at these checkpoints as necessary.

Administering and Supporting Approaches to Meet Organization Leadership Requirements

Organizations often utilize a succession planning method to ensure that future leadership is identified, and any skills gaps in education, experiences, and training can be closed. While it is important to ensure a robust external recruitment strategy when looking for an organization's leadership, it is also important to balance this strategy with a solid succession plan to ensure that top talent within the organization is recognized, rewarded, and promoted appropriately. Depending on the organization and the resources available, an excellent practice is to identify the future leadership or top performers and develop for them a specific training and development plan. Regardless of the method used to meet the needs of the organization's leadership, it is important to ensure that the right person is selected for the right position at the right time. The method to accomplish this could be by either conducting a national, external recruitment, or by promoting an internal high performing employee who was previously identified and trained through the succession plan. HR professionals should gain familiarity with employees and the market to propose a course of action that will meet the organization's needs.

Strategies for Restructuring the Organization's Workforce

Organizations experience change often. Whether the change is due to restructuring, mergers and acquisitions, divestitures, expansions, or outsourcing, each change should be accompanied by a full due diligence process and a communications plan. **Due diligence** is an audit or investigation of the changes being considered. Due diligence should include reviews of multiple facets including legal, financial, process, operations, products, consumers, information technology, human resources, and department functions. Each area will be impacted by the change, and it is important to understand the impacts prior to transitioning. This will ensure that each impact is fully vetted and that liabilities can be minimized. A **communications plan** is the complete plan for all communications that should be delivered, when they should be delivered, and to whom. Multiple platforms may be appropriate including in-person meetings to deliver the same message to multiple employees, written memos or question and answer documents, and frequent updates via email. Each platform should be appropriate to the message and its importance.

Human Resources has a key role in the due diligence process with specific focus being on the organization's employees. Human Resources serves as a business partner to senior leadership in the following areas:

- Identify human resource management risks
- Establish appropriate resolutions and options to mitigate the risks
- Determine costs associated with employment changes such as severance
- Assess the organizational structure
- Assess the HR management process

By fully vetting each of these areas during the due diligence process, senior leadership can make the best, most informed decision possible. Once the decision has been made, this information will also lend to a well-planned workforce transition strategy. This strategy should address all possible personnel actions, including changes in position, supervision and leadership, compensation and benefits, transfers, or layoffs.

Fully vetted and well-planned strategies will assist in the transition by providing the following:

- Fair treatment of all employees impacted by the change
- Strong commitment to the transition
- Transfer of critical knowledge and process
- Minimal disruption to the customer
- Stability to and a smooth transition for employees
- Effective training on new processes and procedures for employees

The goal of any transition is to minimize disruption, liability, and insecurity for employees, customers, investors, or vendors. In order to effectively accomplish this, it is vital that communications are accurate, timely, and targeted. This will assist the organization in keeping rumors, misunderstandings, and misperceptions to a minimum.

In order for HR to address employee concerns and issues related to a transition, it is important to understand the process of managing change. Each individual processes change and transition differently; however, having a plan that addresses each step of managing change can assist employees in successfully moving beyond the change and transition successfully. There are two main phases of managing change: before and after the transition. Before the transition, individuals who receive the news go through various stages of emotion: denial, anxiety, shock, resistance, fear, anger, frustration, confusion, and stress. After the transition, individuals go through new stages of emotion while processing and adjusting to the actual changes. The stages of emotion after the transition are creativity, skepticism, acceptance, impatience, hope, energy, and enthusiasm.

Each stage of emotion and the time that it takes to advance to the next stage are different for every individual. Being understanding and offering resources for employees to deal with each stage can be of great benefit to the organization. This allows employees to process the pending changes while still performing in their current position and accept the new changes while acclimating to their new position. A best practice that many organizations implement during times of change is to provide employees services through an employee assistance program (EAP). EAP services can offer resources through a website or other accessible materials, as well as an on-site counselor that communicates to a large group of employees or allows for one-on-one sessions. Communicating the EAP services and the resources available for employees during the transition may be an excellent starting point to the communications plan.

Individuals are generally intuitive and pick up on cultural, personal, and behavioral changes in others. This can quickly lead to rumors, misperceptions, and misunderstandings if not addressed immediately. While many details are inappropriate to share at certain points in time, it is vital to begin communicating with employees as soon as it becomes appropriate. Employees will understand that some details may not be appropriate to share, but they will appreciate the organization taking a proactive approach in communicating.

The most important technique, one that should be incorporated early and often, is communication. Being open and honest, even if there are details that cannot be provided or questions that cannot be answered, is key to the communications plan. The communication plan should include when meetings will be held, what memos will be distributed, and when there will be individual opportunities for discussions; these steps will assist senior leadership with the transition. This support will lead to a more successful transition for the organization and individual employees. An important element to consider when drafting communications for written memos, presentations, or other formats is that the writer or senior leadership is not the audience of the message. Understanding this element and the fact that employees at various levels of the organization may require a different level of information, it is important to tailor the message to the individuals receiving the message.

It may be appropriate to employ a communications professional to ensure that messages are clear, concise, and specific to those receiving the message. Another practice that organizations can incorporate into the communications plan is to identify champions for each department or area of the organization. The champions are responsible for communicating the approved messages to employees and collecting or answering questions that arise during the meeting. The champions would be available when needed and assist employees working through the stages of emotion when dealing with the upcoming changes. Communicating early, frequently, openly, and honestly can make a substantial difference in how employees process and work through a transition that could have extensive and significant impacts.

Employee and Labor Relations

Employee relations is defined as an organization's commitment to foster a positive working relationship with its employees. Generally, HR manages the relationships between employees to ensure that individual needs are met, including answering questions; providing coaching, counseling, and training opportunities; assisting with career guidance; resolving issues between employees; and being a resource. The best way for HR to manage effective and productive employee relations is to ensure employee involvement, communicate openly and honestly, provide counseling and objective feedback, advocate for employee rights through fair and sound policies, and provide fair and appropriate discipline as needed.

Labor relations is defined as the actual relationship between an organization's leadership and its employees, often through the representation of a bargaining union. Labor relations include establishing, negotiating, and administering bargaining agreements and policies that are negotiated in good faith and that benefit both the organization and the employees. Grievances and disagreements are typically managed and resolved through labor relations; however, if resolution cannot be attained, then other techniques can be employed to resolve the issues.

Interactions with Union and Employee Representatives

Employee and labor relations refers to the maintenance of an effective working relationship with employees and the labor unions that represent them. By working together in various settings, organizations can establish positive working relationships with both labor unions and individual employees. Generally, Human Resources professionals are responsible for maintaining and nurturing the relationship with the labor unions that represent employees; however, it is also the responsibility of management and leadership to ensure strong relationships with employees on a day-to-day basis.

Organizations can implement many best practices to ensure strong and effective partnerships. Most of these best practices fall under the overarching theme of frequent and open communication. Implementing a strong communications plan includes incorporating an open-door policy, meeting regularly, establishing joint committees, providing accurate information and reports, inviting various management and leadership levels to employee meetings, and demonstrating a genuine concern for the employees and their wellbeing. Open-door policies are an excellent practice that can be implemented at all levels of an organization. Open-door policies nurture open communication between employees and managers, resulting in a healthier workplace.

Meeting regularly is important to ensure that all parties are informed and educated on pending issues, the status of project works such as policy development, and employee matters. Providing a standing meeting date and time that occurs regularly is an excellent way to ensure that meetings occur. A best practice to incorporate to ensure that meetings are effective and efficient is to have both parties submit items for an agenda that will be published before the meeting. This allows for all parties to be prepared for discussions and status updates.

Establishing joint committees is also a best practice to incorporate into meeting regularly. Often, certain subjects are not appropriate or necessary to bring into a standing meeting until certain research has been conducted. In these cases, creating a joint committee to discuss, research, and analyze the issue is an excellent way to involve individual employees in the process prior to making a decision. Employees are generally more satisfied with and supportive of programs and actions when they have been involved in the process.

Providing accurate information and reports is also important to ensure that all parties have the same data and are working from the same playbook. Reports may be requested on an as-needed basis or may be part of a regular process and run at a certain time each month or quarter. Having a complete understanding of employee demographics is an important piece of information when working to establish positive employee and labor relations.

Another best practice is to engage employees and management or leadership during standing meetings. Inviting employees to have lunch with leadership to discuss concerns or issues is a great way to connect individuals; however, some employees may not feel comfortable in this setting, so it is important to incorporate other opportunities as well. These may include having leadership attend union or employee meetings to provide information or field questions. Ensuring multiple ways of connection and communication is vital to engaging as many employees as possible. In doing so, leadership also conveys a message that the organization has a genuine concern for employees and their overall wellbeing. All of these best practices support the idea of honest concern for employees, which is the cornerstone of positive employee and labor relations.

Supporting the Organization's Interests in Union-Management Activities

Employee relations refers to the organization's intended strategy for changing relationships with employees and, if applicable, their representative unions. It is also a study of the rules, policies, procedures, and agreements that govern individual employees and departments. Employee relations management is about ensuring that any organizational changes recommended are accepted and successfully implemented. To establish a best-class employee relations program, Human Resources professionals should understand the individual components within employee relations and work to align these components with the overall strategy and vision of the employee relations program. Employee relations includes the following components, which lend to establishing a strong employee relations program:

- Employee involvement
- Employee communication
- Employee counseling
- Employee discipline
- Employee rights

These components build the organizational culture that employees work within. The goal of organizational culture and employee relations strategy is to create an environment in which employees feel like they are being treated fairly. Positive and successful employee relations can have significant impacts to the organization such as improving productivity, ensuring implementation of key initiatives, reducing employee costs, and helping employees to grow and develop. Employees are more likely to have a willingness to perform their job well, maintain a positive attitude, stay motivated and motivate others, and have a high level of satisfaction and commitment to the organization. Additionally, employees are more likely to understand their roles and goals within the organization, with their concerns and needs being addressed quickly and efficiently. Finally, employees have the ability to align their personal goals with the department and organizational goals, which can improve morale, loyalty, and productivity.

Employee involvement refers to creating an environment where employees have an impact on decisions and actions that directly affect their jobs. Every employee is regarded as a unique contributor to the organization; therefore, they are directly involved in helping the organization to meet its goals. Employees' input is sought out and valued by management, even if not implemented. Employee involvement is most effective when individuals are trained in team effectiveness, communication, and problem solving. Additionally, organizations that have robust reward and recognition programs along with effective communication plans are more likely to have strong employee involvement and effective employee relations.

Employee communication refers specifically to two main styles of communication: 1) vertical, and 2) horizontal. Employees should receive and provide communications in a vertical style. **Vertical communications** include upward and downward messaging. **Upward communications** are the messages that flow from the lower levels to the higher levels of an organization. Upward communications include suggestion boxes, employee surveys, open-door policies and procedures, face-to-face conversations, and department meetings to provide insights. **Downward communications** are the messages that flow from the upper levels to the lower levels of an organization. Downward communications include directives from executive leadership, policies and procedures, performance feedback, official memos and instructions, annual reports, and handbooks. Each type of communication is vital to the success of an organization's employee relations program.

Horizontal communication is also important within an organization. **Horizontal communications** are the messages that flow laterally between employees within the same rank. These communications often include problem solving, coordination, and sharing or learning between positions. Horizontal communication is generally informal, but it has a powerful impact within the organization.

Employee counseling refers to the process used when a performance problem cannot be addressed with training or coaching methods. Employee counseling is vital to uncovering the reasons for poor performance and focuses on performance-related behaviors to ensure a positive outcome. Ensuring that the employee understands and accepts the problem is the first goal of employee counseling. Once this has occurred, solutions can be explored to manage the expectations and resolve the issue. Sometimes, the root cause of a performance concern is a personal issue that the employee is dealing with. In these circumstances, once this has been discovered, Human Resources professionals can direct the employee to resources available to assist. **Employee Assistance Programs (EAPs)** are excellent programs to have available to employees to help them work through personal issues so that employees can remain on task while at work.

Employee discipline refers to the tool used by management to improve poor performance and enforce appropriate behavior to ensure a productive and safe workplace. It is vital to ensure that employee discipline is fair and equitable and that employees clearly understand the rules and regulations being enforced, the process to raise concerns and issues, the investigation process, and the penalties involved. If progressive discipline is utilized, employees should understand the intention and when it is appropriate to be used.

Progressive discipline is a discipline system that imposes progressively greater disciplinary measures based on the conduct of an employee. An example of this would be an employee receiving a written warning for attendance issues. If the attendance issues do not change after a stipulated period of time, the employee would receive a day of discipline imposed. Additional future incidents may be given increased disciplinary time off until either the behavior is changed permanently or other corrective action is needed.

Similarly, it is important for employees to understand that some behavior may not warrant progressive discipline, and the corrective action may be immediate termination. An example of this would be engaging in a physical altercation with or sexually harassing a fellow employee. Both of these examples would be appropriate to progress to discipline beyond a written warning after the first offense, including immediate termination after conducting a full investigation. Employees should have clearly defined expectations regarding their behavior and performance as well as what will occur if there are issues with either.

Employee rights refers to the rights that all employees have, including fair and equitable treatment, representation, privacy, grievances, and appeals processes. Employees have the right to know that any investigation conducted was fair and thorough, with sufficient opportunities provided to convey all sides of the situation. Employees should be afforded the right to representation, if applicable. If employees are represented by a union, representation should be offered, especially during disciplinary procedures and investigations. If an employee is not afforded this right, it could interfere with the integrity of the investigation and subsequent discipline. Employees should be afforded the right of privacy. Any disciplinary action, corrective counseling, investigation information, or other details specific to an employee should be held with an appropriate level of confidentiality. Additionally, employees should understand the rights associated with filing a grievance or appeal to resolve an issue or argue a decision such as a disciplinary action.

Ensuring that each of the above components is strong, transparent, and understood will allow an organization to have an effective and productive employee relations program. Employees will more likely be fully engaged, involved, productive, and efficient in their work.

The Collective Bargaining Process

Collective bargaining refers to the process of negotiation between management and union representatives regarding issues such as compensation, benefits, working hours, disciplinary processes, layoffs and terminations, grievance and arbitration processes, union activities, and employee rights. Furthermore, collective bargaining is the continued relationship between management and union representatives that involves the exchange of commitments to resolve conflicts and issues. While collective bargaining is required by law for both parties to negotiate in good faith, success is only achieved when both parties are willing to listen, understand, and compromise. **Good faith bargaining** refers to the duty of both parties to demonstrate a sincere and honest intent to reach agreement, be reasonable, communicate honestly, and negotiate in the best interest of the employees. It is important to note that collective bargaining is a group action that many refer to as an art form. Collective bargaining should not be a competitive process, but rather a continuous and logical process that involves strategy and understanding.

Collective bargaining is the formal process to negotiate contracts and agreements between an employer and union representative. There are various objectives that collective bargaining seeks to achieve:

- Settle disputes or conflicts regarding wages, benefits, working conditions, or safety concerns

- Protect employees' interests

- Resolve differences over difficult and stressful issues

- Negotiate voluntarily and as needed, without the influence or interference of an outside third party who is not as familiar with the organization and employees

- Agree to amicable terms and conditions through a give-and-take strategy

- Co-exist and work together peacefully for the mutual benefit and morale of all employees

- Maintain employee and employer relationships

A best practice that many negotiators utilize at the bargaining table is to establish ground rules at the beginning of the process. **Ground rules** refers to a set of items agreed upon by both parties to assist the negotiations process. Ground rules establish respect for both parties, the time and efforts each puts forth, and other specific areas that may arise during negotiations. Ground rules should establish the following:

- Who speaks for the parties and the individuals representing each party

- When subject matter experts will be called in and the specific purpose

- Where, when, and how long the parties will meet

- A cut-off date for submitting new proposals

- How formal proposals and responses will be made

- Communications plans regarding media or external communications

- What form of agreement will be acceptable: full and complete document or an itemized list of agreed upon changes

- Any other specific details pertinent to the negotiations

There are five basic steps to the collective bargaining process: prepare, discuss, propose, bargain, and settlement. While this process is shown below as a linear process, there can be multiple twists and turns when bargaining in real life. Negotiators should be prepared for surprises and unexpected events that could derail negotiations.

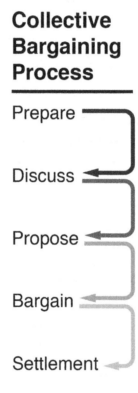

Collective Bargaining Process

Prepare

Discuss

Propose

Bargain

Settlement

Prior to beginning the negotiation process, it is vital for both sides to prepare and determine what needs to be changed, added, updated, deleted, or remain status quo. Each side should come to the negotiation table well prepared and ready to begin discussions. During discussions, new ideas may be presented from the opposing side that require additional preparation before they can be conducted. These should be discussed, and a plan to engage in further discussions should be agreed upon.

Proposals should be given that are thoughtful and based on the needs of the party. They should be clear, concise, and fully communicate the intent of the suggestion as well as provide an understanding of the effects of the change. The employer usually bears the responsibility of costing out a contract and determining the expenses related to new proposals. As each new proposal is discussed, the open dialogue should include transparency regarding the costs associated with each. If an organization only has authorization to spend a certain amount of money to settle a contract, negotiations will need to be conducted about how to spend that money. If every proposal comes with a cost, the sides may have to agree to the proposals that will meet the cost allocation provided and have the most positive impact on the organization and employees.

An example of this is proposing a five percent increase in wages and additional time off that would equate to an additional two percent increase in cost. If the organization is only approved to negotiate an increase of four percent, the parties may want to negotiate a smaller increase to both wages and time so that both areas are receiving an increase, but the overall cost is within the approved cost threshold. When situations like this arise, a vital piece of information is understanding the needs and wants of the employees so that the best decision can be made. When all of the proposals have been discussed and bargaining has occurred for each, the parties can agree to the terms and conditions through a formal settlement.

Each side should have the opportunity to review the final documents before signing. Once the official settlement has occurred, the union representatives must then begin the education and communication process with the membership for ratification of the proposal. **Ratification** is the process in which represented employees vote to approve or deny the proposed settlement. If the settlement is ratified, then the organization will move forward to receiving final approval through a board or executive authority and then finally implementing the terms of the settlement.

Once a final settlement is achieved and ready for implementation, it is important to roll out a communication plan so that employees will understand what will happen and when. Employees should clearly understand what changed, what stayed the same, and, if appropriate, why.

ADR Processes

Alternative dispute resolution (ADR) refers to many different processes and techniques that assist two parties in resolving their issues without filing a lawsuit or going to court. ADR processes include informal and voluntary processes such as negotiation and mediation as well as formal and mandatory processes such as conciliation and arbitration. The more informal the process, the more control each party has regarding recommendations to the resolution. The two parties are generally negotiating between themselves without intervention. As the process becomes more formal, there is less control by either party as an arbitrator, judge, or jury determines the resolution. The goals of ADR are to expedite the exchange of information and decision making, while lowering costs and achieving resolution quickly and confidentially.

The techniques used in ADR are flexible and can be customized to the parties involved and the specific issue that requires resolution. **Negotiation** is a voluntary agreement that works out a solution directly between the two parties involved. **Mediation** is a facilitated negotiation that works out a solution between the two parties through a neutral third party or mediator. **Conciliation** is a non-binding formal process in which a conciliator explains the law and provides the parties with non-binding recommendations to resolve the issue. **Arbitration** is a formal process in which an arbitrator considers evidence presented by each party and determines a solution that is binding and final. It is a common practice to work through the four ADR processes respectively, as described above. Progressing through the four ADR processes above prior to filing a lawsuit or claim is an appropriate path to follow if the matter cannot be resolved. Human Resources is an important resource for each of these steps as HR professionals can provide insights and information that can assist with negotiating an agreement at any of these levels.

Making Recommendations for Addressing Employee Representation

The first major labor statute passed in the United States was the **Norris-LaGuardia Act** of 1932. The Norris-LaGuardia Act endorsed collective bargaining as public policy and established government recognition that the job to a worker is more important than a worker to a corporation. Establishing this relationship was vital in showing that the only real power an employee has is in impacting employers through concerted activity. While this act did not create new rights, it curbed the power of courts to intervene in labor disputes and declared that unions could operate free from corporate control and interference.

The **National Labor Relations Act (NLRA)** is the basic law governing relations between labor unions and employees, giving employees the right to organize and bargain collectively. The NLRA is also known as the **Wagner Act** and was passed in 1935. The NLRA prohibits both employers and unions from violating the basic rights of employees, which include the following:

- The right to self-organize a union to negotiate with the employer
- The right to form, join, or assist labor organizations
- The right to bargain collectively about wages, working conditions, and other subjects
- The right to discuss employment terms and conditions of employment
- The right to choose representatives to bargain
- The right to take action to improve working conditions by raising work-related complaints
- The right to strike and picket, as appropriate
- The right to engage in protected activities
- The right to refrain from any of the above

Additionally, the NLRA stipulates that employers cannot prohibit employees from soliciting for a union during nonwork time or from distributing union literature or communications during nonwork time. The NLRA also prohibits the union from threatening employees with termination or other unjust actions unless union support is given. Finally, the NLRA established the **National Labor Relations Board (NLRB).** The NLRB certifies organized labor unions, supervises elections, and has the power to act against unfair business practices.

The NLRA establishes that both parties must negotiate and bargain in "good faith." **Good faith bargaining** refers to the honest attempt made by both the employer and union to reach an agreement. Good faith bargaining does not obligate either the employer or union to specific concessions or proposals. The basic requirements for bargaining in good faith include approaching negotiations with sincere resolve to reach an agreement, meeting regularly and at reasonable times, putting agreements in writing if requested, and having authorized representatives available and present at the scheduled times. The NLRA also establishes that mandatory subjects of bargaining must be negotiated between labor and management. **Mandatory subjects of bargaining** include wages, benefits, time off, hours, seniority, safety conditions, working conditions, employee testing protocols, disciplinary procedures, and recruitment issues such as promotion and demotion.

In 1947, the **Taft-Hartley Act**, or the **Labor-Management Relations Act,** was passed to amend the NLRA and limit employee labor rights. The Taft-Hartley Act provided protections for employers and stated that they too have the right to go to the NLRB. This act prohibited unions from engaging in the following behavior:

- Forcing employees to support and join the union
- Refusing to bargain in good faith with employers

- Carrying out certain kinds of strikes
- Charging excessive union fees
- Going on strike during certain periods of time

It also provides for a cooling-off period in negotiation. Additionally, this act allowed states to pass "right-to-work laws," banned union contributions to political campaigns, required that union leaders swear they were not communists, and allowed for government intervention in certain circumstances. Finally, the Taft-Hartley Act established the **Federal Mediation and Conciliation Service (FMCS)** to help resolve negotiating disputes.

In 1959, the **Landrum-Griffin Act,** or the **Labor-Management Reporting and Disclosure Act,** was passed to amend the NLRA again. The Landrum-Griffin Act increased reporting requirements, regulated union affairs, and protected union members from improper union leadership to safeguard union member rights and prevent inappropriate practices by employers and union officers. This act is a bill of rights for union members, and it provides election procedures, accounting practices, and leadership oversight. This act was intended to protect the interests of the individual union members. This act provides union members the right to:

- Identify and propose candidates for office
- Vote in elections to select a board of representatives
- Attend and participate in union meetings
- Vote on union business
- Review and audit union accounts and records for transparency and accountability
- File grievances against union officers as appropriate to protect the integrity of the union

The history of unions in the United States goes back to ensuring that employers provide a safe workplace and a fair wage for a day's work. Employees should leave work in the same physical condition that were in when they arrived. While there are various federal laws enacted to protect worker's rights as discussed above, as well as laws that protect wages, working conditions, safety and wellness, and other areas of concern, some individuals still want unions to represent their interest with employers.

While there are many misperceptions about why employees might consider and want a union, the following are the most common reasons for unionizing a workforce:

- Poor communications
- Poor leadership and management
- Supervisors and employee treatment
- Stagnant wages and benefits
- Healthcare and retirement plans
- Safety and working conditions
- Workload and stress
- Job security
- Employee morale
- Lack of employee recognition and appreciation

There is usually not one specific reason that a group of employees may look to unionize, but rather a culmination of multiple factors that lead to a disengaged, unmotivated, and dissatisfied group of employees.

Developing Workplace Policies, Handbooks, and Codes of Conduct

In order for ethical behavior and a company's values to be demonstrated by employees at the lower levels of an organization, these expectations must be modeled by individuals at the top (the members of the board of directors and executive management). Once a company establishes its core values, it is important for management to abide by them because employees are always watching their leaders, especially in difficult times. Management loses credibility with employees when it only "talks the talk" but is not willing to "walk the walk."

The following are some ways management and HR personnel can incorporate a company's values into daily business activities:

- HR can train hiring managers to interview candidates to determine if they are going to be the best cultural fit based on the company's values (in addition to their skills and abilities). For example, if teamwork is one of a company's values, it is important to ask a candidate about their ability to work well as part of a team.

- Managers can reinforce the values during a new hire orientation presentation.

- Managers and HR can reinforce the values in company communications.

- Managers and HR can develop a system to recognize and reward employees for demonstrating the company's values. This may include something as simple as a manager verbally recognizing an employee during a staff meeting, featuring an employee who demonstrates the company's values on the website, or a web-based system where employees nominate their peers for a "spot award," and one lucky winner each month gets a $50 Amazon gift card.

- Managers can integrate the company's values into the performance review process. For example, in addition to evaluating employees on their annual project goals, a manager can also assess them on how well they demonstrate the company's core values. The performance review may be set up so that, even if an employee achieves all of his project goals, he cannot receive an overall review rating of "exceeds" if he has not demonstrated the company's core values over the past year.

- Managers and HR can decide to terminate employees who ultimately fail to exhibit the company's values.

Organizations committed to ethical practices typically develop a code of conduct and/or a code of ethics to communicate the expectations to their employees. Some organizations combine these two codes into a single document. A **code of conduct** details the behaviors a company requires of its employees as well as the behaviors that are prohibited and subsequently result in disciplinary action. A **code of ethics** details the ideal set of standards a company intends to uphold in its business dealings. The following is a list of sections typically found in a company's code of ethics:

- Confidentiality
- Conflicts of interest
- Gifts, entertainment, and contributions
- Personal use of company assets
- Workplace privacy
- Outside employment
- Ownership of intellectual property

- Fair dealing
- Standards of business conduct
- Reporting code violations

Some organizations have hired individuals known as **ethics officers** who are charged with ensuring that employees maintain the ethical standards that were initially developed by executive management and informing the executive team about any ethical issues that may arise.

Some essential job functions of the individuals performing this role include the following:

- Create and distribute ethics statements and supporting documentation.

- Periodically review the company's other policies to ensure consistency with the ethics message.

- Develop and facilitate ethics training for all levels of employees within the company.

- Conduct ethics violation investigations and prepare all associated reports.

- Lead annual corporate governance audits with members of the legal team to minimize company risk.

- Conduct confidential employee hearings about matters concerning conflicts and ethics.

- Stay up to date on corporate governance requirements and the company's compliance and reporting responsibilities.

Providing Employment Agreement Guidance to Employees

Policies and procedures are significant, as they communicate the values and expectations of an organization. They ensure accountability, implement best practices, and facilitate decision making. **Policies** are the standards or guides to the organizational philosophy, mission, and values. **Procedures** are targeted and specific action plans to achieve the organization's goals. Most organizations implement various procedures to ensure consistency, equity, and fairness, including standard operating procedures, employee handbooks, and time/attendance rules.

Standard operating procedures (SOPs) ensure that processes are completed accurately and efficiently every time. SOPs are documents that describe specific details of a task or operation to ensure the quality of work completed. They provide a set of instructions, steps, and guidelines for individuals to follow to ensure safety, compliance, and accuracy each time the process is completed. Additionally, SOPs maximize efficiency and productivity by minimizing errors and rework while maximizing resources and continuous improvement. SOPs can also protect the organization and employees when questions of legality or compliance arise.

Employee handbooks are structured manuals that communicate expectations regarding the employment experience. When provided with a handbook, employees can take ownership of locating answers to commonly asked questions or understanding a specific program. Employee handbooks should strive to achieve the following:

- Introduce employees to the organizational culture, including the mission, values, and goals.

- Communicate expectations for employees and management.

- Ensure that key policies are clearly understood.

- Showcase the benefits offered to employees such as wellness programs, employee assistance programs, discounts, recognition programs, training opportunities, and more.

- Ensure compliance with federal and state laws.

- Provide employees with their rights, responsibilities, and where to go for help.

- Defend against employment claims.

Employee handbooks should also define the standard work schedule, the performance evaluation process, the dress code, and emergency procedures. Employee handbooks serve many purposes, specifically being a reference guide, a communication tool, and an enforcement of company policies. A common best practice is to require all new employees to read the handbook and return a notification that the handbook has been read and understood. This protects the organization from frivolous claims pertaining to not knowing about a particular program or policy.

Time and attendance procedures establish the requirements and expectations of employees regarding reliability and punctuality. Ensuring that employees are available, on time, and at work maintains a productive and fair work environment for all. These procedures should communicate the process for requesting and scheduling time off from work, including vacation and illness leave, as appropriate. Procedures for requesting medical leaves, such as the Family Medical Leave Act (FMLA), should also be detailed in the time and attendance procedures.

Employees should have a clear understanding of their responsibilities when it comes to not being at work. Excessive absenteeism and tardiness create a burden on the company and other employees. When an employee will be late or absent at the last minute, it is important to have an established procedure in which they can call in to report being late or absent due to an emergency or unforeseen circumstance. Time and attendance procedures should also stipulate the consequences for failing to adhere to the expectations of being on time and at work. These consequences could include disciplinary action—up to and including termination—depending on the severity and frequency of the absences and tardiness.

Consulting Managers on How to Supervise and Handle Difficult Employees

Complaints or concerns should always be addressed in a fair and consistent manner regardless of the subject of the complaint. While specific complaints may require different processes due to complexity or legal issues, it is important to have standardized processes and practices. It is also important to understand when to inform leadership of issues and concerns. It may be appropriate to communicate a synopsis, including resolutions, at the end of a process for informational purposes only; however, based on the issue, severity, risks, and impacts, it may be necessary to communicate to leadership immediately after the complaint is received. Leadership may need to be involved in the investigation and process, including the recommendations and action plan to resolve the concerns. It is important to understand the level of communication needed based on the issue.

Handling complaints, either informal or formal, should follow a structured process. Employees should have a full understanding of how and to whom a complaint can be submitted, how the process will unfold, and an estimate of the time needed to complete the process. Seeking to understand as much as possible about the issue should be at the core of the process. This is accomplished by asking questions, researching practices, analyzing data, and following up on additional pieces of information gained throughout the process. Being respectful, responsive, attentive, empathetic, and available will assist in ensuring an effective complaint handling process.

The goal of handling any complaint is to resolve the issue at the lowest level possible. To be successful, employees, especially supervisors, should be trained in conflict resolution methods. **Conflict resolution** involves the following:

- Identifying the problem that is causing the issue
- Identifying the feelings, perceptions, and opinions regarding the issue
- Identifying the potential impacts of the issue as well of any resolution implemented
- Identifying the recommendations and actions to implement to resolve the issue
- Working towards resolution of the issue
- Communicating the resolution with all parties as appropriate

If conflict resolution methods do not resolve the issue, then more formal approaches should be taken to escalate the issue. Ensuring that the issue is resolved in the most effective and efficient way possible is the goal of any process. Filing a grievance, submitting a formal complaint, or reaching out to other oversight organizations that investigate matters such as safety issues (Occupational Safety and Health Administration) or employment practices (Equal Employment Opportunity Commission) may be appropriate as a next step. However, it is important to note that depending on the issue, it may be appropriate to begin the complaint handling process at a more formal level. Examples of these issues would be sexual harassment, workplace violence, discriminatory practices regarding promotions, unsafe working conditions, or other concerns that deserve an escalated response. In each of these examples, leadership should be notified immediately to ensure that the issues are addressed promptly and appropriately. Once a case has been resolved, it may be appropriate to review applicable policies and procedures to ensure that necessary changes are made so that future incidents may be avoided.

Conducting Investigations into Employee Misconduct

Internal investigations are conducted when issues arise or complaints are submitted. Regardless of how an issue comes to the attention of Human Resources, an investigation should be conducted to ensure that any concerns or potential policy violations are corrected and that appropriate responses and actions are delivered. Employees should understand how to submit a complaint regardless of who it is against or what the subject matter. Internal investigations can be both informal and formal, but both should be conducted with good-faith efforts that result in a rational and supported conclusion. Informal investigations could turn into formal investigations to ensure that the issues are fully reviewed and understood. Additionally, a formal investigation could result in an external third-party investigation to ensure impartiality and a full vetting of the issues from an outside perspective. While it is a best practice to attempt to resolve issues and concerns at the lowest level possible, there will always be a need to investigate claims and concerns. Human Resources professionals should be properly and formally trained to investigate complaints.

Internal investigations should always include interviews with the employee making the complaint, the employee who the complaint is against (if any), all witnesses to the incident, and any other party that may have firsthand information and knowledge of the incident. While it is a good practice to have prepared questions for all interviews, it is also appropriate to ask additional questions if new information is presented during the interview to ensure that a full understanding of the incident is gathered. It may be necessary to schedule follow-up interviews based on the information that is gathered or new evidence that is gained. After gathering all information, interviewing all appropriate parties, and assessing the credibility of the investigation, Human Resources professionals should prepare a conclusion and recommendation to resolve the initial complaint.

Investigation conclusions should be rational, specific, and legally defensible based solely on the information gathered during the investigation. Resolution could be conflict resolution between two employees, changing policy or procedure to address a workplace issue, creating training programs for employees to work better together in a team dynamic, and/or discipline if appropriate. Multiple resolutions may be necessary to ensure that the issue is fully addressed and potential future occurrences are eliminated.

When conducting an internal investigation, there are various best practices to incorporate into the process to ensure a thorough and fair investigation. First, it is important to be proactive and not reactive. Investigators should take a proactive approach when gathering information from employees and researching data and details. Being proactive allows the organization to gather the most recent and current information available. Witnesses are more likely to remember details and specifics when the incident is fresh and recent, versus trying to recount information regarding something that happened a while ago. Being proactive also includes being broad and open to identifying new resources that would have information pertinent to the case versus only relying on one individual's account of an incident. A common quote used to describe this is "follow the leads." If an investigator follows the leads and goes where the evidence leads, the investigation is more likely to yield an accurate assessment and conclusion of the incident.

Second, it is important to agree to the purpose and specific issue being investigated. When employees understand what the investigation is attempting to define or discover, they are more likely to be able to provide specifics about the incident. During the investigation, information may arise that is outside of the original scope, and it is important to ensure that either the initial investigation is expanded or a secondary investigation is conducted to review the new information.

Third, investigations should always be independent and impartial. Investigations should be conducted by individuals who can review the evidence and conduct interviews that are unbiased and open-minded. Depending on the professional relationship between the employee complaining and the Human Resources professional conducting the investigation, it may be appropriate to bring in an external investigator who can maintain impartiality. Not only does this allow for a fair and accurate investigation, conclusion, and proposed recommendation, but it also avoids allegations or the perception of conflicts of interest.

Fourth, completed investigations and recommendations should align with the organization's policies, procedures, and goals. If there is not alignment based on the behavior of employees, the investigation may prompt a review and evaluation of the policies, procedures, and goals of the organization. Regularly reviewing these items against the behaviors of employees allows the organization to implement programs that can affect cultural change and promote appropriate and respectful behavior.

Finally, investigations should always consider the consequences and repercussions of the issues being brought forward and the effects of not handling and resolving the issues quickly and completely. Many states have laws that hold supervisors responsible for their behavior, as well as the organization, if appropriate actions are not taken to correct behavior or hold employees responsible. Modern society holds individuals to a higher standard regarding sexual harassment, and many federal statutes are being passed to ensure accountability, transparency, understanding, and consequences. In addition to this, many states are mandating frequent training and requirements regarding training for specific levels of employees. Supervisors may be required to frequently attend expanded training sessions to ensure a thorough knowledge and understanding of the responsibilities when supervising others. However, organizations are responsible for ensuring that training requirements are met and that actions are taken to address issues. By conducting fair, impartial, thorough, and proactive investigations, Human Resources professionals can protect employees and the organization.

Managing Employee Grievance and Discipline Processes

Employees can be terminated from an organization for many reasons. **Involuntary terminations** are separations of an employee and an organization that are warranted due to poor performance, failure of probation, disciplinary actions due to inappropriate conduct or policy violations, or layoffs. **Voluntary terminations** are the separations of an employee due a decision made solely by the employee. Generally, voluntary terminations are resignations due to taking a position with another organization, retirement, or leaving the workforce due to personal reasons such as relocation, choosing to have a family and stay home with the children, or health concerns.

Employees who are involuntarily terminated should be provided with due process based on the reasoning for the separation. If an employee is being terminated for poor performance or failure of probation, the manager should work with Human Resources prior to the termination to ensure that the employee is aware of this issue and given an appropriate amount of time to correct the issues. If sufficient progress is not made within a specified period of time, Human Resources should then work through the appropriate process to terminate employment. In the case of terminating an employee due to inappropriate conduct or policy violations, due process should be afforded. Conducting a proper investigation and determining the appropriate level of discipline should be standard procedure. Depending on the violation, immediate termination may be appropriate; however, if progressive discipline is appropriate, the employee will need to progress through the levels of disciplinary action prior to being terminated.

When an employee is terminated under these circumstances, Human Resources should ensure that a safe and secure environment is provided to deliver the message. A common practice is to terminate an employee at the end of their scheduled shift and/or at the end of the work week. Efforts should be taken to ensure the safety of all employees and may include having a security guard or a police officer on-site and available in the case of emergencies. Employees being terminated should be afforded the opportunity to collect their belongings; however, in some circumstances, it may be more appropriate to mail personal belongings to the individual to expedite leaving the premises. The information technology department should be notified to immediately disable all access to systems, change passwords, and set up out-of-office messages and auto-forwarding of emails.

In the event that an employee is being laid off, Human Resources should ensure that the employee is provided with as much notice as possible and any resources are made available to the employee. On-site counselors may be appropriate to ensure that employees receive the message in a safe environment with readily available resources. When an employee is laid off, it is important to remember that each individual will handle this news differently. Reactions from crying or yelling to no reaction at all are normal. Human Resources professional should be trained and prepared to handle any situation.

When an employee voluntarily resigns, a common practice is to provide a two-week notice to the employer to make arrangements and transition the employee out of the organization. An exit interview is a best practice that many organizations utilize to provide the employee an opportunity to communicate what the organization does well and what the organization could do better. Additionally, questions regarding compensation, benefits, programs, training, opportunities, supervision, and other topics are appropriate to learn more about the impact these items may have had in the decision to leave. Some organizations use this opportunity to ask questions about policy violations, harassment, discrimination, or other inappropriate behaviors that the employee may have witnessed or been subjected to during their employment. This information allows the organization to respond accordingly and take corrective action if necessary. Understanding the reasons why employees voluntarily exit an organization can help determine ways to retain current and future employees and address the gaps and needs to increase retention.

Regardless of the type of termination, all employees should receive exit paperwork that documents information such as the following:

- Final paycheck details, including if a special check will be issued and when
- Leave balance payouts
- Insurance information including when coverage will end
- COBRA and insurance extension information
- Contact information for Human Resources
- Unemployment information

Human Resources professionals should be familiar with state requirements regarding when final paychecks are to be processed. For instance, in the state of California, all private organizations must issue the final paycheck, including all leave balance payouts and any compensation owed, within specific timeframes. If the employer has terminated the employee involuntarily, the final paycheck must be processed and provided to the employee at the time of termination. If an employee resigns and provides no notice, the employer must process the paycheck and provide it to the former employee within three working days. If an employee resigns with a period of notice, the final paycheck must be processed and provided to the employee on their last working day. It is vital to understand these legal requirements as the organization can face penalties and fines if they are not followed accurately.

Resolving Workplace Labor Disputes Internally

It should be the goal of HR professionals to resolve workplace disputes internally and at the lowest level possible. Sometimes, disputes between employees rise to a level that requires a third-party investigation; however, most matters can be resolved through a standard, internal conflict resolution process. As soon as HR is aware of an issue, it is important to act immediately and address the situation so that a resolution can be quickly and amicably achieved. Some issues may be resolved simply by having a conversation with involved individuals to correct any misunderstandings and move forward. Employees may just want to be heard and understood. No matter what approach was deemed appropriate, it is important to the process to ensure that all individuals could express their feelings, concerns, and ideas to resolve the issue and move forward. There may be occasions when issues are of a more serious nature and HR needs to launch a full investigation of the matter. However, when appropriate and necessary, HR should strive to implement conflict resolution techniques to resolve issues internally and at the lowest level possible.

Technology Management

Technology management is a significant tool that can have numerous benefits for the HR department. Most organizations are realizing the benefits that can be seen from utilizing a robust and advanced technology platform to deliver information. These benefits include the following:

- Provides better recordkeeping
- Improves accuracy
- Eliminates bias
- Maintains confidentiality

- Saves time and increases proficiency
- Organizes information
- Updates continually
- Provides a standard of data entry

While not all processes or tasks may have the ability to be automated, it is important to automate as much as possible so that there is less risk for the department. These risks could include providing inaccurate information when important decisions are being made, taking too long to provide information, having disjointed and unorganized reports, or having data stolen. Microsoft spreadsheets are much easier to hack than a professional and secure Human Resources Management System that is generally protected by encryption and security measures.

Technology Solutions for HR Services

Technology management works to enable access to employee information on numerous levels. From self-service portals and filing electronic documents in the onboarding process to managing recruitments and protecting personal data and information, technology management works to provide a solution for each of these initiatives. A common tool that many employees engage with is the self-service portal. This portal is available through an internal website that requires identification and approved access as an employee. Information such as personnel policies, address change forms, benefits documents for open enrollment, and complaint procedures are made available for employees to access at their convenience. Providing employees with the ability to locate important information when needed is vital to ensuring a positive, open, and empowered workforce. Ensuring that employee data is protected is one of the most important functions of technology management. Information such as social security numbers, birth dates, home addresses, and dependent information including minor children must be protected against hackers and leaks. Enabling the most recent and powerful security protocols and safety features helps to ensure that employees feel secure about the protection of their personal information.

Implementing HRIS

A **Human Resource Information System (HRIS)** assists HR with storing information such as employee documents and making effective decisions. This type of system also aids HR personnel with pulling the data needed to compile various reports for federal and state agencies, such as the EEOC. The following is a list of ways a company's HRIS can be used:

- Tracking employees' service awards
- Tracking recruitment efforts
- Allowing for automated benefit administration
- Compliance reporting
- Tracking employees' time and attendance
- Administering training programs
- Eliminating any data entry duplication
- Compensation administration
- Sharing payroll information with the finance group

When selecting and implementing an HRIS, it is important to consider if it will need to be integrated with other company systems and to make decisions as to who will see what information, which determines the number of levels of access.

Policies for Maintaining Confidentiality of Employee Data and Using Technology to Protect Privacy

Data security is defined as the security relating to the confidentiality, availability, and integrity of data. Data security focuses on a location's physical security as well as the logical security of data and digital information. Data security includes issues such as the confidentiality, integrity, and availability of data; network protection; and the physical security of facilities, equipment, transport, and employees. **Data privacy** is defined as the appropriate use and control of the data. Data privacy focuses on protocols that employees have over their personal and work-related data and how to protect it from unwanted or harmful uses. Data privacy includes issues such as how data are processed, where data are held, and how long data will be retained. Data security and privacy are vitally important, and both relate to the protection of data and assurance that information is safe and secure.

Data security and privacy are critically important to protect through robust policies and procedures, knowledge and training, and continued vigilance on an everyday basis. New efforts are constantly being identified to undermine and hack organizational systems to gain access to personal information such as social security numbers, dates of birth, health information, and banking information. Additionally, organizational information such as account information and access, credit cards, and sensitive and proprietary information is also at risk with these security breaches. Security breaches can allow unauthorized individuals access to private information. Not only can this have an impact to the employees and the organization, but it can have a negative impact regarding publicity and social media, which can result in decreased customer loyalty and business. It is crucial for organizations to manage privacy and security issues effectively and as a core competency. Employees should have a feeling of security and not worry that their personal information could be stolen through a data breach.

Organizations can implement many best practices to ensure that data are safe and secure. First, organizations can fully evaluate, approve, and protect data. A great example is the compliance and procedures set in place for the **Health Insurance Portability and Accountability Act (HIPAA)** data, or medical information. A data breach of HIPAA data could be cause for serious concern as well as violate the legal statutes. This violation could include fees and fines for violating the law.

Second, organizations can control and limit access to data and the networks, ensuring that only authorized individuals can gain access. Encryption is an excellent practice that many organizations utilize. **Encryption** for emails ensures that only the sender and authorized recipient can access the email and information included. If a recipient does not have the proper encryption software, the information cannot be accessed.

Third, organizations can secure devices and install privacy and control mechanisms such as compliance proof and identification software to ensure that only the authorized employee can gain access. Many organizations require a double authentication, or two-factor verification, to ensure the identity of the individual accessing the information. Employees' access to information can be aligned with their position and role within the organization to ensure access is only granted to the information necessary for the work being conducted.

Finally, organizations can ensure that all employees receive regular and frequent compliance training. Training programs should be included for all employees to understand how to create and update an appropriate password to ensure that if their computers are stolen, information is protected. Additionally, employees should be trained in how to identify malware, suspicious emails and requests, and viruses sent through emails. Reports should not include social security numbers, dates of birth, or other confidential information. In the case that this information is required to report, the report should be monitored to ensure that the hard copies are controlled and maintained.

While most data and security breaches are unintentional, there are very real consequences that can impact the employees and the organization. For example, consider a full employee roster that includes social security numbers, home addresses, and dates of birth that is printed and then disposed of in a regular trash receptacle. This report could easily be discovered in a garbage bin, and identities could be stolen. While this may have been a simple oversight, the consequences could be tremendous. Employees could now face having to monitor their credit and identity, and the organization could need to arrange to provide and fund credit monitoring for a period of time to ensure that the impact to employees is minimal. Procedures should be put in place to ensure that data are secure. Personnel files should be kept under lock and key, printed reports and documents should be disposed of in a confidential and private manner, and passwords should be strong.

If a data breach does occur, it is important to report the incident immediately so that appropriate responses and necessary actions can be deployed as soon as possible. Initiating immediate action can limit the exposure and liability of the organization. Executive leadership should be informed of the issue, and corrective action should be taken. Additionally, a communication plan should be created and deployed to ensure that employees understand the breach and what it means on a professional, work-related basis and, if applicable, a personal basis. A best practice would be to incorporate an emergency management and action plan specific to a data breach that ensures appropriate actions are taken to address the issue.

Providing Guidance to Stakeholders on Policies for Technology Usage

Human Resources is responsible for ensuring that personnel policies are appropriate, detailed, clear, and fully understood. In addition to personnel policies, HR should work together with Information Technology to ensure that strong policies are put in place that protect both the organization and the employees regarding technology in the workplace. Policies should not only define appropriate usage of company equipment and resources such as the internet, but they should also define a code of conduct and ethical use of technology. Many employees experience an overlap between personal and professional lives. Technology can blur this line even further. As technology continues to advance, so should the policies that are implemented. Organizations must implement policies that define appropriate social media usage, specific timelines and usage guidelines for utilizing the internet and computer for personal use, and more. Many organizations include the technology policies in the new hire orientation process and require employees to sign an acknowledgement form.

Manages Vendors Implementing HR Technology Solutions

Many HR technology solutions are provided and supported by outside vendors. From payroll programs that manage timekeeping and issue paychecks to HR management systems that track performance evaluations and job progression within a career, HR professionals can manage several vendors at any given time. From issuing requests for proposals, to identifying a new solution or vendor, to maintaining and updating current contracts, HR should strive to work with vendors that evolve their solutions and programs to meet the organization's needs. Vendors should work to maintain flexibility and creativity in delivering solutions that manage and resolve the issues that each organization faces. It is important that HR professionals stay abreast in the latest technology and tools so that the organization is confident they are receiving the best services. Attending conferences and conventions allows for new products to be viewed and tested. Having knowledge of what services and products are available in the open market is extremely important in ensuring that the HR solutions are the best available.

Using Technologies that Collect and Analyze Data

Some technology platforms are excellent online storage facilities of information. The most effective technology platforms can hold multiple pieces of information and provide reports that allow for evaluation and assessment of the information. Using data in this fashion allows for trends to be seen and decisions to be made. These trends may identify new and unique challenges that need to be addressed such as high turnover or excessive absenteeism. It is important to understand that the reports and evaluation models that are created from a technology system are only as good as the data that is entered into the system. Bad data in equals bad information out. Recommendations that are based on data and backed up by evidence are much more likely to be supported and implemented versus recommendations that are based on emotion or feelings. It should be noted that using a Microsoft Excel spreadsheet may be a more useful tool than a fancy high-tech program. Tools can vary in ease of use, cost, and abilities; however, understanding the audience and the recommendations should determine the technology and tools used to present the information.

Workplace Knowledge

Managing a Global Workforce

When an organization has a presence in more than one country, it is important to understand how this global context affects the HR strategic plan. Incorporating global elements into HR plans helps to support the organization's overall initiatives and provide opportunities for employees. Providing training to employees that develops multicultural learning and awareness as well as relationship building provides for a more well-rounded workforce that can approach situations that are uniquely tailored to the specific country and culture. Being aware of and understanding the cultural differences, language barriers, acceptable norms, and appropriate practices is only one component of working in a global context. Having an awareness of the political, economic, societal, technological, legal, and environmental aspects are also important, as they will have an impact on the organization and its business model. Ensuring that the employees are trained in these areas will allow for a more effective and productive workforce in these different countries.

Addressing Global Issues that Influence HR Activities

HR professionals will need to address specific issues when working in a global environment. In general, most of the issues will be the same—compensation, benefits, work-life balance; however, there are also other issues that may arise due to the complexity of managing a global workforce. These issues include cultural differences, management styles, communication or language barriers, and staff values that differ from the organization. Because of these types of issues, it is imperative that the organization conduct a complete and comprehensive analysis of the environment and the current policies and programs offered. If there are discrepancies, HR should work to address these by updating the policies. If possible, HR should engage the workforce to assist with recommending and implementing the changes. Initiating surveys to employees as a way to provide feedback is an excellent way to engage employees in the process and solicit feedback on potential changes. Once this information is received and analyzed, HR should present recommendations to the leadership to make appropriate and needed changes within the organization's policies and procedures.

Maintaining Current Knowledge of PESTLE Factors

HR professionals often use the PESTLE analysis when working to provide recommendations to address concerns, updates, or new resolutions within an organization. When operating in a global environment, a

PESTLE analysis is a vital tool that can be used to identify specific factors that can allow for a more effective and efficient organization. Comparing the information from two countries provided through the PESTLE tool can also provide insight into the gaps that an organization may have regarding policy and allow for recommendations that are supported by data. The PESTLE factors include the areas of political, economic, social, technological, legal, and environmental. Below provides a list of example items that should be analyzed within the PESTLE tool when reviewing the global environment:

- Political: tax policy, tariffs, trade restrictions
- Economic: exchange rates, inflation rates
- Social: workforce demographics, career attitudes
- Technological: automation, research, development
- Legal: employment law, safety laws
- Environmental: climate change

Each topic above should have a policy directly related to it. Understanding how each country handles the above items and its relation to policies within an organization can help to identify necessary adjustments to policies and procedures. A gap analysis can be conducted by taking the information from two separate countries, reviewing the differences, and identifying recommended actions.

Administering HR Activities Associated with a Global Workforce

Human Resources supports various activities throughout an organization from recruiting and training to benefits and leave administration. Human Resources is also responsible for implementing policies and practices that will align with the organization's mission and goals, adhere to all local laws and regulations, and provide a positive and healthy working environment. There are four strategic areas that HR professionals can deploy to ensure an engaged and motivated global workforce. First, HR can create a process to identify specific career paths and progressions that provide job security, satisfaction, and growth. Using individual development plans and succession planning can ensure that employees have a path forward with the organization that provides challenges while expanding skills and knowledge.

Second, HR can establish a cross-training program that allows employees to learn new areas of the business and organization. A cross-training program can align with the employee's career path identified earlier and assist in expanding the opportunities available for the future. Third, HR can assign specific individuals to short-term projects that deal with a specific issue or concern. Again, this allows for a training opportunity while learning more about the lines of business. Finally, HR can work with the Information Technology department to implement new solutions to connect employees in new ways that allow for a more transparent relationship. From Zoom and Skype programs to webinars and online learning, establishing new ways of communicating with each other allows for growth and the exchange of ideas in a more convenient and timely manner.

Conducting Audits of Global HR Practices

The Human Resources department is responsible for conducting audits in four main areas: policies, systems, procedures, and documentation. Regardless of working in a global environment, an HR audit should be fair, consistent, detailed, and timely. While the findings of an audit may vary based on the country, it is important to understand how the organization is performing in each of these areas so that specific and appropriate corrective action can be taken if necessary. The goal of an HR audit should be to determine if the policies, systems, procedures, and documentation are 1) in alignment with the organizational strategy, mission, and values; 2) in compliance with legal requirements; and 3) provide a positive and healthy work environment that results in employee satisfaction. Once the findings of an audit are finalized, HR should work to address issues that have been identified quickly and effectively.

Maintaining Knowledge of Global HR Trends and Best Practices

Now more than ever, it is necessary for HR professionals to have an awareness and understanding of global trends and best practices. This knowledge is necessary due to the diverse and inclusive workforce that many organizations employ. HR professionals should understand how these global trends might be necessary to develop and implement in order to attract diverse candidates from around the globe. The two primary areas where this could have a large impact are employee engagement and employee productivity. When HR professionals understand workforce demographics, they can gain insight and create connections, which lead to knowledge of different trends and practices across the globe. For example, if the majority of an organization's workforce has roots in Western Europe, then it may be best to learn more about the employment initiatives in those countries and align the current practices with some of these techniques and strategies. Additionally, learning which resources are best to gain this knowledge is important. Using networks such as LinkedIn can encourage professional relationships with employees across the globe. There are also reports, publications, and other information resources available through organizations such as Deloitte, Global HR Research, and SHRM.

Balancing Desire for Standardization of HR Policies with Local Needs

Most organizations have complete standardization of Human Resources policies, programs, and practices; however, when operating in multiple countries, it is important to balance the need for standardization with the local laws, customs, and principles. This is called localization. **Standardization** works to ensure consistent, transparent, effective, efficient, and equitable practices. **Localization**, however, works to respect the local culture and traditions, understand the educational system, adapt to the legislation and government, and acclimate to the expectations that employees hold for the workplace. Human Resources should ensure a complete understanding of the localization needs and work to implement policies and practices that adhere to both the organizational standards as well as the local needs and expectations. This is not an easy task, and HR should work to engage the legal team to ensure that any recommendations meet all necessary legal requirements.

Building Relationships with Global Stakeholders

Building relationships with local and global stakeholders is based on having a shared understanding of what is important. While there may be unique challenges or issues for each location, there should be a fundamental goal that everyone is working to accomplish. Once this is understood, Human Resources can work to develop policies, programs, and initiatives that work to achieve this goal while incorporating the specific and unique needs of the location. An example of a core goal that a global organization may want to achieve is to have the most satisfied customers in every country that business is conducted. Each location will have its own culture, workforce, concerns, and needs. It is important to align any actions with the fundamental goal so that each issue is addressed while also continuing on the course to achieve the primary goals of the organization. Brainstorming and sharing ideas, maintaining a two-way dialogue, asking questions, providing information, and creating unique resolutions and actions that have realized impacts is a streamlined approach to building relationships with global stakeholders.

Managing Activities Associated with International Assignments

Organizations that have locations across the globe require dedicated HR professionals that provide exceptional support to the employees who have been assigned to these locations. When a specific employee is needed for a special assignment in another country, there are various elements of an expatriate assignment that should be handled. From compensation and benefits, to travel and relocation, the employee will need a substantial amount of support from the assigned HR professional. The primary focus of HR in these situations is to assist the employee in this international assignment however possible. This could include providing assistance with paperwork, locating medical facilities and school locations, assisting with spousal employment, providing moving companies, or ensuring short-term housing. An HR professional should assist in all of the areas related to the international assignment for the employee and their family. Once the employee is settled in the new location, the HR professional remains the primary contact to answer questions, research information, and maintain the connection to the organization's home country. Additionally, at the end of the assignment, the HR professional should work to repatriate the employee and their family back to their home country, or in some cases, to another country based on assignment.

Diversity and Inclusion

When diversity and inclusion are incorporated into an organization's culture, values, and policies, the result is a highly engaged and extremely productive workforce. **Diversity** specifically refers to the identities of the employees within a workforce. **Inclusion** refers to the acceptance of thoughts, ideas, and perspectives from every employee. When diversity and inclusion are valued in an organization, and there is equity in responsibility, opportunity, and resources, the organization establishes a culture of belonging. This sense of belonging within an organization provides employees with an effective environment that helps them to thrive and allows for different thoughts, beliefs, and views to be integrated into the workplace dynamics. Employees do their best work when they are valued, supported, and have a commitment from leadership.

Mentoring and Coaching Employees on Cultural Differences

A robust and holistic diversity and inclusion strategy must focus on the following areas:

- Effective leadership
- Employee engagement
- Inclusive culture
- Competitive talent

Effective leadership is achieved by ensuring consistency, commitment, and initiative. Building leaders at all levels of the organization allows for a deep and diverse leadership talent pipeline. Additionally, ensuring a strong succession planning program can identify talent for development in key leadership roles.

Employee engagement is achieved by implementing and facilitating programs that allow employees to have a shared purpose and community within the organization. By providing training and resources to every leader, the organization can build and sustain a diverse internal talent pool. **Inclusive culture** is achieved by aligning the business strategy and high-level goals and leveraging the knowledge of employees with the diversity and inclusion strategy. Expanding engagement encourages recruitment efforts and ensures leadership capabilities within employees, resulting in a culture of transparency and openness for new ideas and innovation. **Competitive talent** is achieved by developing a diversity recruiting strategy that addresses skills gaps within the current workforce. By making targeted and specific decisions relative to recruiting and hiring, an organization can optimize the workforce, innovation, and overall effectiveness.

Employee resource groups (ERGs) are groups of individuals who participate in initiatives, programs, and activities with others of a shared background, common interest, or other similarity. ERGs foster diversity and inclusiveness within the organization and provide an opportunity for employees to discuss valuable viewpoints regarding programs, concerns, and other issues. ERGs are an excellent way to engage the community as well. By inviting community members to participate in an ERG, new viewpoints and perspectives can be gained and discussed. New ideas can be shared through brainstorming sessions and potentially implemented as new programs. Additionally, by engaging community members within an ERG, corporate responsibility can be enhanced by ensuring an understanding from all sides. Employees who have the opportunity to hear directly from the community can incorporate this feedback into their work and recommendations. Similarly, community members who have the opportunity to hear directly from the employees can have a deeper understanding of the daily work and responsibilities of the organization.

Consulting with Managers about Performance Issues vs. Cultural Differences

With a global workforce, HR professionals must be acquainted with cultural differences that could cause difficulties in the working environment. In some cases, untrained managers may interpret a situation incorrectly and address what is believed to be a performance issue; however, the concern may be cultural and inherently a case of not understanding or realizing the true cause of the issue. While the manager is working toward a resolution to performance issues, the actual issue of understanding the cultural differences and providing training and awareness may go unnoticed or unresolved. Without addressing the true nature of the concern, the issue will only progress and persist. Some areas that managers should be familiar with related to cultural differences and how employees work differently include the following:

1. Communication
2. Conflict resolution
3. Workload and task prioritization
4. Decision making
5. Information sharing

Each employee brings a unique skill set as well as a unique background. These backgrounds include individual beliefs, values, perceptions, expectations, attitudes, and assumptions that have evolved over time with each experience and insight gained. It is vital to the success of an organization, department, and team to have an awareness of these differences while also establishing expectations for all employees. While one employee may not be comfortable sharing information or communicating with the team about the status of a project assignment due to their individual culture, it may be necessary to in order to engage the team and ensure that the tasks are being done effectively and efficiently. If one task is reliant on another, it should be an established expectation that employees communicate clearly with each other.

Knowledge of Current Diversity and Inclusion HR Best Practices

Human Resources professionals are responsible for understanding Equal Employment Opportunity, Affirmative Action, and Diversity and Inclusion when assessing and implementing employee programs. **Equal Employment Opportunity** refers to the enforcement of statutes, laws, and regulations to prevent employment discrimination. **Affirmative Action** refers to the effort to achieve equity and equality in the workforce through outreach to eliminate barriers in the recruitment process. **Diversity and Inclusion** refers to leveraging differences within the workforce to achieve better results and higher levels of productivity and efficiency. By creating and maintaining an inclusive work environment where all employees are respected, an organization can effectively improve performance and enhance the customer and employee experience. By incorporating programs that align with the diversity and inclusion vision, an organization is able to support employee performance successfully, recruit the best talent, develop talent and expand skills, strengthen the employer brand, motivate employees with a positive employment experience, and strengthen the organization's market position.

Contributing to an Organizational Culture that Values a Diverse and Inclusive Workforce

The impacts of a strong diversity and inclusion strategy are far reaching, beyond the internal employees and organization. The culture and core values of the organization are the foundation for the framework of an organization's mission and align with achieving the overall objectives.

There are four main areas that an organization's diversity and inclusion strategy will impact:

- Workplace
- Workforce
- Marketplace
- Community

Diversity and inclusion within the workplace foster an inclusive environment in which different backgrounds, perspectives, behaviors, and experiences are valued and respected. Diversity and inclusion within the workforce build a diverse talent pipeline and provide high impact engagement, innovation, involvement, and development programs. Diversity and inclusion within the marketplace serve the diverse needs of customers, shareholders, and executive leadership through the products and services provided. Diversity and inclusion within the community shows the organization as a good corporate "citizen" with demonstrated social responsibility through community leadership, involvement, philanthropy, and volunteering. Overall, the organization is able to build and sustain a culture and environment where all employees are embraced and valued for who they are. This allows each employee to reach their full potential and enables the organization to meet and exceed their identified goals and achievements.

Opportunities to Enhance the Fairness of Policies to All Employees

Historically, diversity initiatives were incorporated into organizations based on a moral imperative to have the workforce reflect the external labor market and community population. Recruitment programs and methods were incorporated to attract and hire individuals from various backgrounds. The issue that has become apparent over the years, however, is that simply hiring more diverse individuals is not enough and should not be the ending point for establishing a diverse working environment. Currently, organizations are focusing on inclusion and establishing an inclusive working environment for all employees. Organizations establish inclusion by:

- Utilizing diverse perspectives and opinions to broaden problem solving, innovation, and creativity
- Encouraging collaboration and learning from differences, flexibility, and fairness
- Embedding inclusive values in organizational structures, policies, and practices

Each individual has a distinct and unique set of skills, values, goals, and motivations for both their professional and personal life. For an organization to attract a diverse, talented, and best-in-class workforce, an inclusive environment and culture must be present.

To establish an inclusive workplace, four pillars must be created, supported, and functional: awareness, mobilization, action, and alignment.

Awareness is the pillar that raises the understanding and mindfulness of the organization and employees toward the diversity and inclusion initiatives. Awareness prepares employees for the acceptance of the culture and the willingness to accept changes that increase inclusion. Activities that encourage awareness include education, bias training, cultural immersion, and job training.

Mobilization is the pillar that sets up the policies, processes, procedures, and systems that allow for accountability for all employees at all levels.

Action is the pillar that implements the strategies through specific efforts and tactics. Activities within the action pillar include working with diverse suppliers and vendors, actively engaging employees to build an inclusive workplace, and structuring programs that align with inclusion.

Alignment is the pillar that is essential to ensuring a successful implementation of all diversity and inclusion strategies. Alignment focuses on analyzing, reviewing, and revising strategies, policies, and ways of conducting business to meet employee and customer expectations. Additionally, alignment strengthens innovation, engagement, and loyalty from both employees and customers.

For diversity and inclusion strategies to be successful, organizations must have leaders who understand and value a diverse workforce, while simultaneously recognizing the challenges that come with different perspectives. The organizational culture must create a high standard of performance for all employees, and the culture must encourage openness, honesty, and transparency. The culture must stimulate personal development, make employees feel valued, and be clear in the commitment to employees. Finally, the organization must have a clear vision and define success related to diversity and inclusion.

Organizations that value and commit to diversity and inclusion see real and high-impact benefits. Diverse thinking and bringing in different opinions and perspectives leads to an almost seventy percent increase in innovation. Inclusivity within leadership and management increases the likelihood of new customers and employees, leading to an almost fifty percent increase in the likelihood of growing market share and market presence. When teams are motivated, employees remain engaged and motivated to provide input and affect change. Overall, performance at all levels within the organization is stronger when diverse leadership and experiences are available.

Workplace Accommodations

The Americans with Disabilities Act (ADA) requires that employers make reasonable accommodations to support an employee in the workplace, as long as the request does not cause an undue hardship to the organization. An undue hardship could be excessive cost or substantially changing the core functions of the job. Most requested accommodations are either implemented fully or partially to address the main concern of the employee. Typical accommodations can include:

- Increasing accessibility to the workspace
- Modifying work schedules
- Reassigning the employee to another position
- Modifying or acquiring new equipment or devices
- Providing interpretation services

Workplace accommodations can be informal or formal, and they can be based on ergonomic, religious, or medical needs. Typically, a workplace accommodation begins with an employee making a request to the HR department. Depending on the request, further documentation may be required from a medical provider or religious leader. Some common examples of workplace accommodations are:

- Purchasing a new ergonomic chair that provides lumbar support
- Allowing for additional breaks and a secure, private area to allow for nursing mothers to lactate
- Modifying the work schedule to allow for regular physical or mental therapy appointments

- Installing a sit/stand ergonomic desk to allow for wheelchair access
- Approving a telecommuting arrangement to work from home due to an injury

There are numerous types of workplace accommodations, and HR should evaluate each based on the needs of the employee and the specific circumstances. While a specific request may not be feasible, HR can work with the individual to determine what can be provided that may still meet their needs.

Supporting Stakeholders for the Organization's Diversity and Inclusion Efforts

An organization establishes a foundation of diversity and inclusion by incorporating these principles in its vision, strategy, core business, leadership style, infrastructure, and policies. Once the foundation is securely established, HR professionals should work to ensure that the principles are implemented throughout all employee-related policies. Diversity and inclusion principles should be included in the following programs related to internal stakeholders (employees): recruitment, both internal and external; training and development; total rewards including compensation, benefits, and work-life balance; position descriptions and job design; and diversity and inclusion education to ensure that employees understand how to bring these principles to their own work every day.

Diversity and inclusion principles should also be core values when working with external stakeholders, such as the community, customers, and local leaders. Corporate social responsibility is an area in which organizations have had to increase their focus, and aligning this program with diversity and inclusion allows for a larger impact within the community. Diversity and inclusion principles should also be incorporated into marketing materials, customer service, product distribution, and vendor selection. Ensuring that customers, vendors, leaders, and the community are aware of the commitment to diversity and inclusion will enable the organization to be viewed more favorably. HR professionals can assist with recommending and writing the policies that will allow for the successful implementation of diversity and inclusion principles across the organization.

Risk Management

Risk management is the strategic process that an organization engages in to identify, address, mitigate, and eliminate potential risks and challenges. The risk management process works through four specific steps:

1. Identify and Define
2. Assess and Recommend
3. Implement and Resolve
4. Monitor and Evaluate

Working through these steps will allow for thoughtful and engaged conversation to occur and ensure that appropriate actions are taken to address the specific challenges or dangers that are being or will be faced. It is important to note that this process may need to be repeated to address risks, as the proposed recommendations may not have allowed for a full resolution, or the dynamics may have changed.

Monitoring PESTLE Factors and their Influence on the Organization

Many variables influence the decisions that organizations make. As mentioned previously, six trends that should be frequently reviewed and understood are represented by the acronym **PESTLE**: political, economic, social, technological, legal, and environmental. Knowledge of these variables allows the HR team to identify risks, challenges, and dangers that must be addressed within a robust and strategic risk management process. All of these factors can present the organization with various challenges at different times. Ensuring a consistent risk management process to address each challenge as needed and respond with appropriate and necessary action allows an organization to work through issues and concerns while ensuring a productive and engaged workforce.

Administering HR Programs and Policies that Mitigate Workplace Risk

HR policies and practices should always support a workplace that minimizes risk. When risks are identified—either through being proactive or reactive due to a specific incident—it is imperative that HR takes appropriate action quickly and effectively. HR can be proactive in minimizing risk by establishing strong documentation, procedures, and processes in the following areas:

- Job descriptions
- Personnel policies
- New hire orientations
- Safety procedures
- Training and learning
- Internal audits
- Complaint procedures
- Investigations

Each of these areas can present a substantial amount of risk to an organization. If these areas lack strong policies and procedures, the organization might be at high risk of employee issues, conflicts, low morale, high turnover, ineffective performance, claims, and even lawsuits. Human Resources should audit these areas on a regular basis to ensure that they align with current laws and the organization's strategic plan, and that they are thorough and applicable to the workforce.

Implementing Crisis Management

When an organization experiences a crisis such as a natural disaster, it is vital that HR works with the leadership and management to ensure that appropriate emergency management plans are immediately implemented. In many cases, revisions or additions must be made to address specific concerns that have arisen due to the crisis. The most recent example of this is the COVID-19 pandemic. Most organizations have emergency plans to address natural disasters but may not have a plan prepared specifically to address the safety, health, and employment issues specific to a virus. When this occurs, it is important to use the plans that have been prepared and approved for other events and use them as a template while making modifications as appropriate.

Throughout the global pandemic, most organizations were forced to offer telecommuting options when they were prohibited from gathering in the office. Should a similar health and safety concern arise, organizations are now equipped to offer that option for employees as part of their disaster management plan. In this case, HR should work directly with leadership and Information Technology to ensure that the available technology supports telecommuting efforts. Additionally, a new policy and application would need to be prepared for distribution to those employees who are able to telecommute. By providing this option, the organization can continue to provide business services to customers while also ensuring that employees can continue to work and receive a paycheck to provide for their families.

Communicating Information About Risks

HR is usually responsible for communicating with employees. This includes information regarding leave administration, benefits enrollment, safety procedures, worker's compensation programs, and training opportunities. Additionally, when there is a safety or security concern, HR plays a critical role in ensuring that all employees have appropriate and important information related to the issue, including how to work through the concern. It is important to understand what information should be gathered and disseminated to employees, supervisors, leadership, and stakeholders. HR should strive to ensure that any distributed information is accurate and updated. Sending information that is dated, unclear, or complicated can cause confusion, frustration, and in some cases, fear. It is also important to send appropriate information. Maintenance workers do not necessarily need to have information related to how revenue will be impacted due to a pandemic; however, all employees, including leadership and stakeholders, should have information about how to stay healthy during a pandemic. When writing communications, it is important to remember who will be receiving the message and write specifically to that audience. Communication at all levels requires an understanding of what each level needs to know and when.

Conducting Due Diligence Investigations

A **due diligence investigation** is a detailed risk assessment that provides insight and information regarding a specific concern or issue. The investigation results provide insight into the issues, root cause of the concern, and recommendations to implement. Due diligence investigations should be thorough, and they should fully assess the situation. Individuals who have firsthand knowledge should be interviewed, and all appropriate and necessary documentation should be fully reviewed. Investigators should run down every lead and work to answer every question to ensure that a complete picture is painted. With a full view of the issue, recommendations will most likely make an impact and correct the issue. HR professionals should be trained in conducting investigations. Active listening and asking targeted questions are vital components to conducting a thorough due diligence investigation.

Conducting Workplace Safety- and Health-Related Investigations

HR professionals often conduct workplace safety investigations, especially when an injury occurs. The goal of this type of investigation is to ensure that the workplace is safe for employees and if not, that changes are made immediately so that another employee is not injured. Employees should receive information during their new hire orientation training on how to report a workplace injury. Additionally, reminders should be sent via email and posted in common areas to ensure that employees understand what to do if an injury occurs. If an accident or injury does occur, the first priority is to ensure that the employee receives the care needed to treat the injury. This could include first aid, sending the employee to the hospital, or calling an ambulance. Once the employee has been treated, an investigation should occur immediately.

Statements should be taken from the employee, supervisor, and any witnesses. Photographs should be taken, and the standard operating procedures should be reviewed. Once all of the of the information has been gathered, the cause of the injury should be determined. If the cause was due to employee negligence, HR should work with the supervisor to determine the appropriate action needed. This could include training, coaching, or even discipline depending on the severity of the violation and the employee's history. If the cause was due to the inadequate safety procedures, equipment malfunctions, or other issue not related to the employee's actions, corrective action should be identified and immediately implemented. Employees should be trained in the corrective actions to ensure that all individuals understand the changes. Once the change has been made, HR should check in with the supervisor and employees to ensure that the changes have in fact corrected the situation and if not, work to identify new actions.

Auditing Risk Management Activities and Plans

Human Resources is responsible for auditing various programs, policies, and plans, including those related to risk management. Auditing risk management processes is critical to ensuring that the efforts in place are still appropriate to address potential risks that the organization may face. Risks evolve and change, and the plans to address and manage these risks should also evolve and change to meet the needs. Auditing the risk management plans and programs allows for the organization to understand how these risks have changed and work to address them so that the risks do not become a liability for the organization.

HR should follow a standard auditing practice when assessing risk management plans. A standard audit process includes three general steps: planning, execution, finalizing. The **planning phase** includes defining the scope and objective of the audit, or what will be investigated. The **execution phase** includes interviewing individuals, gathering and reviewing reports and procedures, and conducting the actual audit. The **finalizing phase** includes preparing a report that summarizes the findings, highlights the strengths, identifies the weaknesses, and provides recommendations to address the weaknesses. Risk management audits should occur on a regular or as-needed basis.

Accurate Reporting of Workplace Health and Safety Standards

Workplace health and safety standards will vary depending on where the operations are being performed. Each country will have specific standards, and it is important to understand them and ensure that they are followed. International standards have been implemented through the Occupational Health and Safety Management System; however, there have been numerous updates and revisions to the systems and standards that must be incorporated into the daily operations and procedures of an organization. In the United States, the Occupational Safety and Health Administration is responsible for ensuring that organizations adhere to all required health and safety standards. Because there may be differences in standards between countries, it is vital to ensure that there is appropriate tracking and reporting of the requirements for each location. This will ensure that audits can be conducted with updated information and that the organization is in compliance with all standards.

Incorporating the Anticipated Level of Risk into Business Cases

One important perspective that HR brings to the organization is understanding anticipated levels of risk and how to incorporate controls and systems into the operational procedures to minimize these risks. Areas such as recruiting and hiring, compensation and benefits, training and safety protocols, and workforce efficiency and effectiveness are all areas that can create risk or liability to an organization in the form of complaints, claims, injuries, or lawsuits. HR is an integral part of the team that works to implement successful strategies to ensure that goals are achieved. Employees are the backbone of the organization working to accomplish these goals. Ensuring fair and equitable hiring and promotion practices, aligning the compensation philosophy to pay a fair wage while recognizing employees for their performance, training employees on safe procedures within the workplace, and providing adequate tools, training, and resources to perform the job well are all areas that HR can work with leadership to accomplish. In doing so, HR is also working to minimize the level of risk that the organization could experience.

Corporate Social Responsibility

Corporate social responsibility (CSR) is a sustainable, operational strategy that should be incorporated into policies, processes, and practices to ensure that the business operates in a socially acceptable manner to employees, leadership, stakeholders, and the public. CSR principles address social issues that are important to the workplace, marketplace, environment, and community beyond the concept of being a philanthropic organization. Many organizations have implemented environmental programs that limit printing to save paper or provide additional leave time for employees to perform charitable work; however, CSR goes beyond these concepts by working to incorporate these same types of principles throughout the organization at a deeper level. CSR incorporates the initiatives of values, commitment, integrity, honesty, collaboration, sensitivity, partnership, charity, and environmental focus at every level within the organization. In doing so, the organization will see numerous benefits such as increased employment engagement, lower turnover rates, higher productivity, stronger profitability, increased customer satisfaction, and more.

Acting as a Professional Role Model

All employees are representatives of an organization; however, Human Resources professionals are often the face of the organization to new employees and candidates. Additionally, when working with the community in philanthropic efforts or coordinated events, employees represent the values and ethics of the organization to the public. It is important to understand the significance of these interactions and behave in a manner that is consistent to the organization's expectations. This reflects positively not only on the organization to the public, but also on the employees to their supervisors and leadership. Representing an organization with integrity and honor allows for an engaged community that understands not only the business and services available, but also the commitment to and impact on the public.

Engaging in Community-Based Volunteer and Philanthropic Activities

Most organizations are involved and engaged in the community. By working together in philanthropic efforts and engaging the community, organizations can work to make the community more prosperous, while also seeing benefits within the organization. Many employees live and work in the same communities, so when efforts are made by the organization to improve the community, employees feel the benefits at both work and home. Lower turnover rates, increased satisfaction and morale, and excellent representation are all examples of how these activities can impact the workforce. From Habitat for Humanity and Second Harvest food drives to paper shredding and local business events, an organization can have a large and far-reaching impact on many levels.

Promotes Opportunities to Engage in CSR Activities

Human Resources is most effective when the department has an awareness and understanding of what is important to the employees. This includes knowing which philanthropic events and opportunities would be valued and therefore should be encouraged within the organization. Many organizations provide a separate leave allowance for employees to participate in volunteer work; however, when an organization decides to organize, sponsor, or be substantially involved in an effort, employees can see firsthand the organization's commitment to social responsibility. Surveys are an excellent way to source ideas from employees for ideas of different events that are meaningful to the workforce. While it is not realistic to commit to all opportunities, surveying the workforce for ideas is an excellent way to involve them in the planning stages and will most likely result in higher levels of participation. Many companies have a specific charity or organization that they sponsor with donated time, resources, or staff support. HR can work to determine if new opportunities exist and should be explored to align with the overall philosophy of CSR.

Helping Staff Understand the Role of the Organization's CSR Activities

The most effective way for Human Resources to ensure that all employees understand the organization's role in corporate social responsibility is to create policies and programs that align with and support this effort. These policies and programs should be fully communicated during the onboarding process with reminders and updates provided throughout the year on the activities that are ongoing. When goals and objectives are reached, leadership should ensure that employees receive this information so that every employee understands the significance of the actions being taken on a daily basis that help support the achievements. Additionally, HR can train employees in the four responsibilities of CSR as defined by Archie B. Carroll. These four responsibilities are represented in the Pyramid of Corporate Social Responsibility, as depicted below:

Employees should be educated in these four responsibilities and how their specific role aligns with them. It is vital to understand that all CSR philosophies and strategies must align with and be supported by a strong economic responsibility and profitability. An organization is able to do more for employees, customers, and the community when it is profitable and has strong economic principles. This foundation then allows for the pyramid to be built using legal and ethical responsibilities that fully support philanthropic efforts with organizational backing.

Maintaining Transparency

One of the most important and fundamental principles of a strong Human Resources department should be transparency. Being open and honest with policies, programs, practices, and initiatives is vital to the success of the department and individual employees. While there are situations where confidentiality and privacy must be maintained, it is vital to understand when full transparency should be implemented. Employees should have full access to information as appropriate regarding internal items such as personnel policies, employee training, and complaint procedures. External communications should be tailored to employees to reflect how the information is applicable as well. An example of this would be a social responsibility report that is available to the public showing the philanthropic efforts that the organization has committed to and the outcomes. This information should be provided to employees as well with a specific communication from leadership that discusses how this information applies to employees. This would be a good opportunity to recognize employees for going above and beyond or for other accomplishments that resulted in the success of the programs.

Coaching Managers to Achieve an Appropriate Level of Transparency

A critical need within any organization is for managers to be trained, educated, and coached in effective and appropriate communication practices. How, what, and when to communicate with employees is not an easy task. Individuals hear things differently, interpret words differently, and can have completely different understandings of the same message. Communication is a skill that needs to be practiced. Managers have a unique role as they can be the gatekeepers regarding organizational information and decisions. HR can work to ensure that managers have the skills needed to communicate the best message possible and minimize confusion and misunderstandings.

Opportunities for Incorporation Environmentally-Responsible Business Practices

Human Resources often networks with other professionals to discuss best practices, creative solutions, current concerns and issues, and other HR specific topics. Each organization will have unique programs specific to the business needs, community, and workforce. It is an excellent practice to network with HR professionals to learn what others are doing and bring those ideas back to the organization to see if they would be appropriate to implement. Some of the best ideas initiated within an organization were first being practiced within another organization. It is not always necessary to reinvent the wheel. If an organization has seen success with a particular program, practice, or concept, it is worth the time and effort to look into the idea and determine if it would be successful or at least worth piloting to gain further insight and data. Bringing these ideas to leadership prior to implementation is important because without support from leadership, new programs are less likely to be successful.

U.S. Employment Laws and Regulations

The United States has many federal and state laws and regulations regarding the rights of employees and the responsibilities of employers. These laws are in the primary areas of discrimination, pay, employee privacy, and workplace safety. Each of these areas have specific government agencies working to enforce the laws—the Equal Employment Opportunity Commission (EEOC) enforces the laws regarding discrimination, the Department of Labor (DOL) enforces the laws regarding compensation, the Department of Justice (DOJ) enforces the laws regarding employee privacy, and the Occupational Safety and Health Administration (OSHA) enforces the laws regarding workplace safety. As an HR professional, it is vital to have an awareness and full understanding of these laws and regulations at both the federal and state levels. Many state laws have elements that are more expansive and inclusive than the federal laws. In these cases, the law that provides the higher level of benefit to the employee should be followed.

A general rule of thumb is that the federal law is the minimum level of benefit afforded to an employee. If state legislation creates a more comprehensive law that provides additional benefits, those standards should be followed. Additionally, HR professionals should know how these laws and regulations are applied to an organization's policies, practices, and procedures. While there are some businesses that may be exempt from particular laws due to the size of the organization or other factors, most organizations must adhere to all components of these areas that are dictated in the law. If an organization does not comply with these laws and regulations, the penalties could be severe.

Maintaining Current Knowledge of Employment Laws

One of the most critical proficiencies for an HR professional is being up-to-date and well educated on all relevant laws, case law, legal rulings, regulations, and on-going litigation regarding employment. Working within HR is not just about conflict resolution, benefits orientation, and recruiting. The fundamental foundation to establishing expertise in HR is being aware of, having an understanding of, and being able to apply laws, legal findings, and regulations that have been, are being, and will be implemented in the local, state, and federal government levels. When working within a global organization, it is critical to include all applicable employment laws so that the organization can ensure that the policies and practices align with all of the appropriate laws and regulations. Employment laws and regulations encompass a large number of topics, including discipline and unfair termination, minimum wage requirements, overtime calculations and payment, human rights, health and safety, and workers' compensation.

Ensuring that HR Programs and Policies Align with Laws and Regulations

HR professionals must ensure that all programs, practices, policies, and initiatives comply with federal and state laws and regulations. The only exception to this is if the organization wants to increase the benefits afforded to employees and provide a more lucrative program than what is required under the law. An example of this would be regarding the Family Medical Leave Act (FMLA) and maternity leave. While FMLA leave is unpaid, an organization could provide a paid maternity leave benefit, which would be considered an additional benefit while also remaining in compliance with the requirement of the law. HR professionals should regularly audit the policies and procedures to ensure compliance with both current and new laws and regulations. Not doing so can put the organization at risk. In some states, individual employees can also be held personally responsible for not adhering to the laws, even if they were following policy at the time.

Coaching Employees in Illegal and Noncompliant HR-Related Behaviors

Human Resources is responsible for ensuring that employees understand the policies and practices of an organization. HR should ensure that employees understand the expectations regarding behavior, as well as what constitutes an inappropriate action that violates policy. HR should adhere to best practices such as:

- Providing an employee handbook to all new employees during the new hire orientation process

- Displaying labor law posters in break rooms

- Maintaining policies and procedures that are easily accessible to all employees

- Providing training opportunities to ensure that all employees have the knowledge, skills, and understanding to avoid behavior that is inappropriate, or even illegal

HR should be proactive when coaching and training employees on the policies regarding appropriate behavior. Many organizations react to situations as they occur and provide training only after an issue has been reported. While it is important to address situations as they arise, it is also important to be proactive and work to avoid inappropriate behaviors within an organization. A best practice that can be deployed to ensure proactivity is to require annual regulatory and policy training for all employees. This training can be used as an excellent tool to remind employees of the expectations and requirements, as well as communicate new laws or policies. This type of training also allows an organization to have a record regarding training in the case of audits or lawsuits.

Legal Services for Interpreting Employment Laws

Some organizations have internal legal departments that provide support regarding Human Resources issues, including employment law. When an organization does not have this internal support, HR is responsible for ensuring that the organization has these resources available through external legal support. Organizations that have internal legal departments may also have a need to acquire external legal support as well due to potential conflicts of interest or requiring a specialized field of the law. HR should assess the situation and the needs of the organization to determine which course of action is most appropriate. HR may determine that multiple contracts are entered into for external legal services based on the needs identified. One law firm may specialize in labor negotiations while another law firm may focus on leave administration policy. HR should ensure that the most appropriate legal services are available for each unique need.

Practice Quiz

1. During which phase of Kurt Lewin's Change Model is the motivation for change created?
    a. Unfreezing
    b. Changing
    c. Refreezing
    d. Monitoring

2. In John Kotter's Change Model, which step involves identifying the key stakeholders and true leaders in the organization who can guide the change effort with their influence and authority?
    a. Create a clear vision for the change.
    b. Communicate the vision.
    c. Create short-term wins.
    d. Form the change coalition.

3. During which step of the strategic planning process does environmental scanning take place?
    a. Strategy Formulation
    b. Strategy Development
    c. Strategy Implementation
    d. Strategy Evaluation

4. Which of the following is an example of a weakness that may be uncovered during a SWOT analysis that can affect an organization's ability to reach its objectives?
    a. Outdated equipment
    b. Consumer trends
    c. A labor shortage
    d. A changing political climate

5. Which of the following is used to determine if targeted outcomes have occurred as a result of employees completing a training program?
    a. Pretests
    b. Participant surveys
    c. Performance metrics
    d. Posttests

Answer Explanations

1. A: During the unfreezing phase of Kurt Lewin's Change Model, the motivation for change is created. During the changing phase of Kurt Lewin's Change Model, resistance to the change is managed, and the organization comes into alignment with the change. During the refreezing phase of Kurt Lewin's Change Model, evaluation of the outcome takes place, which may lead to some additional fine-tuning.

2. D: In John Kotter's Change Model, during the "form the change coalition" step, key stakeholders and true leaders in the organization who will be able to lead the change effort with their influence and authority are identified. The coalition should be made up of a mix of individuals from various levels and departments throughout the organization.

3. B: Environmental scanning and a SWOT analysis are performed during the Strategy Development step of the strategic planning process. During this step, long-range plans are also established that will set the company's direction for the next three to five years.

4. A: Outdated equipment, unreliable suppliers, ineffective leadership, and insufficient marketing campaigns are examples of weaknesses that can be uncovered during a SWOT analysis. Internal weaknesses can potentially reduce a company's ability to reach its objectives and place it at a competitive disadvantage. Consumer trends are examples of opportunities. A labor shortage and a changing political climate are examples of threats.

5. C: Performance metrics, such as an increase in sales, are utilized to determine the degree that targeted outcomes have occurred as a result of employees completing a training program. Participant surveys are used to find out the degree to which participants react favorably to a training program. Pretests assess the knowledge of learners prior to the start of a training program, and posttests determine the knowledge students have acquired following a training program.

Practice Test

Behavioral Competencies

Leadership

1. Which of the following is NOT a component of effective leadership?
    a. Directing and overseeing work
    b. Motivating and encouraging individuals
    c. Directing and managing people
    d. Engaging and motivating employees

2. Which of the following statements is TRUE regarding leadership within an organization?
    a. Leaders exist at every level and in every department of an organization.
    b. Leadership is most important at the highest levels within the executive team.
    c. Leadership is best received by employees when it is formal and structured.
    d. Leadership can only be truly displayed at the highest levels of the organization.

3. Jack is working on implementing a new health and wellness program for employees. As a part of the process, he has been asked to prepare and communicate a presentation for the leadership team to receive final approval to move forward. Jack has already begun to create various communications pieces and wants to use these in his presentation. How should Jack proceed?
    a. Provide a packet of the communications already prepared to roll out the program to all employees.
    b. Provide the program documents created by the vendor that include the platform information and necessary resources.
    c. Give a verbal presentation of the program and respond to any questions asked by the team.
    d. Prepare a specific presentation that provides the details that the executive team would need to make a decision.

4. Angela is preparing her performance measures for her annual performance objectives. These measures will be the focus of her work for the next year and what she will be evaluated on for her annual performance review. All of her performance measures are specific, achievable, and realistic to accomplish for the next year. What elements are missing to ensure the objectives are SMART?
    a. Metrics and Teamwork
    b. Maintenance and Targets
    c. Measurable and Time-Targeted
    d. Methods and Tools

5. Which of the following allows for conversation and exchange of new ideas and solutions?
    a. Teamwork
    b. Brainstorming
    c. Leadership
    d. Collaboration

6. What is the single MOST effective method to achieve engaged stakeholders and commitment to HR initiatives?
    a. Emailing frequent status updates and providing answers to questions
    b. Establishing credibility as an HR leader and moving forward with the initiative
    c. Hiring an unbiased, outside party to engage stakeholders and accomplish the initiatives
    d. Bringing stakeholders together and communicating the benefits

7. Angelina is working on a status report for a project that she is managing. She finds that certain milestones have not been met and that the project is now tracking to be several months behind schedule. What should Angelina do?
    a. Review the goals and timing originally set and ensure that proper resources were allocated.
    b. Immediately discuss the schedule with her boss to determine what went wrong.
    c. Call a team meeting to determine who allowed the project to get off track.
    d. Continue to report that the project is on track and strive to catch up later.

8. Why is adaptability an important skill for an HR professional?
    a. Policies and procedures should be adapted for each situation and each employee.
    b. Organizations and employees continue to evolve and change over time.
    c. Adaptability should be a honed skill, but it is not used in the course of daily operations.
    d. Flexibility should be a skill utilized only when programs are not meeting objectives.

9. Which of the following is NOT a way to increase credibility as an HR expert within an organization?
    a. Education and experience
    b. Certifications and training programs
    c. Accomplishing objectives and achieving results
    d. Working with numerous companies

10. Latoya has formally recognized her team as both a workgroup and as individuals during the annual recognition awards. She noticed that some team members did not seem encouraged or happy with the recognition. What should Latoya do to ensure that all of the employees are recognized and motivated?
    a. Latoya should work to understand how each employee is motivated, which could include informal recognition.
    b. Latoya should initiate additional formal recognition with the leadership team to ensure that employees know they are appreciated.
    c. Latoya should stop recognizing her team in the formal recognition awards program in the future because it made some employees uncomfortable.
    d. Latoya should not take any actions regarding this concern and should continue to move forward with the goals and objectives for the team.

11. Which leadership quality is defined as being honest with yourself and determining actions based on personal values and beliefs?
    a. Ethics
    b. Authenticity
    c. Personal integrity
    d. Accountability

12. Blanca has made a mistake in the entry of a benefits change. This error caused an issue for the insurance company, the payroll department, and the employee. What is the first thing that Blanca should do?

    a. Correct the issue and put measures in place to ensure that the error does not happen again.

    b. Discuss the issue with the employee and correct the error during the next enrollment.

    c. Wait for the employee to come to HR and request a correction to the issue.

    d. Admit the mistake to her supervisor, take ownership of the error, and discuss corrections.

13. Which of the following statements about confidentiality is FALSE?

    a. Confidentiality and privacy should be provided for all employees, including those reporting bad behavior and those who may have engaged in the behavior.

    b. Confidentiality should be protected at all costs and under no circumstance compromised.

    c. Confidentiality is vital to an employee reporting unethical or inappropriate behavior.

    d. Confidentiality allows for an unbiased and fair investigation to occur.

14. Joseph recently completed a long and complex investigation in which an employee was found to have acted inappropriately toward other coworkers, resulting in a hostile work environment. Joseph has followed up with all of the employees who were interviewed to let them know that the investigation was concluded, appropriate action was taken, and the matter is resolved and closed. Additionally, he met with the individual who came forward with the initial complaint to ensure that they were comfortable with the results, including the level of discipline given to the employee who behaved inappropriately. The next day, Joseph's supervisor schedules a meeting to discuss the investigation and inappropriate activity on Joseph's part. What did Joseph do that needs to be addressed by his supervisor?

    a. Joseph should have completed his investigation sooner and worked in a more expeditious manner.

    b. Joseph should not have followed up with all of the interviewed employees regarding the closure of the investigation as this is not necessary.

    c. Joseph discussed the discipline given to the employee with another.

    d. Joseph did everything appropriately, and his supervisor may just want a debrief of the situation.

15. What does a SWOT Analysis tool evaluate?

    a. Strategy, Weaknesses, Outlook, Training

    b. Strengths, Weaknesses, Opportunities, Threats

    c. Strategy, Willingness, Outlook, Threats

    d. Strengths, Willingness, Opportunities, Training

16. When should HR provide an employee with the handbook, policies, procedures, and expectations of employment?

    a. During new employee orientation, typically scheduled for the first day of employment

    b. When a situation arises and the employee needs the information

    c. After applying for an open position

    d. The information should be accessible online for the employee to locate when needed

17. There are many benefits of hiring an outside, third-party investigator when handling employee issues. All BUT which of the choices below is one of these benefits?

    a. It enhances credibility and trust in HR.

    b. It allows for a quicker and speedier investigation.

    c. It ensures a fair and unbiased investigation.

    d. It provides an accurate representation of the issue.

18. There are numerous ways to communicate policies, programs, and changes to practices. Employees should have multiple ways of accessing this information so that they are informed, educated, and aware. Which of the below is the easiest way for misunderstandings and inaccuracies to occur?
- a. Town halls and employee meetings with leadership
- b. Formal handbooks and brochures
- c. Printed webpages and electronic documents
- d. Word of mouth and employee-to-employee communication

19. In which of the following cases should HR notify the organization's leadership immediately?
- a. Payroll discrepancies
- b. Benefits changes and enrollment
- c. Potential ethics violations
- d. Classification requests and reviews

20. A candidate's first look at how an organization behaves and what is expected from employees is presented in what?
- a. Job description brochure
- b. Benefits overview
- c. Vision, mission, and values statements
- d. Company background

21. Roger recently joined a new organization and is currently working on a new recognition program. At his previous company, he implemented a new program that was extremely successful, and he plans on using the same design for his new company, including the forms, process, and flyers. What should Roger take into consideration prior to implementing this new program?
- a. That his new company will have a unique culture and identity and that the program may not be received in the same way
- b. That the supervisors and managers will not want a formal recognition program and only want to utilize an informal program
- c. That employees will not want to see a change in how things are being done and want to continue using the same programs
- d. That the program will be received in the same way by the new company and employees, resulting in success

22. Which of the following is an example of a training opportunity that should be extended to all employees?
- a. Writing a request for proposal
- b. Diversity and inclusion
- c. General accounting practices
- d. Conducting investigations

23. Linda recently attended a symposium on new HR trends, programs, challenges, and legislation. She believes several of her organization's policies to be outdated and not in compliance with the new legislation. She has formulated a new policy to review with her director that she believes addresses the discrepancies and inconsistencies between the current policy and new legislation. Why is this such an important function of Linda's position?

    a. Without alignment between policy and legislation, the organization could be at risk, including costly lawsuits and legal action.

    b. This is an element of Linda's job description and without this duty, her role is not a full-time position and could be reduced to a part-time position.

    c. Linda should justify the cost to attend the symposium by recommending actions and changes specific to what was presented.

    d. Linda needs to contribute on a higher level, and recommending policy changes for the entire organization is an example of this.

24. Which of the following SWOT analysis factors are internal factors to the organization?

    a. Strengths and Opportunities

    b. Weaknesses and Threats

    c. Opportunities and Threats

    d. Strengths and Weaknesses

25. Which of the following SWOT analysis factors are external factors to the organization?

    a. Strengths and Opportunities

    b. Weaknesses and Threats

    c. Opportunities and Threats

    d. Strengths and Weaknesses

Interpersonal

26. What is the first step in ensuring successful relationship management?

    a. Delivering solutions that resolve the needs

    b. Creating solutions that address the needs

    c. Allowing for introductions and conversations

    d. Understanding the needs of the other party

27. Allowing for the exchange of ideas, sharing insights, soliciting advice, and relating to others are all descriptions of what?

    a. Relationship management

    b. Conflict resolution

    c. Networking

    d. Brainstorming

28. Which of the following is NOT a helpful tip when building relationships?

    a. Frequently engage with others

    b. Be selective and exclusive

    c. Be honest and encouraging to others

    d. Express thankfulness

29. Which of the following statements regarding sincerity is accurate?
    a. Sincerity can be complicated and overwhelming.
    b. Being honest about your own weaknesses while asking for help shows sincerity.
    c. Sincerity is not necessary when building trust and relationships.
    d. Sincerity can only be shown in formal and structured ways.

30. Eliza is managing a project to initiate a new complaint intake system and process for investigating employee concerns. As part of her development process, she met with department leaders to listen to their concerns and discuss specific needs that both the leaders and employees would want in this new system. One of the concerns raised was confidentiality and ensuring 100 percent privacy no matter the issue. Eliza is unable to fully address this due to reporting requirements when certain subjects are discussed during an investigation. What should Eliza do?
    a. Move forward with the project as confidentiality can be maintained during most cases.
    b. Update the policy requirements with the legal department to allow for 100 percent confidentiality in all cases.
    c. Halt the project and continue with the current intake system and investigation process.
    d. Communicate to the group when confidentiality cannot be maintained and why.

31. Which of the following statements is accurate regarding teamwork?
    a. Teamwork can occur at all levels within an organization, on both small and large scales.
    b. Teamwork occurs when each employee identifies their unique vision and goals.
    c. Engaging a team to be a functional group is not a difficult process.
    d. Working toward a common vision is applicable for teamwork within the leadership group.

32. A leader has many roles and responsibilities when creating and developing a team. What is the most important thing that a leader can do in order to accomplish the goals?
    a. Assign employees based on their job titles
    b. Reassign weaker employees to different teams
    c. Identify the specific skills and needs that are necessary
    d. Develop a strong and robust plan

33. The simple statement "increase the positive while decreasing the negative" describes which of the following?
    a. Conflict management
    b. Conflict resolution
    c. Relationship management
    d. Relationship resolution

Please use the model presented below to answer questions 34–36.

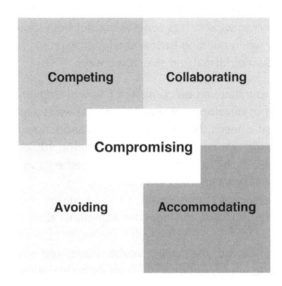

34. The model above shows the relationships between high and low levels of cooperation and assertiveness based on conflict. What is this model called?
   a. Transactional Analysis
   b. Lencioni's 5 Dysfunctions of a Team
   c. Drama Triangle
   d. Thomas-Kilmann Conflict Modes

35. Kyle cooperates with his teammates, but only when there are issues. For most of a project, he does not participate with the group and awaits direction from others. In which quadrant would Kyle fall?
   a. Competing
   b. Collaborating
   c. Avoiding
   d. Accommodating

36. Tamika is a leader within her workgroup and frequently engages other employees in solutions, cooperates with others to get the job done, and asserts herself when appropriate. Into which quadrant would Tamika fall?
   a. Competing
   b. Collaborating
   c. Avoiding
   d. Accommodating

37. What is the only thing that will help two conflicted employees work to resolve the issues and move to a point of compromise or resolution?
   a. Discipline and counseling
   b. Open and clear communication
   c. Training and development
   d. Root cause analysis

38. How can conflict be positive and productive?
    a. Conflict causes creative thinking and brainstorming by engaging employees in different ways.
    b. Conflict can never be positive or productive and should be eliminated from the organization.
    c. Conflict allows for more problems between employees that can include legal issues.
    d. Conflict encourages employees to look for other employment to increase their skillsets.

39. Which of the following statements is FALSE regarding destructive conflict?
    a. Destructive conflict should be addressed as soon as possible.
    b. It may be appropriate to call in a third-party investigator to address the issue.
    c. Employees should "hammer out" their issues and handle their conflicts on their own.
    d. It should be handled quickly and effectively, not allowing issues to linger.

40. Rachel recently issued a new policy to all employees. She has since received multiple questions about the same issues regarding the policy. What is the best way for Rachel to respond?
    a. Answer each question separately to the individual asking the question.
    b. Reference the policy to locate answers so that the employee becomes familiar with the details.
    c. Create a Frequently Asked Questions document and distribute it to all employees.
    d. Direct employees to their supervisor for answers to their questions.

41. What type of communication strategy is used when the leader of an organization issues a communication to their direct reports, who then relay this message to the next level of the organization until the message has been relayed to all employees?
    a. Pyramid Method
    b. Triangle Method
    c. Cascading Method
    d. Top-Down Method

42. Which of the following statements regarding listening is accurate?
    a. Listening is an active and engaged skill.
    b. Listening is the simple skill of hearing what someone says.
    c. Listening requires being nonresponsive to the speaker.
    d. Listening does not require a conscious effort.

43. Being skilled in global and cultural effectiveness means that an HR professional values what?
    a. Different education majors, universities, and social experiences
    b. Different industry experience and unique job roles
    c. Different perspectives, backgrounds, experiences, and personalities
    d. Different values, visions, ethics, and behavior

44. There are many benefits when working with a group of diverse employees. Which of the following is NOT something that an organization typically faces when there is diversity among employees?
    a. Recruiting and retention
    b. Turnover and attrition
    c. Growth and development
    d. Creativity and innovation

45. Louisa wants to promote a new diversity and inclusion initiative within her organization. She has researched other programs with various industries and has many models as examples. She has also reviewed a training program to roll out to the employees. What should Louisa do first to promote diverse and inclusive characteristics within the organization?
   a. Finalize the communications of the new program and submit it to leadership for approval.
   b. Create a training program and pilot it with the supervisors and managers.
   c. Meet with every employee to discuss the expectations and tools available to employees.
   d. Establish a diversity and inclusion policy that provides expectations and strategies.

46. Which of the following is an excellent way to gain key insights into an organization's lines of business?
   a. Apply for any positions within the organization when they become available to learn more about the business.
   b. Become a customer of the organization, use the product, and become familiar with the customer service provided.
   c. Create informal workgroups and discuss daily activities and supervisory issues that employees are facing.
   d. Sign up for all training and development opportunities to gain skills and education to promote further up in the organization.

47. Paul has recently taken a new assignment in another country. He has been reviewing the policies and procedures for the new office and finds that many of the policies lack the same information and detail as those from his previous role in his home country. What could be the reason for this?
   a. The local workforce has different opinions on the policies.
   b. The leadership team did not want to update the policies and upset their employees.
   c. Local laws may be different, and the policies need to consider this.
   d. The previous HR professional may have been derelict in their duties when creating the policy.

48. Which of the following is NOT a solution to ensure harmony between employees while encouraging and fostering a positive work environment?
   a. Sensitivity training
   b. Coaching sessions
   c. Cultural education
   d. Mentoring opportunities

49. Which term describes the intentional planning to engage all employees in the achievement of objectives that align with the overall success of an organization?
   a. Diversity
   b. Strategic planning
   c. Inclusion
   d. Business acumen

50. Eugene recently conducted an employee survey that requested information about the current workplace, including supervisory relationships, issues, concerns, and other problems that employees are experiencing. This survey was initiated to ensure that the policies and practices are appropriate and address the current needs of the workplace. Eugene only received a 23 percent response rate, which was exceptionally low. What could be a reason for this?

    a. Employees were simply not interested in providing information for the survey, as they were too busy with work.

    b. Surveys are not an effective way to gather information from employees, and the response rate was around the average.

    c. Eugene did not send out the survey multiple times or provide multiple ways to respond and should have allowed a much longer response time.

    d. Employees had to provide their department, job title, and other identifying information, which did not allow for anonymity.

Business

51. Which of the following is a representation of how to process information and develop competitive awareness?

    a. The Situational Awareness Triangle

    b. The Awareness Triangle

    c. The Top-Down Triangle

    d. The Competitive Intelligence Triangle

52. When working to determine competitive intelligence, which factor should have the largest focus?

    a. Action

    b. Analyze

    c. Adaptation

    d. Aware

53. Jake is interested in learning more about his organization's products and revenue opportunities. He has recently started reading annual reports and other resources. What type of resource is Jake utilizing?

    a. Physical

    b. Human

    c. Financial

    d. Organizational

54. Which of the following are NOT trends that are analyzed when using the PESTLE method?

    a. Social and Environmental

    b. Economic and Technological

    c. People and Sustainability

    d. Political and Legal

55. Which tool reviews all of the expenses and results to determine if a project has a positive return on investment and is worth the organization's financial support?

    a. Key performance indicators

    b. Cost-benefit analysis

    c. SWOT analysis

    d. Business analysis

56. Which of the following terms is defined as the strategic process of connecting an organization's resources, capital, tools, and workforce to achieve the goals and objectives at the highest levels?

    a. Strategic alignment

    b. Strategic planning

    c. Decision making

    d. Resource allocation

57. Julie has recently joined an organization as a recruitment coordinator. As part of her position, she is responsible for ensuring a robust, qualified candidate pool for hiring managers to interview. Julie is new to the organization, as well as the industry. What should Julie do to ensure that she provides strong candidates for consideration in the hiring process?

    a. Memorize the job descriptions for each position to ensure an understanding of the roles in the organization.

    b. Engage in training sessions to become familiar with each of the jobs that are performed in the organization.

    c. Engage in discussions with the HR staff of their knowledge and opinions of roles in the organization.

    d. Spend time with employees across the organization to understand the core business and what they do.

58. What data point calculates how much employees are absent from work?

    a. Attrition

    b. Human capital

    c. Presenteeism

    d. Absenteeism

59. What data point calculates how many employees are leaving an organization?

    a. Attrition

    b. Human capital

    c. Presenteeism

    d. Absenteeism

Please use the model presented below to answer questions 60–62.

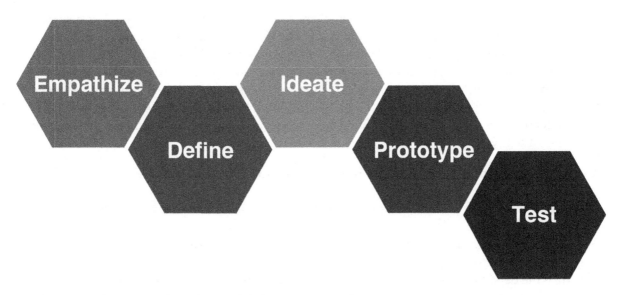

60. What strategic process does the model above represent?
    a. Innovative thinking
    b. Creative thinking
    c. Design thinking
    d. Strategic thinking

61. Which step in the model above refers to establishing the issue or concern broadly and specifically to ensure that the actual issues are being addressed?
    a. Empathize
    b. Define
    c. Prototype
    d. Test

62. Which step in the model above refers to implementing and evaluating the recommendations?
    a. Empathize
    b. Define
    c. Prototype
    d. Test

63. What is one of the most important things that an HR team and department should encourage and facilitate?
    a. Department meetings
    b. Open and honest dialogue
    c. Monthly employee newsletters
    d. Continuous growth and development

Please use the below scenario to answer questions 64–65.

Erin recently worked with the team to implement a new HR and Payroll system. This new system has many features and reporting options that will allow for department managers to access information easily and quickly. When the system is rolled out, she is surprised to see that not many managers are excited about the new platform. They are reluctant to use the system and submit requests for HR to run and provide the reports needed instead of using the system directly. During the planning phase, she was confident that this system would meet all of the department's needs as well as HR and Payroll, and she relied on external sources and feedback to select the system.

64. What should Erin have done during the planning phase to ensure buy-in and support from the departments?

a. Involve them in the planning phase and ask direct and specific questions to identify their needs, concerns, and wants.

b. Email the department managers letting them know that a new system was being selected and to submit recommended vendors.

c. Train the department managers on how new HR and Payroll systems are selected, how they operate, and the reports the provide.

d. Request an all-employee meeting to communicate to all employees that a new system would be selected.

65. What can Erin do to engage the department managers in the new system?

a. Provide specific, relevant, and useful training in how to navigate the system, run reports, and locate information.

b. Request that the executive leadership speak to the department managers and require their participation.

c. Indicate in the department manager's performance reviews their reluctance to use the system.

d. Review the decision and request that the old platform be reinstalled while the team works out a solution.

66. What is the first step when implementing a change management process?

a. Prepare for the change

b. Implement the change

c. Identify the need for change

d. Reinforce the change

67. Which of the following statements is TRUE when providing guidance to managers in departments other than Human Resources?

a. HR should train supervisors in all areas of HR so they can handle every complaint.

b. HR should train supervisors to understand when HR should be immediately involved.

c. HR should not train supervisors in how to coach and counsel employees.

d. HR should train supervisors in how to write a job description and recruitment flyer.

68. Why is it important to allow for anonymity when conducting employee surveys?

a. Anonymity does not provide any benefits to the employee when completing a survey.

b. Anonymity should not be provided so that management can know where the issues are.

c. Anonymity does not require management to communicate results or action plans.

d. Anonymity provides a safe and secure way to communicate true and honest feedback.

69. Which of the following statements regarding customers is NOT accurate?

    a. Customers each have a unique need, and understanding this need is required to provide excellent customer service.

    b. Customers are always external to the organization, with services being provided outside of the organization.

    c. Customer requests should be responded to quickly and accurately, with a high priority given to ensuring high satisfaction.

    d. Communication is the basis of a relationship with a customer and should be prioritized.

70. What process is defined as reviewing, analyzing, and auditing a program or initiative with a fair, balanced, and unbiased mindset?

    a. Critical evaluation

    b. Situational awareness

    c. Customer interaction

    d. Business acumen

71. What is the ultimate goal of handling any complaint?

    a. Following a structured process to resolve the issues

    b. Informing leadership immediately of the issues

    c. Resolving the issue at the lowest level possible

    d. Being respectful and responsive

72. Which of the following statements is TRUE regarding employee and labor relations?

    a. Employee and labor relations is the sole responsibility of Human Resources.

    b. Employee and labor relations is the maintenance of effective working relationships with employees and the labor unions that represent them.

    c. Employee and labor relations manage themselves and require attention only as needed.

    d. The cornerstone of positive employee and labor relations is joint committees.

73. Which of the following should be the core basis in selecting a position for job elimination?

    a. Employee information such as age, years of service, and retirement eligibility

    b. Employee performance

    c. Employee disciplinary history

    d. Job duties and organizational need

74. What is one of the most important and fundamental recordkeeping functions within Human Resources?

    a. New hire documents

    b. Offer letters

    c. Personnel files

    d. Timecards

75. Which of the following is a best practice regarding employee surveys?

    a. Committed leadership is not necessary for an effective survey.

    b. Surveys should require employees to identify themselves to ensure appropriate actions are taken.

    c. Commit to surveying employees every six to twelve months.

    d. Share data consistently at all levels of the organization.

Functional Areas

People Knowledge

1. Carl has recently joined a new organization as the Human Resources Director. He quickly realizes that the department does not have a strategic plan and the team, while knowledgeable and technically proficient, does not have a clear direction. What should Carl do first to begin strategic planning for the HR department?

    a. Tailor the strategic plan from his previous organization, and implement it immediately throughout the department

    b. Develop a plan based on the knowledge gained through the onboarding process and the research conducted during the new hire process

    c. Review the organization's mission, goals, and objectives against the HR mission, goals, and objectives to ensure alignment

    d. Hire an outside consultant to determine the best strategic plan for the department and ensure an unbiased and fair review

2. Which of the following is an INACCURATE statement about strategic planning?

    a. Strategic planning is critical to ensure that employees are working toward the goals and objectives of the organization.

    b. Strategic planning is the formal assessment of available resources, work force, knowledge, and skills within an organization.

    c. Strategic planning ensures that the organization is aware of and in possession of the resources necessary to succeed.

    d. Strategic planning plays a vital role in the success of an organization at all levels, including each individual department.

3. Strategic planning is dependent on which of the following?

    a. HR professionals who are proficiently trained in process mapping and assessment

    b. Robust and thorough recruitment, selection, hiring, and onboarding practices

    c. Knowledge and awareness of the organizational and departmental goals and objectives

    d. Outsourced HR staff who are unbiased and separate from the organizational culture

4. Why is it important to ensure that any action plans and items are aligned with the SMART methodology?

    a. It ensures that success can be defined, measured, and achieved.

    b. It allows for the quickest and most effective path to success.

    c. It identifies weaknesses and what is needed to be successful.

    d. It facilitates the resources needed for the plans.

5. What does the SMART methodology stand for?

    a. Simple, measurable, actions, resources, time-targeted

    b. Specific, milestones, achievable, resources, technology

    c. Simple, milestones, actions, realistic, technology

    d. Specific, measurable, achievable, realistic, time-targeted

6. Andrea is working on a project to create a more well-rounded and informational experience for employees when working with Human Resources. Additionally, she is hoping this new experience will give the organization an edge with the competition and attract the most qualified candidates for open positions. In addition to assessing the compensation, benefits, retirement, promotion opportunities, and work-life balance programs, what should Andrea also incorporate in her review?

    a. Products and services offered

    b. Total rewards package

    c. State benefit plans such as disability

    d. Executive leadership profiles

7. Which of the following is NOT a component of the 7 C's when working to effectively communicate?

    a. Considerate

    b. Concise

    c. Courteous

    d. Complex

8. What are the two most important factors when presenting information that will be used for making decisions?

    a. Timeliness and complexity

    b. Timeliness and accuracy

    c. Financial data and accuracy

    d. References and data research

9. Which of the following is described as the strategic process that takes into account the holistic view of the workforce needs, both current and future?

    a. Recruitment process

    b. Talent acquisition process

    c. Onboarding process

    d. Workforce planning

10. Which of the following is described as the tactical process of filling a vacancy?

    a. Recruitment process

    b. Talent acquisition process

    c. Onboarding process

    d. Workforce planning

11. The overall brand that an organization provides to its current and future workforce is referred to as what?

    a. Organizational branding

    b. Total rewards package

    c. Employee value proposition

    d. Compensation and benefits

12. Liang is working on the organization's employee value proposition. She is excited to roll out a brand-new program, including a new online portal that provides access to information on compensation, benefits, career, and culture. What element is she missing?
    a. Turnover rates
    b. Key performance indicators
    c. Work environment
    d. Employee forms

13. Which of the following is NOT a benefit of having a strong, robust EVP?
    a. Increased candidate referrals and talent pools
    b. Fewer job vacancies and lower absenteeism
    c. Trust in leadership and increased productivity
    d. Increased turnover and higher cost per hire

14. According to a survey conducted by the Corporate Leadership Council, what is the biggest benefit of employee engagement?
    a. Productivity
    b. Workforce retention
    c. Customer retention
    d. Overall profit

15. Armando is working to make several changes to HR programs that will improve the employee experience. He has implemented the same changes at his previous organization and saw great success. Armando has finalized all of his recommendations and is rolling out a soft launch of the programs. He is surprised to find that most employees do not have a strong response, or one at all, to his new program ideas. What should Armando have done to ensure that employees would be more receptive to the program ideas?
    a. He should have conducted a survey to find out specific employee needs and implemented changes that meet those needs.
    b. He should have conducted a market survey to determine what other organizations are doing and implemented those ideas.
    c. He should have discussed with the HR team what has been done in the past and reimplemented previous programs that were not successful.
    d. Armando did everything necessary to implement changes, and he should work to communicate the changes frequently.

16. Which of the following options is NOT considered a unique program that can enhance employee engagement?
    a. Safety and security protocols
    b. Training and learning opportunities
    c. Recognition and achievement programs
    d. Telecommuting and alternate work schedules

17. Which of the following job redesign processes occur when new tasks related to the current job roles and responsibilities are added to increase motivation and engagement?
    a. Job design
    b. Job enrichment
    c. Job enlargement
    d. Job rotation

18. Which of the following job redesign processes occur when employees trade off positions or alternate duties and assignments between individuals?
   a. Job design
   b. Job enrichment
   c. Job enlargement
   d. Job rotation

19. Maggie is working with Steven, an accountant who wants to increase his knowledge and skill set in other areas of finance so that he will be eligible for additional promotional opportunities in the future. Maggie has identified several new tasks and assignments for Steven that are outside of his normal workload and standard role; however, these tasks will enable him to expand his role within the organization. What job redesign process has Maggie worked through in this situation?
   a. Job design
   b. Job enrichment
   c. Job enlargement
   d. Job rotation

20. What term refers to the entire package that employees receive when joining an organization?
   a. Offer letter
   b. Employee value proposition
   c. Total rewards
   d. New employee orientation

21. What are the five components that make up the total rewards package?
   a. Offer letter, health insurance providers, supervisor information, training schedule, and policies
   b. Pay, health insurance providers, work-life, training schedule, and policies
   c. Offer letter, safety procedures, supervisor information, training schedule, and recognition
   d. Pay, benefits, work-life, learning and development, and performance and recognition

22. Which of the following benefits is government mandated to be offered to employees?
   a. Long-term care coverage
   b. Health care coverage
   c. Legal protection coverage
   d. Pet insurance coverage

23. The Family Medical Leave Act provides an employee how much time of protected leave to care for a family member or for the birth of a child?
   a. Six months
   b. Twelve weeks
   c. Six weeks
   d. Four months

24. What is the one standard that should be adhered to regarding benefits plans, whether government mandated or voluntary?
   a. Clear and concise communication containing contact information
   b. Least expensive plans with the maximum benefit allowed
   c. Services with an online portal and customer service options
   d. Fully funded by the employer regardless of the cost for all dependents

25. Amelia is working on improving the performance evaluation process and would like to create a tool that can chart out the growth, development, and potential career paths for employees. This tool would also identify the areas of improvement and needed skills to reach these goals. What tool should Amelia use in order to accomplish this?
    a. Strategic plan
    b. Succession plan
    c. Individual action plan
    d. Employee value proposition

26. Which of the following is a standard, efficient, and effective method to identify employee needs, wants, or concerns?
    a. Comment cards
    b. Individual meetings
    c. Employee surveys
    d. Market research

27. Which component of the employee value proposition (EVP) encourages an understanding throughout the entire organization of the overarching goals and objectives, including trust, support, teamwork, collaboration, and social responsibility?
    a. Culture
    b. Work environment
    c. Career
    d. Benefits

28. Which component of the employee value proposition (EVP) encourages employees to know and understand how their performance aligns with the expectations of the position and future opportunities?
    a. Culture
    b. Work environment
    c. Career
    d. Benefits

29. Which of the following statements is INACCURATE regarding talent acquisition?
    a. Talent acquisition is the entire process from when a vacancy occurs to the hiring of a new employee.
    b. Talent acquisition is a strategic process that includes assessing the workforce needs and recruiting talent.
    c. Talent acquisition aims to hire individuals with specific skills and abilities that align with the organization's needs.
    d. Talent acquisition deals only with the initial hiring of an employee and not the future opportunities.

30. When establishing goals and objectives in a performance review or individual action plan, what methodology ensures that success can be accurately defined and described?
    a. SWOT
    b. SMART
    c. 7 C's
    d. EVP

Organization Knowledge

31. Which of the following is a tool that presents how an organizational group is designed, how work is assigned, and how positions report to each other?
    a. Organization chart
    b. Organization structure
    c. Organization design
    d. Organization function

32. Darcie is creating a new organization chart for the Human Resources department that provides in-depth and detailed information such as who is responsible for training, benefits, orientation, safety, and other functions within the department. What benefit can Darcie realize with this new organization chart?
    a. Darcie can provide her team with the updated organization chart to ensure that employees know their roles and scope of duties.
    b. Darcie can use the organization chart to defend staffing levels and funding during budget preparation.
    c. Darcie can keep the organization chart in her files to reference in the future, but there are no real benefits.
    d. Darcie can use this organization chart as a tool to educate departments on the appropriate contacts for specific topics.

33. Human Resources should be structured in a way that provides the best customer service to the organization, departments, and employees. The two most common forms of structure are decentralized and centralized models. What is the difference between these two models?
    a. A decentralized model allows for HR staff to report to the HR department, while a centralized model allows for HR staff to report to external department leaders.
    b. Both models allow for HR staff to report to the HR department, with a decentralized model providing services to external customers.
    c. A decentralized model allows for HR staff to report to external department leaders, while a centralized model allows for all HR staff to report to the HR department.
    d. Both models allow for HR staff to report to the HR department, with a centralized model providing services to internal customers.

34. Which of the following methodologies is used to eliminate the need for a customer to search for the right person to call for a specific question?
    a. SPOC
    b. SWOT
    c. SMART
    d. ADR

35. Amelia is researching an answer for Bob regarding his FMLA leave request and the amount of remaining time in the calendar year that he is eligible for. The standard policy in HR is to provide an answer within twenty-four hours of receiving the initial request, but Amelia will not be able to provide a response in that timeframe. What should Amelia do?

    a. She should continue to research the request and communicate with Bob when all of the information is available, regardless of the timeframe.

    b. She should communicate directly with Bob that she is working on the request and will need some additional time to prepare the final response.

    c. She should provide Bob with the contact information for the state offices so that he can follow up with them directly.

    d. She should request that another employee manage Bob's FMLA leave request due to her inability to provide a response with the twenty-four hour timeframe.

36. According to Richard Beckhard, an American organizational theorist and pioneer in the field, there are three factors in the organizational development process. Which of the following is NOT one of those factors?

    a. Organizational development is implemented organization-wide.

    b. Organizational development is managed from the top levels of leadership.

    c. Organizational development is planned.

    d. Organizational development is managed within each department.

37. Which of the following is a concern when departments other than Human Resources maintain an employee file?

    a. Department files on employees can create efficiencies.

    b. Department files are subject to different retention schedules.

    c. Documents may not be secured or filed in a confidential manner.

    d. Departments should maintain the master employee file.

38. What term is defined as the organization's commitment to foster a positive working relationship with its employees?

    a. Labor relations

    b. Workforce planning

    c. Employee relations

    d. Mission statement

39. What term below includes the establishment, negotiation, and administration of bargaining agreements and policies as well as managing grievances and disagreements?

    a. Labor relations

    b. Workforce planning

    c. Employee relations

    d. Mediation

40. Which of the following statements about alternative dispute resolution (ADR) is NOT accurate?

    a. ADR processes progress from more formal to less formal.

    b. ADR processes include negotiation, mediation, conciliation, and arbitration.

    c. ADR processes include both formal and informal methods to resolve concerns.

    d. ADR processes work to expedite the exchange of information and decision-making processes.

41. Lisa has been identified as the HR specialist for employees to call for all questions related to benefits and leave administration. From making changes to dependents or health insurance plans, to applying for family medical leave, Lisa is the HR specialist who should be contacted. What term would best describe Lisa?

    a. Customer service
    b. SPOC
    c. HR representative
    d. CSR

42. Self-service portals, accessibility to employee information, filing electronic documents, and internal websites are all examples of solutions provided by what?

    a. HR management system
    b. Policies and procedures
    c. Recordkeeping program
    d. Technology management

43. Harry, an HR specialist, is working with a manager to counsel an employee on their frequent personal internet usage. The employee has spent an unusually large amount of time on the internet for personal use. This use has negatively affected the amount of work that is being performed. The employee has responded that they now understand the internet use was excessive but were unaware that there was a policy regarding internet use. The employee has accepted responsibility and agreed to manage time better to complete work tasks. Harry has reviewed the policies and procedures and found that the most recent policy regarding internet usage was implemented five years ago. What should Harry do next?

    a. He should provide the employee with the current policy so they know what the expectations are regarding internet usage.
    b. He should update the policies and procedures to accurately reflect new technology, including social media and usage guidelines.
    c. He should prepare a written reprimand and formally discipline the employee for the inappropriate usage of company resources.
    d. He should request that Information Technology block external sites so that no employee has access to the internet for personal use.

44. Which of the following would NOT be a standard component to include in a workplace technology policy?

    a. Specific daily usage limit
    b. Code of conduct
    c. Examples of ethical use
    d. Appropriate guidelines

45. Michael attends a Human Resources conference annually to stay up-to-date with new trends, resources, and legal changes. Additionally, he uses these conferences to network with other professionals and talk to vendors that provide services such as payroll software, recruiting and onboarding tools, and other technology. Why is it important for Michael to keep abreast of the new technology available to HR?

    a. So that he can shop pricing and change vendors if he sees a better price tag in order to save the organization money

    b. So that he can receive free tutorials and trial subscriptions to sample the products and pull resources for future use

    c. So that he can convey to his department and organization that they are receiving the best services available at a competitive price

    d. So that he can discuss his future career plans with the vendors and provide them with his resume and references

46. Which of the following statements is INACCURATE regarding data, data storage, and reporting?

    a. A simple and low-cost tool such as Microsoft Excel® may be more useful than a high-cost, high-tech program.

    b. The technology and tools needed should be determined by the end user or audience, as well as the organizational needs.

    c. If inaccurate data is entered into the system, a useful and informative report can still be generated.

    d. Effective technology platforms should be able to hold many pieces of information and provide detailed reports.

47. Which alternative dispute resolution methods is a non-binding formal process in which a negotiator explains the law and provides the two parties with a non-binding recommendation to resolve the issue?

    a. Arbitration

    b. Negotiation

    c. Mediation

    d. Conciliation

48. Which alternative dispute resolution method is a voluntary agreement that works out a solution directly between the two parties involved?

    a. Arbitration

    b. Negotiation

    c. Mediation

    d. Conciliation

49. Why is it important to communicate an organization's mission, values, goals, and objectives to an outside vendor who is providing a technology platform?

    a. To ensure a fair and competitive pricing schedule based on the organization's level of affordability

    b. To ensure alignment between the services offered and the strategic plan, which will support the overall organizational goals

    c. To ensure that the outside vendor is structured in the same manner as the organization, centralized or decentralized

    d. It is not important to communicate this information, as the outside vendor will have their own mission, values, goals, and objectives.

50. When organizational development and effectiveness is not being realized within an organization, it could be due to many factors, such as lack of resources, ineffective technology, low motivation, mental fatigue, or increased workload. What are these factors known as?
   a. Barriers
   b. Threats
   c. Opportunities
   d. Weaknesses

51. When all of the Human Resources employees report to the HR leader and provide services to assigned customers, how is the department structured?
   a. Decentralized
   b. SPOC
   c. Centralized
   d. SMART

52. Human Resources data is typically organized in six specific, key areas. Which of the following is NOT one of those areas?
   a. Technology management
   b. Employee data and job history
   c. Training, growth, and development
   d. Operational and departmental information

53. Lucille is auditing the HR process of new employee paperwork and filing protocols. She finds that some paperwork is scanned and stored electronically, some paperwork is filed in a master filing system, and some paperwork is sent to the department for storage in a departmental file. This practice has been in place for many years and many employees who have been with the organization are hesitant to implement a new practice. What should Lucille do?
   a. She should recommend that the current practice be continued until a new electronic system can be purchased and all paperwork can be scanned and saved electronically.
   b. She should recommend that the current practice be continued until the current employees retire or leave the organization; afterward, she should implement a new practice for all new employees.
   c. She should recommend that the director establish a training session for employees regarding change and how it can benefit an organization and its practices.
   d. She should recommend that HR implement a standardized process, communicate this change to departments, and update all current files to reflect this new standard.

54. How can an organization help to ensure that employees feel protected regarding their personal information, such as home addresses, social security numbers, and dates of birth?
   a. Allow employees to review their personnel file regularly
   b. Maintain master personnel files off-site at a remote location
   c. Implement a paperless filing system for all employment records
   d. Enable the most recent, powerful security protocols and safety features

55. Why is it important to automate as many processes and tasks as possible?
   a. It maximizes risks associated with hackers and data leaks.
   b. It eliminates the need for data entry and auditing.
   c. It minimizes risks associated with providing inaccurate information.
   d. It allows for the system to locate, identify, and manage trends.

56. When does HR have an integral role in organizational development?
   a. During the career planning and training of an employee
   b. During the entire lifecycle of an employee
   c. During the hiring and selection of an employee
   d. During the recognition and promotion of an employee

57. Courtney is an HR Manager who is working to resolve a dispute between two employees. She has been unable to resolve the issue herself and has entered into a contract with a neutral, third party to work with the two employees and resolve the issue. What process is Courtney utilizing to resolve the dispute?
   a. Conciliation
   b. Arbitration
   c. Mediation
   d. Negotiation

58. There are numerous benefits that can be realized with a robust and advanced technology platform to deliver information. Which of the following is NOT one of these benefits?
   a. It increases proficiency and saves time.
   b. It organizes information and provides a standard of data entry.
   c. It maintains confidentiality and eliminates bias.
   d. It incorporates external market data for trend analysis.

59. Which of the following describes how a department is designed and how work is assigned?
   a. Organization structure
   b. Organization chart
   c. Organization policy
   d. Organization system

60. Which of the following is an indicator of a technology platform being the most effective available?
   a. Ability to hold multiple pieces of information and provide reports to perform analysis
   b. Understanding of the audience and the recommendations needed for the concerns
   c. Identifies inaccurate or inappropriate data entered into the system
   d. It is the most cost-effective solution provided by an outside vendor

Workplace Knowledge

61. Having awareness and understanding of which of the following components is vital specifically in a global organization?
   a. Organizational structure, leadership, and mission
   b. Cultural differences and language barriers
   c. Corporate policy, practices, and procedures
   d. Compensation, benefits, and training

62. Comparing information from two countries through the PESTLE tool can provide insight into gaps between policies and practices, allowing for recommendations to address these gaps. What factors does the PESTLE tool analyze?
   a. Political, economic, social, technological, legal, and environmental
   b. Process, equipment, social, teamwork, lawsuits, and environmental
   c. Process, economic, structure, technological, lawsuits, and ergonomic
   d. Political, ergonomic, structure, teamwork, legal, and efficiency

63. Karen is working with the leadership to identify potential issues or concerns that need to be addressed prior to initiating a satellite office in a new country. She has reviewed various pieces of information and data to prepare her findings. Karen is providing three recommendations to address gaps discovered. Her recommendations include updating the employee training models, providing new opportunities and development, and hiring new employees who support the organization's goals and values. Which PESTLE factor has Karen identified as a concern?

    a. Economic

    b. Social

    c. Environmental

    d. Technological

64. When conducting an HR audit of policies, systems, procedures, and documentation, there are three specific goals to achieve. Which of the following is NOT one of these goals?

    a. To provide a positive and healthy work environment

    b. To align with the organizational strategy and values

    c. To comply with legal requirements and statutes

    d. To finalize the audit as quickly as possible

65. Which of the following works to ensure consistent, transparent, effective, efficient, and equitable practices?

    a. Localization

    b. Compliance

    c. Standardization

    d. Adaptation

66. Which of the following works to respect the local culture and traditions, understand the educational system, and adapt to the legislation and government?

    a. Localization

    b. Compliance

    c. Standardization

    d. Adaptation

67. Miguel is an HR generalist who is working with Emily, a customer service manager who will be relocating to the Philippines from the United States. Emily has received a promotion to lead a new customer service center that will provide services to clients. She will be responsible for hiring new employees, training existing employees who have transferred to this new location, and working to accomplish the goals of the new service center. Miguel is Emily's primary contact to assist with the relocation and transfer to the new position and country. Which of the following situations will Miguel NOT assist Emily with?

    a. Assisting Emily's spouse with employment

    b. Locating medical facilities and short-term housing

    c. Repatriating back to the United States

    d. Recruiting new employees for the service center

68. Which of the following refers to the identities of the employees within a workforce?

    a. Demographics

    b. Integration

    c. Inclusion

    d. Diversity

69. Which of the following refers to the acceptance of thoughts, ideas, and perspectives from every employee?
    a. Demographics
    b. Integration
    c. Inclusion
    d. Diversity

70. Which of the following workplace accommodations would be considered UNREASONABLE?
    a. Purchasing interpretation software
    b. Creating a new job and role for the employee
    c. Reassigning the employee to a new job
    d. Acquiring new office equipment and special devices

71. Which of the following workplace accommodations would be considered UNREASONABLE?
    a. Installing a sit/stand ergonomic desk to allow for wheelchair access
    b. Approving a telecommuting arrangement to work from home due to an injury
    c. Modifying the work schedule to allow for unlimited paid breaks
    d. Providing additional breaks and a secure, private area to allow nursing mothers to lactate

72. Rita is working to identify, address, and eliminate challenges and threats that the HR department may encounter. She is auditing policies, programs, and practices to ensure that the department is in compliance with regulations and that fairness, equity, and efficiency is applied to every case. What process is Rita working through?
    a. Risk management
    b. SWOT analysis
    c. PESTLE analysis
    d. Root cause analysis

73. Which of the following statements is NOT correct regarding risk management within the HR department?
    a. HR policies and practices should always support a workplace that minimizes risk.
    b. HR should identify risks only when a specific incident occurs, or in a reactive setting.
    c. HR can be proactive in minimizing risk by establishing strong documentation and process.
    d. HR should conduct regular audits to ensure compliance with laws and updates.

74. Brandon is the HR director for a local company that provides consultant services for land use. A recent earthquake has hit the area, and Brandon is working to ensure that employees are safe and understand the protocols for when a natural disaster occurs. Brandon implements the appropriate emergency management plan immediately but realizes that under the current circumstances, there are elements that are not included or need to be revised to address the immediate needs of the employees and organization. What should Brandon do?
    a. He should implement the current plan with no changes or deviations, but after the current disaster is over, he should make changes for the future.
    b. He should immediately make arrangements for all employees to telecommute, pending further notice, until the disaster is over.
    c. He should implement the current plan and recommend modifications for approval that address the current needs.
    d. He should request plans from other agencies and work to develop a new plan that addresses all of the current needs.

75. Which of the following is a detailed risk assessment that provides insight and information regarding a specific concern or issue?
    a. Due diligence investigation
    b. Policy audit
    c. Workplace safety investigation
    d. Benefit audit

76. When a workplace accident or injury occurs, what is the first priority?
    a. To initiate an investigation and begin taking statements
    b. To ensure that the employee receives the care needed to treat the injury
    c. To work with the supervisor to ensure any safety violation has been resolved
    d. To take photographs of the incident, including those of the injured employee

77. What are the three standard steps in an audit process?
    a. Review, assessment, and results
    b. Discussion, evaluation, and finalizing
    c. Assessment, analyzing, and execution
    d. Planning, execution, and finalizing

78. Which of the following steps in a risk management audit would include mapping out the scope of the investigation and defining the objective?
    a. Preparation
    b. Planning
    c. Execution
    d. Finalizing

79. Which of the following steps in a risk management audit would include preparing a report that summarizes the findings, highlights strengths, identifies weaknesses, and provides recommendations?
    a. Preparation
    b. Planning
    c. Execution
    d. Finalizing

80. Rosalie is updating the HR personnel policies and is working to include strategies and elements that will increase social awareness for employees regarding the environment, community, marketplace, and workplace. One new policy provides employees with an additional ten hours of paid leave to work with a charity such as a food bank or home building program. What strategy is Rosalie working to incorporate into the policies?
    a. Corporate social responsibility
    b. Environmental programs
    c. Sustainable strategy
    d. Social justice practices

81. What is the appropriate alignment, or order, of the four responsibilities of corporate social responsibility?
    a. Economic, legal, ethical, and philanthropic
    b. Legal, economic, philanthropic, and ethical
    c. Philanthropic, legal, economic, and ethical
    d. Ethical, philanthropic, legal, and economic

82. Which of the following statements regarding communication is NOT accurate?

    a. Communication should be practiced, and managers should be coached on effective techniques often.

    b. Many individuals hear information differently and will have separate understandings of the message.

    c. Most individuals hear the same information and will have the same understanding of the message.

    d. Communication is a critical need within an organization that managers should be trained and educated in.

83. Which of the following agencies enforces the laws regarding employee privacy?

    a. Occupational Safety and Health Administration (OSHA)

    b. Equal Employment Opportunity Commission (EEOC)

    c. Department of Justice (DOJ)

    d. Department of Labor (DOL)

84. When can an organization offer a benefit to employees that is different from the federal or state requirement?

    a. If the offered benefit is more lucrative, or greater than the requirement in the law

    b. Under no circumstances can a benefit be different from the requirement in the law

    c. If the offered benefit is less lucrative, or less than the requirement due to finances

    d. If the employee signs a release waiving their rights under the law

85. Which of the following examples would be an INAPPOPRIATE reason to enter into a contract with an outside legal service?

    a. To negotiate a new contract with a union, and the team currently does not have this experience

    b. The current staff does not want to audit the safety practices because they are uninteresting.

    c. To resolve a conflict between two employees after multiple attempts with the current staff

    d. To review and update leave administration policies based on updated state legislation

Answer Explanations

Behavioral Competencies

Leadership

1. C: Directing and managing people is NOT a component of effective leadership. Choices *A*, *B*, and *D* are incorrect answers because they are all components of effective leadership. Directing and overseeing work, motivating and encouraging individuals, and engaging and motivating employees are all key elements of being an effective leader within an organization. Choice *C* is the correct answer because while directing and managing people is an important function of an organization, supervisors or managers within the organization usually handle these responsibilities. Leaders should be focused on strategic goals and how the employees will work to support the organization in accomplishing these goals.

2. A: Leaders exist at each and every level within an organization and within every department. Choice *B* is incorrect because leadership is important at all levels within an organization, not just within the executive team. Choice *C* is incorrect because while formal leadership is important, so is informal leadership, and many employees respond differently to a structured versus an unstructured approach to leadership. Choice *D* is incorrect because leadership is consistently displayed on a day-to-day basis by all employees within an organization, regardless of job titles and formal work roles.

3. D: Jack should prepare a specific presentation for the executive team that communicates the details needed to approve the program. Choices *A*, *B*, and *C* are incorrect because on their own, they do not provide the information that an executive would need to approve a new program. While samples of employee communications and program documents would be excellent reference materials, Jack should focus on communicating the relationship between this new program and how it can impact both the employees and the organization. Jack should also be able to answer questions that arise, and if he does not have the answer, he should commit to responding later.

4. C: For an objective to be SMART, it must meet each of the following attributes: Specific, Measurable, Achievable, Realistic, and Time-Targeted. Choices *A*, *B*, and *D* are incorrect as they each identify the means to achieve the elements indicated within a SMART objective. Metrics provide the data to measure. Teamwork will allow larger objectives to be accomplished. Maintenance is vital once an objective is achieved to ensure sustainability. Methods are needed to provide the roadmap to achieve success. Tools and resources should be identified to ensure the objectives can be met.

5. B: Brainstorming is the process in which employees converse and exchange new ideas and solutions. Choice *A*, teamwork, is important to an organization and allows for employees to work together. Teamwork is important for brainstorming to be effective. Choice *C*, leadership, defines the objectives of an organization that brainstorming then works to create solutions to achieve. Choice *D*, collaboration, is another term for teamwork, which allows for brainstorming to work effectively.

6. D: The single most effective way to engage stakeholders and ensure a commitment to HR initiatives is to bring stakeholders together and communicate the benefits that employees and the organization will realize. While Choices *A*, *B*, and *C* are all important and potential steps to take, they should be done in alignment with engaging the stakeholders.

7. A: Angelina should review the goals and timing originally set when the project was designed and then ensure that the proper resources were identified and allocated to achieve success. Choice *B* is inaccurate because Angelina should first determine what occurred before going to her boss. After she has figured out how the project got off track, then she should seek out her boss for assistance. Choice *C* is inaccurate because as the project manager, Angelina is responsible for the project and ensuring that the team is working toward the goals and has the proper resources. Looking for someone to blame is not the way to move forward. Choice *D* is inaccurate because deliberately reporting dishonestly and inaccurately is an unethical behavior that could not only result in the project failing but in Angelina having to face serious consequences for her actions.

8. B: HR professionals should develop skills related to adaptability and flexibility because over time, organizations and employees will evolve and change frequently. To ensure equity and fairness, policies and procedures should not be changed for any reason, so Choice *A* is incorrect. Choice *C* is incorrect because adaptability should be used when needed and could be needed during the course of operations on a daily basis. Choice *D* is incorrect because flexibility should be used when needed and appropriate, not just for when a program is not meeting objectives or timeframes.

9. D: While working with numerous companies builds a resume, it is not the most effective way to build credibility within an organization and with others. Choices *A*, *B*, and *C* are incorrect because they are, in fact, ways to establish credibility with an organization. Education and experience, certification and training programs, and most importantly, accomplishing objectives and achieving results will work to establish a credible and solid reputation within an organization.

10. A: Each employee is motivated differently, and some may not feel comfortable with formal recognition. Some employees may preferentially receive their encouragement and motivation from informal recognition. Latoya should strive to understand each employee's needs and work to recognize them in the most appropriate way. Choice *B* is incorrect because employees who are not comfortable with formal recognition should not be pushed into even more formal situations. This choice doesn't show an understanding of those employees and their needs. Choice *C* is incorrect because Latoya should not simply stop formal recognition, as some employees do find motivation through formal programs. Latoya shouldn't stop one form of recognition altogether, but should work to establish numerous ways of recognition, so that each employee is valued. Choice *D* is incorrect because Latoya should take some action to ensure that all employees' needs are met.

11. C: Personal integrity is the leadership quality of being honest with yourself and taking actions based on personal values and beliefs. Personal integrity has the most impact to an organization. Choices *A*, *B*, and *D* are incorrect because they are all elements of leadership qualities, including personal integrity. Personal integrity includes ethics, authenticity, and accountability.

12. D: The first thing that Blanca should do is immediately admit the mistake to her supervisor, take ownership of the error, and have a discussion about what can be one to correct the mistake. Choice *A* is incorrect because it should not be the first thing that Blanca does. While she will need to correct the issue and put measures in place to ensure that the mistake does not happen again, she should first take ownership of the mistake and then work with her supervisor on the next steps. Choice *B* is incorrect because the error should be corrected immediately and should not wait until the next enrollment. Choice *C* is incorrect because HR should not wait for an employee to come forward when a mistake has been identified. HR should work to correct the matter immediately.

13. B: The correct answer in this case is Choice *B*, as confidentiality may need to be broken due to the information received. In cases in which a law has been broken or abuse has been reported, HR professionals may need to involve law enforcement or a legal advisor. Employees should understand this during the process of reporting to HR. Choice *A* is an incorrect answer, as providing confidentiality and privacy to all employees involved is true and should be extended to all individuals, including those who have allegedly engaged in the behavior. Choice *C* is an incorrect answer, as confidentiality is in fact vital to employees who may need to report unethical behavior. Choice *D* is also incorrect, because confidentiality does allow for a fair and unbiased investigation.

14. C: Joseph should not have discussed the issued discipline with the employee who made the complaint. This is not appropriate, and this type of information should only be discussed with the subject employee. The complainant has no say in the discipline issued, and their satisfaction with the resolution is not a matter for HR to consider. Choice *A* is not the correct answer because investigations may take time to be fully completed, depending on the number of witnesses, the complexity of the complaint, and potential second interviews. Investigations should take as long as necessary to ensure that they are complete and accurate while getting to the core issue that needs to be addressed.

Choice *B* is not the correct answer because Joseph should follow up with any employee who was interviewed to let them know that the matter has been fully investigated, resolved, and closed. This conversation also allows Joseph to remind employees about retaliation not being condoned following the matter. Choice *D* is not the correct answer because Joseph did breach confidentiality and ethics when discussing the discipline of one employee with another. Joseph's supervisor should receive a debrief of the matter and what the next steps are to provide awareness of the situation and resolutions needed, but Joseph also needs to be counseled on his inappropriate action.

15. B: A SWOT analysis tool works to address an organization's issues by evaluating strengths, weaknesses, opportunities, and threats. Choices *A*, *C*, and *D* are incorrect answers. While strategy, outlook, training, and willingness are all elements that are important to an organization and may be a variable of the SWOT analysis, they are not the actual criteria that are used for evaluation.

16. A: Employees should receive the employee handbook, policies, procedures, and expectations of employment on their first day with the organization. Typically, this information is provided during the new hire orientation. Choice *B* is incorrect in that employees should have this information before an issue arises; however, it may be a best practice to provide this information when a new issue is brought forward so that the employee can refamiliarize themselves with the policies. Choice *C* is incorrect because candidates are not usually provided with this level of information. The organization's vision, mission, and values can be made available, but an employee handbook and the policies, procedures, and expectations of an employee are for employees, not candidates. Choice *D* is incorrect because while this is a best practice for accessibility of information for employees to seek out when needed, it should be provided during an orientation session to allow for questions and not just available for an employee to find.

17. B: Hiring a third-party investigator will most likely not allow for a quicker and speedier investigation. A proper and thorough investigation should take the amount of time needed to process all of the information and interview all potential witnesses or others who may have information in relation to the complaint. Choices *A*, *C*, and *D* are incorrect because they are all items that can be accomplished when an outside investigator is hired to handle complaints. These include enhanced credibility and trust in the HR department, a fair and unbiased investigation, and an accurate representation of the issue and concerns.

18. D: While there are numerous communications methods and techniques, it is important to remember that consistent communications should always be the goal. Employees should not learn about policies, programs, and changes from word of mouth and one-on-one communication as the primary means of learning. Choices *A*, *B*, and *C* are incorrect answers because town halls, employee meetings, formal handbooks, brochures, webpages, and electronic documents are all best practices to ensure that employees receive the same message and information. Consistency, clarity, and specific information are vital to ensure that all employees understand and are aware of the organization's policies.

19. C: When HR becomes aware of a potential ethics violation, the organization's leadership should be immediately notified. Ethics violations could have far-reaching impacts to the organization, and leadership should be informed so that the issue can be resolved, and any necessary actions can be taken. Choices *A*, *B*, and *D* are incorrect, as issues regarding payroll, benefits, or classifications should be handled at the department level. Unless these issues could create substantial liability for the organization, leadership should not have to be involved.

20. C: A candidate can learn about an organization, its behavior toward process, and expectations regarding employees from the vision, mission, and values statements usually presented on the website. While Choices *A*, *B*, and *D* all provide information about the position, benefits, and company, they do not necessarily identify how work is done and how employees should conduct themselves. This information is usually contained with the vision, mission, and values statements.

21. A: Roger should take into account that his new company has its own identity and culture, with different employees who will have different needs and wants, such as recognition, in programs. Roger should work to understand these differences and adjust his program accordingly to ensure the acceptance of the new recognition program. Choice *B* is incorrect because supervisors and managers generally do want new ways to recognize their employees to ensure that they understand how valued they are. Choice *C* is incorrect because usually employees want to see and encourage change, especially when it relates to recognizing their accomplishments. Choice *D* is incorrect because the company and employees are unique, and their responses to the program will most likely differ from those at his previous company.

22. B: There are several training opportunities that should be extended to all employees, one of which is diversity and inclusion. Choices *A*, *C*, and *D* are incorrect as they are all training specific to a particular job or role within an organization. Not all employees will need to know how to write a request for proposal nor will they work with accounting practices or conduct investigations.

23. A: Updating policies to accurately align with new legislation is vital because if there are discrepancies between policy and legislation, the organization could be at risk for incurring lawsuits and legal action, along with penalties, fines, and back payments for errors in payroll. Choices *B*, *C*, and *D* are incorrect answers because they are all irrelevant to ensuring alignment between policy and laws. Changes in policy should not be made to justify a full-time position or attendance at a conference, nor should they be made for the sake of change. Policy changes should be clear, strategic, concise, and they should align with the applicable laws, as necessary.

24. D: The SWOT analysis evaluates several factors; the internal factors reviewed are Strengths and Weaknesses. Strengths and Opportunities, Choice *A*, are positive factors that include an internal and external factor. Weaknesses and Threats, Choice *B*, are negative factors that include an internal and external factor. Opportunities and Threats, Choice *C*, are external factors that an organization takes into account during the SWOT analysis.

25. C: The SWOT analysis evaluates several factors; the external factors reviewed are Opportunities and Threats. Strengths and Opportunities, Choice *A*, are positive factors that include an internal and external factor. Weaknesses and Threats, Choice *B*, are negative factors that include an internal and external factor. Strengths and Weaknesses, Choice *D*, are internal factors that an organization takes into account during the SWOT analysis.

Interpersonal

26. D: The first step in ensuring successful relationship management is to understand the needs of the other party. Choice *A* is incorrect because delivering solutions is the result of relationship management. Choice *B* is incorrect because creating solutions that address the needs should only occur after first understanding what the needs actually are. Choice *C* is incorrect because, while important, allowing for introductions and conversation should be included in the initial step of understanding the needs of the parties involved.

27. C: Networking is a tool that allows for the exchange of ideas, sharing insights, soliciting advice, and relating to others. Choice *A* is incorrect because relationship management is defined as the maintenance of relationships between two parties—company and clients, employees and supervisors, company and employees. Networking is a component of relationship management. Choice *B* is incorrect because conflict resolution is the process of working to a peaceful and appropriate conclusion that resolves the issue identified. Conflict management may be needed during the relationship management process. Choice *D* is incorrect because brainstorming is when employees come together to think out loud, create solutions, and formulate ideas as a group.

28. B: When building relationships, it is important to NOT be selective and exclusive. Building relationships should allow for inclusivity, and individuals should avoid cliques and being selective. Choices *A*, *C*, and *D* are incorrect as they are all excellent tips that should be followed when building relationships. Frequently engaging with others, being honest and encouraging, and expressing thankfulness are all key components to establishing a strong relationship with others.

29. B: Being sincere includes being honest about both your strengths and weaknesses, while offering or asking for help. Choice *A* is inaccurate because sincerity is absolutely not complicated or overwhelming. Sincerity is simply being meaningful, honest, and kind. Choice *C* is inaccurate because sincerity is actually the cornerstone of building trust and relationships with others. Choice *D* is inaccurate because sincerity should be simple, informal, and unstructured, not complicated or overwhelming.

30. D: Eliza should communicate to the group that confidentiality can be maintained in most cases; however, in some cases, such as those that include issues such as domestic violence or criminal activity, law enforcement would need to be notified. Additionally, if ethical violations are discovered, it may be necessary to disclose some information to executive leadership to promote change within policy. Choice *A* is incorrect because it does not address the actual issue raised by leadership and allow for a dialogue. While Eliza should move forward with the project, leadership should know why this particular concern couldn't be fully resolved. Choice *B* is incorrect because updating a policy will not nullify the duties of an investigator to report information that is illegal. Choice *C* is inaccurate because there is no reason to stop the project due to this particular issue. There just needs to be communication as to why the concern cannot be fully addressed.

31. A: Teamwork occurs on small scales with simple changes as well as large scales with policy and practice changes. Additionally, teamwork can happen at any level within an organization and should be encouraged. Choice *B* is inaccurate because teamwork should always incorporate a common vision and goal that all employees are working to accomplish. Choice *C* is inaccurate because engaging a team to be a functional working group is actually a difficult process. Bringing individuals together physically may be simple but achieving engagement is quite complex. Choice *D* is inaccurate because teamwork, regardless of the level, should always be pointed toward a common vision and direction.

32. C: The most important thing that a leader can do in order to accomplish the goals created for a team is to identify the specific skills and needs necessary. Employees who possess these skills can then be given specific duties and assignments based on the needs of the project. Choice *A* is incorrect because job titles do not fully describe an individual's skills, strengths, or weaknesses. Choice *B* is incorrect because a leader should work to identify the strengths that an employee does have and then provide training to address the deficiencies in other areas. Choice *D* is incorrect because even with a strong and robust plan, if the right individuals with the right skillsets are not given the proper roles, the plan will most likely fail.

33. A: Conflict management is a difficult process in which problems and struggles are managed and resolved. Simply put, conflict management works to "increase the positive while decreasing the negative." Choice *B* is incorrect because conflict resolution is specific to the final steps and specific actions taken to resolve the issues. Choice *C* is incorrect because relationship management is the process in which an individual facilitates partnerships and connections with others. Choice *D* is incorrect because relationship resolution is a made-up term that could refer to how one repairs a relationship with another.

34. D: The Thomas-Kilmann Conflict Modes show the relationships between high and low levels of cooperation and assertiveness based on conflict. Choices *A*, *B*, and *C* are incorrect because, while they are all other models for managing conflict, the model presented is specifically the Thomas-Kilmann Conflict Mode.

35. D: Based on this model, with the *x*-axis measuring cooperation and the *y*-axis measuring assertiveness, Kyle would fall in the Accommodating quadrant. The Accommodating quadrant indicates a high level of cooperation but low level of assertiveness. Choice *A* is incorrect because the Competing quadrant indicates a low level of cooperation and a high level of assertiveness. Choice *B* is incorrect because the Collaborating quadrant indicates a high level of cooperation and a high level of assertiveness. Choice *C* is incorrect because the Avoiding quadrant indicates a low level of cooperation and a low level of assertiveness.

36. B: Based on this model, with the *x*-axis measuring cooperation and the *y*-axis measuring assertiveness, Tamika would fall in the Collaborating quadrant. The Collaborating quadrant indicates a high level of cooperation and a high level of assertiveness. Choice *A* is incorrect because the Competing quadrant indicates a low level of cooperation and a high level of assertiveness. Choice *C* is incorrect because the Avoiding quadrant indicates a low level of cooperation and a low level of assertiveness. Choice *D* is incorrect because the Accommodating quadrant indicates a high level of cooperation but low level of assertiveness.

37. B: Open and clear communication is the only thing that will help two conflicted employees work to resolve the issues and move to a point of compromise or resolution. While compromise may not happen immediately or even quickly, when employees are open, honest, and clear in discussions, it is easier to resolve the issues between individuals. Choice *A* is incorrect because while discipline and counseling may be necessary and appropriate due to the particular circumstances, they might not necessarily lead to compromise between the employees. Choice *C* is incorrect because while training and development may help the employees to better understand tools or resources to use, as mentioned with Choice *A*, it might not lead to compromise between the employees. Choice *D* is incorrect because a root cause analysis will allow the actual issue to be identified; it will not bring resolution or compromise. This information may be helpful when working toward compromise.

38. A: Conflict can be positive and productive for an organization by encouraging employees to think creatively and brainstorm. Engaging employees in different ways can allow for new ideas and innovation. Choice *B* is not correct as conflict can in fact be positive and productive. Negative conflict such as problems or issues between employees should be eliminated and resolved when appropriate, but conflict can be positive in some cases. Choice *C* is not a correct answer for this specific question. This statement is in fact true that conflict can create more problems between employees, including legal actions, but it is not relevant to this particular question. Choice *D* is not a correct answer because employees should not be encouraged to look for other employment simply due to the conflict that exists in the organization. Conflict can lead to innovation.

39. C: Destructive conflict should not be handled by allowing employees to simply "hammer it out" and try to work out their conflicts and issues on their own. Choices *A*, *B*, and *D* are incorrect answers as they are in fact true statements regarding destructive conflict. Destructive conflict should be addressed as soon as possible, may require a third-party investigator, and should not be allowed to linger.

40. C: Rachel should create a Frequently Asked Questions document including all of the questions asked with their respective answers. This document should then be distributed to all employees so that everyone has the same information. Choice *A* is incorrect because while Rachel should respond to each individual, the information needs to be disseminated to all employees. If there is one random question that the policy clearly answers, then this choice may have been appropriate; however, if several questions are received about the same issues, the policy may not have been clear on this item. Choice *B* is incorrect because this choice again does not provide this information to all employees, which should always be the goal. Rachel may want to incorporate policy references in the Frequently Asked Questions document to cite the specific language that answers the question. Choice *D* is incorrect because Rachel is the subject matter expert and should be responsible for responding to questions regarding this policy.

41. D: When a leader issues a communication that is then relayed to each level of the organization by the next level, they are using the Top-Down Method of communication. Choices *A*, *B*, and *C* are incorrect, as they are fictitious terms to create an image of how the message is relayed. Creating a picture of the Top-Down Method would look like a pyramid or triangle and could be synonymous with the term *cascading*.

42. A: Listening is an active and engaged skill that requires an involved, conscious, and physically engaged participant. Choices *B*, *C*, and *D* are incorrect answers because they do not express the engagement, involvement, or physical responsiveness that is required of listening. Choice *B* is inaccurate because listening is complex and complicated and involves far more than just hearing what someone says. Listening involves asking questions, repeating statements, and engaging with the individual. Choice *C* is inaccurate because listening requires being physically responsive to the speaker. Choice *D* is inaccurate because listening absolutely requires a conscious effort to remain engaged and involved in the conversation.

43. C: When an HR professional values different perspectives, backgrounds, experiences, and personalities, they are skilled in global and cultural effectiveness. Choices *A* and *B* are not correct because global and cultural effectiveness encompasses much more educational experience, social experience, and work experience. Choice *D* is incorrect because the elements of values, vision, ethics, and behavior are not indicative of cultural effectiveness. In fact, these qualities should most align with the organization's efforts to ensure a good employment match.

44. B: Turnover and attrition are not usually issues in an organization that encourages and maintains a diverse workforce. The primary benefits of diversity include Choices *A, C,* and *D,* and with them, an organization will see better recruitment, retention, growth, development, creativity, and innovation. More candidates will want to join the organization; employees will want to stay with the organization; employees will seek growth and development; and employees will engage with each other with creativity and innovation to resolve issues and seek out new solutions.

45. D: Louisa should first establish a diversity and inclusion policy for the entire organization that includes the specific expectations, strategies, tools, and responsibilities for each employee. The policy is the foundation of all program elements and without it, the program will lack structure and most likely fail. Choices *A, B,* and *C* are inaccurate because these actions should not be the first thing that is done to initiate a new program, including one that addresses diversity and inclusion. These choices are best practices that should be implemented after the policy has been created and rolled out.

46. B: An excellent way to gain key insights into an organization's line of business is to become a customer. By using the product and becoming familiar with the customer service provided, an employee will become intimately aware of how an organization treats customers as well as customer expectations. Having this knowledge will allow for a deeper understanding of the lines of business and can also allow for a more involved and integrated approach to performing work. Choice *A* is inaccurate because it is unreasonable to expect that an individual will be qualified for any position and that an organization will move employees around frequently. Choice *C* is inaccurate because this type of activity, while in some cases can be beneficial as a sounding board, can quickly turn to gossip and rumor spreading. Choice *D* is inaccurate because training and development opportunities develop new skills that can create promotional opportunities but will not typically educate individuals in the lines of business.

47. C: Paul is experiencing a common occurrence when moving to another country. Each country has their own laws and regulations that must be adhered to within policies and practices, regardless of where the headquarters are located. Policies should take into account local laws, regulations, accepted practices, and culture. Choice *A* is incorrect because opinions should not be taken into account when writing policy. While practices and norms should be reviewed and discussed, opinions should not hold the same weight. Choice *B* is incorrect because the leadership team should update policies that adhere to local laws as well as the organization's overall holistic expectations. Some employees may be upset at the changes but with the proper communication and training, leadership should strive to create awareness and understanding of the policies. Choice *D* is incorrect because while dereliction of duty by a predecessor may be the reason for weak policies, it is most likely not the case.

48. D: A mentoring opportunity is not a solution that ensures harmony between employees. Mentoring has many positive impacts, but the best solutions to encourage and foster a positive work environment are Choices *A, B,* and *C.* Sensitivity training, coaching sessions, and cultural education are best practices that encourage effective and productive environments.

49. C: Inclusion is the specific and intentional planning that engages every employee in the achievement of the organization's success by aligning individual objectives to the overall goals. Choice *A* is not the correct answer because diversity is the actual inclusion of individuals who are different—backgrounds, educations, perspectives, experiences, and more. Choice *B* is not the correct answer because strategic planning is the holistic and overarching planning that incorporates inclusion within the overall plan. Choice *D* is not the correct answer because business acumen is the ability to identify, understand, and resolve situations that result in positive outcomes.

50. D: Eugene should have ensured that the survey was completely anonymous so that employees could feel empowered as well as safe to be open and honest with their feedback. Employees should feel secure that the information provided will not be used in a negative way. Choices *A*, *B*, and *C* are incorrect because employees are always interested in providing feedback and insight to better the workplace. Additionally, surveys are an extremely effective way to gather information when done effectively and in the right manner. Surveys that have both an electronic and hard copy method of submission along with a reminder is adequate to allow for employees to submit their information. Employees should be held accountable for reading their emails and following the directions on the survey.

Business

51. B: The Awareness Triangle is the tool that provides a representation of how to process information and develop competitive awareness. Choices *A* and *C* are incorrect because they are fictitious terms. Situational awareness and top-down methods are terms that are important to many processes but do not provide insight into competitive intelligence. Choice *D* is incorrect because The Awareness Triangle is the actual name of the tool that defines competitive intelligence, which is gaining insight into other organizations.

52. D: The step that should have the largest focus when determining competitive intelligence is "Aware." Ensuring awareness of as much data as possible is vital to allow for a full and holistic view of the situation. Choice *A* is incorrect, as the "Action" step is the final step of the process, and the actions taken should be specific and clear based on the information gathered during the "Aware" step. Choice *B* is incorrect because the "Analyze" step is the second step of the process, and the analysis should take into account the possibilities that exist due to the information gathered in the "Aware" step. Choice *C* is incorrect because Adaptation is not a step in the process.

53. C: Jake is utilizing the organization's financial resources to learn more about its products and revenues. Financial Resources can include annual reports, cash flow statements, and compliance reports. Choice *A* is incorrect, as physical resources include actual locations such as call centers, administrative offices, or retail stores. Choice *B* is incorrect because human resources include employees at all levels of the organization. Choice *D* is incorrect because organizational resources include policies, procedures, and practices.

54. C: The PESTLE method does not analyze People and Sustainability. Choices *A*, *B*, and *D* are not correct because they are all factors that should be analyzed when using the PESTLE method. PESTLE analyzes the Political, Economic, Social, Technological, Legal, and Environmental trends that may influence an organization.

55. B: A cost-benefit analysis reviews all of the costs or expenses and all of the benefits and results of a project to determine if the project should be supported. Choice *A* is not the correct answer because key performance indicators are specific pieces of data such as attrition, staffing costs, headcount, training costs, and net profits. A cost-benefit analysis could actually be considered a key performance indicator. Choice *C* is not the correct answer because a SWOT analysis identifies the Strengths, Weaknesses, Opportunities, and Threats that a project or organization is facing. Choice *D* is not the correct answer because business analysis is an overarching strategic practice that focuses on functions, processes, methods, procedures, and performance in order to identify issues, create and implement solutions, and monitor the results.

56. A: Strategic alignment is the process by which an organization's resources, funding, human capital, and tools are aligned with the goals and objectives identified. This alignment ensures that resources are specifically directed to reach necessary achievements. Choice *B* is incorrect because strategic planning is the overall planning that would include strategic alignment. Choice *C* is incorrect because decision making is the process by which choices are made based on the information available. Choice *D* is incorrect because resource allocation is the specific distribution of tools to achieve a goal. Resource allocation is an important component of strategic alignment.

57. D: For Julie to provide the strongest candidate pools in the hiring process, she should spend time with the employees across the organization to understand the core business and what each employee does. Choice *A* is not correct because simply memorizing a job description will not allow a full understanding of the actual work being done. Additionally, the job may have changed, and the document may be outdated and not accurate. Choice *B* is not correct because it is unreasonable to expect an HR professional to become a subject matter expert in every position and role within an organization. Choice *C* is not correct because while information from other staff members may be beneficial in some cases, it should not be the primary way of learning about the organization and positions.

58. D: Absenteeism is the data point that calculates how much employees are absent from work. Choice *A* is incorrect because attrition is the data point that calculates how many employees are leaving an organization. Choice *B* is incorrect because human capital is the data point that compares the costs of employees to the organization's revenues. Choice *C* is incorrect because presenteeism is the data point that calculates how many employees are not absent from work. Presenteeism is the data point used to calculate perfect attendance awards.

59. A: Attrition is the data point that calculates how many employees are leaving an organization. Choice *B* is incorrect because human capital is the data point that compares the costs of employees to the organization's revenues. Choice *C* is incorrect because presenteeism is the data point that calculates employees who are not absent from work. Choice *D* is incorrect because absenteeism is the data point that calculates how many employees are absent from work.

60. C: Design thinking is the strategic process that can be used to navigate a new solution or process. The model presented shows the specific five steps in the design thinking process. Choices *A*, *B*, and *D* are incorrect answers as they are all fictitious terms; however, these terms do represent the types of thinking that design thinking incorporates—innovation, creativity, and strategy.

61. B: The Define step in Design Thinking establishes the issue or concern broadly and specifically to ensure the actual issues are being addressed. Choice *A* is not the answer as the Empathize step works to understand the situation and ensure others know the commitment being established with the process. Choice *C* is not the answer as the Prototype step works to finalize a proposed recommendation to implement along with a timeframe. Choice *D* is not the answer as the Test step works to implement and evaluate the recommendations.

62. D: The Test step in Design Thinking works to implement and evaluate the recommendations. Choice *A* is incorrect because the Empathize step works to understand the situation and ensure others know the commitment being established with the process. Choice *B* is incorrect because the Define step establishes the issue or concern broadly and specifically, to ensure the actual issues are being addressed. Choice *C* is incorrect, as the Prototype step works to finalize a proposed recommendation to implement along with a timeframe.

63. B: One of the most important things that an HR team and department should encourage and facilitate among all employees is open and honest dialogue. Without this, many communication efforts will not be successful. Employees will not feel safe and secure in voicing opinions and may believe their opinions are not valued. Choice *A* is an incorrect answer because department meetings are a form of communication and interaction between employees, which are more successful when there is open and honest dialogue. Choice *C* is an incorrect answer because employee newsletters are a great way of communicating to employees about programs, benefits, and changes. Choice *D* is an incorrect answer because continuous growth and development should be part of employees' training plans. Many practices and initiatives, regardless of how amazing they are, will not be successful without open and honest dialogue.

64. A: To ensure engagement and buy-in to the new HR and Payroll platform, Erin should have involved the department managers in the planning phase. In doing so, she could have then asked direct and specific questions to identify their needs, concerns, and wants. The department managers should have been afforded the opportunity to have this discussion, which would also allow them to be engaged in the process. Choice *B* is incorrect because asking department managers of non-HR or non-Payroll departments for HR and Payroll vendors is neither appropriate nor productive. If there were certain functions of previously used systems that were helpful or would be useful in the current environment, this information should be gathered during the planning process. Choice *C* is incorrect because training department managers on how a new system should be selected, operated, or the functions it provides would not address the need of involving them earlier in the process. Choice *D* is incorrect because a decision of this nature would not be appropriate to share with all employees at this stage in the process.

65. A: Erin should provide training to the department managers that is specific to their needs, relevant to what they need to do their job, and useful for day-to-day operations. Teaching them how to navigate the system, run reports, and locate information will be vital to engaging them in using the system on their own. Additionally, providing training manuals or cheat sheets would be helpful. Choice *B* is incorrect because even executive leadership cannot mandate engagement and buy-in from others. If anything, this could backfire and create even more disconnection. Choice *C* is incorrect because this will not have the intended effect of creating engagement and support for the program. As with Choice *B*, this could also cause more disconnection and have a negative impact. Choice *D* is incorrect because backtracking on the decision is not an appropriate response. The decision has been made and the new platform installed. Going backward could cost the organization substantially, and not just financially.

66. C: The first step in a change management process, regardless of whether it is a simple or complex change, is to identify the need for change. Choice *A* is inaccurate because preparing for the change is the second step. Preparation for a change should only occur after first identifying the change needed. Choice *B* is inaccurate because implementation of change should occur after first identifying and then preparing for a change. Preparation is the third step in the change management process. Choice *D* is inaccurate because reinforcing the change is the final step in this process.

67. B: When providing guidance to managers in non-HR departments, HR should ensure that supervisors are trained to understand when HR should be immediately involved. Reports of sexual harassment, discrimination, or employee conflicts are examples of urgent employment matters that should immediately be forwarded to HR. Choice *A* is incorrect, as HR should be responsible for investigating certain complaints and serve as a resource to managers. While some complaints should be handled and resolved with the supervisor directly, most complaints need HR involvement. Choice *C* is incorrect because supervisors should absolutely be trained in how to coach and counsel employees. Choice *D* is incorrect because non-HR supervisors do not need the skillset of writing job descriptions and recruitment flyers. This responsibility lies within HR, and while supervisors may assist with providing information that should be included or deleted in these documents, they should not be the writers of the documents.

68. D: Anonymity is important when conducting an employee survey because it allows for a safe and secure way to communicate true and honest feedback. Employees may fear repercussions when providing feedback on certain issues. Anonymity removes this fear and allows management to receive information that accurately represents the current state. Choice *A* is inaccurate because, as indicated, anonymity does provide the benefit of providing safety and security. Choice *B* is inaccurate because anonymity should be provided. While it would be helpful to know specific departments that have certain issues versus other departments, the data may not be truly accurate if anonymity is removed. Choice *C* is inaccurate because management should always communicate the conclusions and action plans that result from an employee survey. Anonymity does not remove management's responsibility to communicate with the employees.

69. B: Customers are not only external; customers can also be internal, especially with Human Resources. Employees are customers, department managers are customers, and leadership personnel are customers. Services are not only provided outside of the organization but inside of the organization to these internal customers. These services could be information, assistance with benefits changes, or asking for advice. Choices *A*, *C*, and *D* are incorrect because they are all accurate statements regarding customers. Each customer has a unique need that must be understood so that the best service can be provided. Customers should receive responses quickly and accurately, while being given high priority. Communication is always the basis of a relationship, especially with a customer.

70. A: Critical evaluation is the process that reviews, analyzes, and audits a program or initiative. Critical evaluation is conducted with a fair, balanced, and unbiased mindset. Choice *B* is incorrect because situational awareness is a concept that refers to having complete attentiveness to an individual's circumstances. Choice *C* is incorrect because customer interaction is the communication between an individual and a party that is receiving services. Choice *D* is incorrect because business acumen is the ability to identify, understand, and resolve situations that will result in positive outcomes.

71. C: The ultimate goal of handling any complaint is to resolve the issue at the lowest level possible. While it is important to follow a structured process to resolve issues and inform leadership of the issues, effective resolution of the issue with the lowest amount of intervention is the goal. Resolving complaints does require being respectful and responsive, as do all other issues and concerns brought forward and in day-to-day interactions with others, not just in handling a complaint. Please note that some complaints must proceed directly to a formal and escalated response due to the complaint.

72. B: Employee and labor relations is the maintenance of effective working relationships with employees and the labor unions that represent them. Employee and labor relations is the responsibility of management, leadership, and Human Resources and requires frequent communication and attention for maximum success. Additionally, multiple best practices such as open-door policies, joint committees, frequent meetings, and accurate information exchanges are all cornerstones of positive employee and labor relations.

73. D: Job duties and organizational need should be the core basis in selecting a position for job elimination. Under no circumstances should employee information, performance, or disciplinary history be considered when making decisions regarding which positions to eliminate.

74. C: Personnel files are one of the most important and fundamental recordkeeping functions within Human Resources. New hire documents and offer letters are components of the personnel file, and timecards are generally retained within Payroll.

75. D: Survey data should be shared consistently with all levels of the organization. Committed leadership is essential for an effective survey. Surveys should always ensure confidentiality and anonymity for employees. There is no set timeline for administering employee surveys; however, a standard recommendation is at least once per year.

HR Expertise

People

1. C: Carl should first review the organizational and departmental mission, goals, and objectives to ensure that they are aligned. Strategic planning always begins with the review of what the organization and departments want to accomplish. Without this information, plans can be disjointed and waste resources. Choice *A* is incorrect because another organization's strategic plan was developed for that specific organization. While there may be elements that can be incorporated from Carl's previous work assignments and experiences, it is important to remember that each organization and department is unique. Strategic plans should be designed to support the specific organization. Choice *B* is incorrect because a strategic plan should not use data or information from one sole source or one specific area of a process.

There may be improvements needed or best practices that can be implemented, which would be a component to an overall strategic plan; however, an entire strategic plan for a department should not be singularly focused. Choice *D* is incorrect because typically an outside consultant is not the best resource to manage a strategic planning process. Internal resources work best in this process as employees have insight and knowledge to the culture, history, and organizational specifics that work together to create a robust strategic plan. Since Carl is new to the organization, he would benefit from engaging other employees to create a dialogue and tap into this information.

2. B: While strategic planning includes the formal assessment of available resources, workforce, knowledge, and skills within an organization, strategic planning also encompasses much more. Strategic planning includes reviewing the mission, goals, and objectives of the organization and departments, assessing the resources available, forecasting the gaps and needs, and developing a plan. Choices *A, C,* and *D* are incorrect because they are all accurate statements of strategic planning. Strategic planning is critical to ensure that employees are all working together to accomplish the goals and objectives defined by the department and organization. Strategic planning ensures that the organization, department, and individual employees are aware of the resources needed to succeed. Strategic planning plays a vital role in the success of individual employees, departments, and an organization.

3. C: Strategic planning is dependent on the knowledge and awareness of the goals and objectives that have been developed for both the organization and the department. Aligning these two is vital to the strategic planning process. Choice *A* is incorrect because while having HR professionals trained in process mapping and assessment is beneficial and considered a resource in the process, strategic planning is not dependent on this. Choice *B* is incorrect because strategic planning is not dependent on strong recruitment and selection processes. Strong recruitment and hiring practices may actually be dependent on strategic planning, as this process clarifies the needs of the department and areas for improvement.

Choice *D* is incorrect because, once again, strategic planning is not dependent on staff location or the actual employer, whether within or outside an organization. Strategic planning may actually be more productive with internal staff members who are aware of the history, culture, information, and organizational specifics that an outsourced resource would not have access to.

4. A: It is important to align action plans and items with the SMART technique to ensure that success can be defined, measured, and achieved. If goals are broad and general, it will be more difficult to assess whether the objective was met. When goals are SMART—specific, measurable, achievable, realistic, and time-targeted—it is much easier to determine what needs to be done and when, as well as when the goal has been achieved. Choice *B* is incorrect because the SMART methodology does not provide the actual path to achieve objectives. Other tools such as Six Sigma or lean methods can be incorporated into the plan to create an effective path. Choice *C* is incorrect because the SMART method does not define weakness or plan to address them. The SWOT analysis tool would be the best tool to provide this insight. Choice *D* is incorrect because the SMART methodology does not facilitate resources needed. The strategic planning process would be used to make these determinations. Once this is done, then SMART elements can be used to properly define the needs and how success will be achieved.

5. D: The SMART methodology stands for specific, measurable, achievable, realistic, and time-targeted. In order for an objective to be SMART, all of these components must be identified in the objective. Choices *A, B,* and *C* are incorrect because each is missing one of the strategic components of the actual methodology, and some of the components are incorrect. While some objectives may be simple, this is not a component of SMART. Milestones is another term for time-targeted. Additionally, resources and technology are elements that will work to accomplish the SMART objectives.

6. A: Andrea should include a review of the products and services that are offered by the organization. When identifying opportunities to establish a competitive advantage, it is important to look at the organization holistically to ensure that all opportunities are captured. Choice *B* is incorrect because the items that make up the total rewards package are compensation, benefits, retirement, promotion opportunities, and work-life balance programs. Choice *C* is incorrect because state benefits plans are standard for all organizations that meet the eligibility requirements and would not necessarily be an item that could create a competitive edge. Choice *D* is incorrect because the executive leadership profiles are informational, and while this could be used in a portfolio to promote the top talent and the organizational leadership, this information is static and only changes with individuals leaving or joining the team. These profiles do not represent a trend or benchmark that can be adjusted to create competitive advantage.

7. D: In order to communicate effectively, communication should NOT be complex. Choices *A, B,* and *C* are incorrect because they are all components of effective communication. Being considerate, concise, and courteous are all elements in effectively communicating with others.

8. B: When presenting information that will be used for making decisions, the two most important factors are timeliness and accuracy. Choice *A* is incorrect because the information should not be complicated and complex. This can cause confusion and frustration, potentially resulting in poor decisions being made. Choices *C* and *D* are incorrect because regardless of what is being presented—financial data, references, or data research—all information should be timely and accurate. Outdated information or data that is not accurate will also lead to poor decisions being made, or no decisions at all.

9. B: Talent acquisition is a strategic process that reviews the current and future needs of the workforce to ensure implantation of a holistic and complete process. Choice *A* is incorrect because recruitment is the tactical process of filling an open position. Recruitment is a component of talent acquisition. Choice *C* is incorrect because onboarding is the process of bringing a new employee into the organization and acquainting them with the day-to-day operations, training them in the policies such as safety, and finalizing new paperwork. Choice *D* is incorrect because workforce planning is the practice of reviewing all positions within an organization and determining the needs to accomplish the work. Workforce planning feeds the talent acquisition process by identifying the jobs and positions needed first.

10. A: Recruitment is the tactical process of filling an open position. Recruitment is a component of talent acquisition. Choice *B* is incorrect because talent acquisition is the strategic process that reviews the current and future needs of the workforce to ensure a holistic and complete process is implemented. Choice *C* is incorrect because onboarding is the process of bringing a new employee into the organization and acquainting them with the day-to-day operations, training them in the policies such as safety, and finalizing new paperwork. Choice *D* is incorrect because workforce planning is the practice of reviewing all positions within an organization and determining the needs to accomplish the work. Workforce planning feeds the talent acquisition process by identifying the jobs and positions needed first.

11. C: The employee value proposition (EVP) is the organization's brand that is presented to both the current and future workforce. The EVP answers the question "what's in it for me?" to prospective candidates and allows for current employees to be aware of their total rewards. Choice *A* is incorrect because organizational branding is specific to the product branding presented to customers, not to employees. Choice *B* is incorrect because the total rewards package is a component of the EVP and is comprised of compensation, benefits, policies, flexible work schedules, retirement, training, promotional opportunities, and more. Choice *D* is incorrect because compensation and benefits are a component of the total rewards package, which is a component of EVP.

12. C: The employee value proposition is comprised of five elements—compensation, benefits, career, culture, and work environment. Choices *A* and *B* are incorrect. While they are all important pieces of data, they do not play a role in the EVP. Turnover rates and key performance indicators would be data presented in a metrics dashboard for HR strategic planning and status in reaching objectives. Lastly, while employee forms would most likely be available within the EVP portal, they are not considered an element of the EVP. Employee forms could be included in all of the five components from benefit enrollment forms to promotional job applications. Therefore, Choice *D* is incorrect.

13. D: An organization that has a strong, robust EVP will NOT experience high turnover or a higher cost per hire. On the contrary, a strong EVP will allow an organization to see higher retention rates and lower costs per hire. Choices *A, B,* and *C* are incorrect because they are all benefits that an organization will experience with a strong EVP. Employees making referrals, larger and more qualified talent pools, few vacancies, lower absenteeism, increased productivity and trust in leadership are all benefits that an organization will see when having a strong EVP.

14. B: Workforce retention, or lower attrition rates, is the biggest benefit of employee engagement. High employee engagement shows an 87% increase in employee retention in the Corporate Leadership Council survey. Choices *A, C,* and *D* are incorrect because while they are benefits of having high employee engagement, they are not the largest benefit realized. Productivity increased by 21% in the survey, customer retention by 10%, and overall profit by 22%. All of these benefits are significant and can have a major impact to an organization; however, the largest impact of employee engagement is in workforce retention.

15. A: Armando should have conducted an employee survey to engage those in the workforce and find out what their specific needs are. Once this information was collected, he could then work to provide specific solutions to the needs identified. In doing this, employees will feel engaged in the process, and the new ideas and changes will most likely be more successful. Choice *B* is incorrect because Armando should not solely rely on a market survey to determine what is in the best interest of his organization and employees.

Each organization is unique, a fact that he should be sure to consider. While there may be some excellent ideas and best practices that come from a market survey, these ideas should be weighed against what the employees need. Choice *C* is incorrect because Armando is only gauging the feedback from a few team members, not the workforce. While reestablishing a former program may be a great idea, he needs to ensure that this program actually meets the needs of the current employees. Choice *D* is incorrect because Armando should have engaged the employees to determine what their needs and wants are prior to implementing changes. Simply communicating the changes more will not engage employees or motivate them to accept the new changes.

16. A: Safety and security protocols are a necessary and vital requirement for an organization. They are not considered a unique program due to many specific regulations that must be adhered to in order to achieve compliance. Choices *B, C,* and *D* are incorrect as they are all examples of programs that can be uniquely tailored to the organization and employees to increase engagement and satisfaction. Training and learning opportunities, recognition and achievement programs, and telecommuting and alternate work schedules are all examples of programs that can be developed and tailored to maximize employee satisfaction and the employee experience within an organization.

17. C: Job enlargement is the redesign process that occurs when new tasks and assignments are added to the current job roles and responsibilities. Job enlargement increases the duties being performed by the employee with tasks that are specifically aligned with and related to the current work being performed. Choice *A* is incorrect because job design is the process of creating a new position that is different than the current roles already defined within the organization. Choice *B* is incorrect because job enrichment is the process of adding unrelated and brand-new tasks to an employee's workload that may not be aligned with the current work being performed. Choice *D* is incorrect because job rotation is the process of allowing employees to trade positions or rotate duties.

18. D: Job rotation is the process of allowing employees to trade off positions or alternate duties and assignments between individuals. This job redesign process is also known as cross training, and it allows for a stronger bench strength within the organization. Choice *A* is incorrect because job design is the process of creating a new position that is different than the current roles already defined within the organization. Choice *B* is incorrect because job enrichment is the process of adding unrelated and brand-new tasks to an employee's workload that may not be aligned with the current work being performed. Choice *C* is incorrect because job enlargement is the redesign process that occurs when new tasks and assignments are added to the current job roles and responsibilities.

19. B: Maggie has worked through the job enrichment process by adding tasks and responsibilities that are outside of the normal scope of Steven's workload. Job enrichment provides an employee the ability to increase knowledge and skills, which can provide for more promotional opportunities in the future. Choice *A* is incorrect because job design is the process of creating a new position that is different than the current roles already defined within the organization. Choice *C* is incorrect because job enlargement is the redesign process that occurs when new tasks and assignments are added to the current job roles and responsibilities. Choice *D* is incorrect because job rotation is the process of allowing employees to trade positions or rotate duties.

20. C: Total rewards is the term utilized to describe the entire package that an employee receives when joining an organization. The total rewards package includes the offer of employment, compensation details, benefits, work-life programs, learning opportunities, and recognition. Choice *A* is incorrect because the offer letter generally includes information related to the offered job, salary, supervisor information, and information specific to the position. Each organization will have a different way of communicating terms in the offer letter; however, this letter is only one component of the total rewards package. Choice *B* is incorrect because the employee value proposition, or EVP, is the overall brand that an organization provides to the workforce. The EVP communicates the programs that the organization offers to all employees but does not provide specifics to the individual employee. Choice *D* is incorrect because new employee orientation refers to the training an employee receives once hired into an organization. This training acclimates the new employee to the organization relative to the policies, procedures, standards, and expectations.

21. D: The total rewards package is made up of five specific components: pay, benefits, work-life programs, learning and development, and performance and recognition. Choices *A, B,* and *C* are incorrect because they do not fully incorporate all of the components required for the total rewards package. Some of these items may be incorporated into the package such as the offer letter, training schedule, supervisor information, and health insurance providers. It is important to include all of the components to ensure a full awareness and understanding of all programs available to a new employee.

22. B: The Affordable Care Act (ACA) requires that all employers that meet certain standards provide health care coverage to their employees. Choices *A, C,* and *D* are incorrect because there is no government regulation that requires an employer to provide long-term care, legal protection, or pet insurance coverage. These benefits are considered voluntary, and employers may offer these benefits to employees at their own cost. Organizations may be able to offer discount pricing to employees on these programs, but there is not a requirement to provide them to employees.

23. B: An employee is eligible to receive twelve weeks of protected leave under the Family Medical Leave Act (FMLA) to care for a family member or for the birth of a child. There are additional eligible circumstances for an employee to take FMLA. Choices *A, C,* and *D* are incorrect because the FMLA allows for only twelve weeks of leave. While there are other circumstances that may allow for additional leave, such as caring for a servicemember, the standard leave time is twelve weeks.

24. A: The one standard that should be applied and adhered to regarding any benefit plan, government mandated or voluntary, is to ensure clear and concise communications. Employees should be able to access this information, along with contact information and forms in a convenient and understandable manner. Choice *B* is incorrect because the best benefit plan should be selected based on the needs of the employees and organization, as well as the costs and benefits provided; however, this may not mean that the least expensive plan is the best option. It may be in the best interest of the organization to offer employees multiple options for plans with varying cost and benefit levels. Choice *C* is incorrect because not all services are available online. By applying the general standard, an organization may eliminate excellent vendors with plans that would be beneficial to an employee. Choice *D* is incorrect because covering all costs for insurance may not be feasible, and typically, voluntary benefits are paid for fully by the employees.

25. C: Amelia should work to implement an individual action plan. The individual action plan is a tool that can chart out an employee's growth, development, and career paths while also identifying gaps in skills and experience. Choice *A* is incorrect because a strategic plan is an overall plan that can be used for multiple areas of need. The individual action plan could be considered a strategic plan because this tool does use strategy to define and assess the career path and how to succeed. Choice *B* is incorrect because a succession plan is a tool that is used to chart out the employees who could potentially fill key positions within an organization in the near and long-term future of the organization. The individual action plan should align with the succession plan. Choice *D* is incorrect because the employee value proposition is the overall brand that an organization communicates to the workforce, both current and future. The EVP includes the commitment toward compensation, benefits, work-life programs, training, opportunities, and more.

26. C: Employee surveys are a standard, efficient, and effective method used to identify employee needs, wants, or concerns. These surveys can provide an opportunity for employees to communicate what the organization is doing well, what needs to be improved or changed, and any ideas or concerns they may have. Choice *A* is incorrect because comment cards are not effective, and employees may not feel a sense of confidence when utilizing this old-school method. Choice *B* is incorrect because meeting individually with every employee is not efficient, and employees may not want to communicate their true feelings to Human Resources. Choice *D* is incorrect because market research does not indicate the specific needs of the internal employees. This information may be beneficial to have to benchmark new ideas and what the competition offers, but it will not provide insight into the needs of the current employees.

27. A: The culture component of the EVP encourages the entire organization to understand the overarching goals and objectives, including the values of trust, support, teamwork, collaboration, and social responsibility. Choice *B* is incorrect because the work environment component of the EVP includes the recognition of performance, balancing work life and home life, and encouraging engagement and involvement across all levels of the organization. Choice *C* is incorrect because the career component of the EVP includes the stability, training, education, coaching, evaluation, and feedback. Choice *D* is incorrect because the benefits component of the EVP includes the retirement programs, health insurance programs, time off, holiday schedule, telecommuting options, and educational reimbursements.

28. C: The career component of the EVP encourages employees to know and understand how their performance aligns with the expectations of the position and future opportunities. Additionally, the career component includes the stability, training, education, coaching, evaluation, and feedback. Choice *A* is incorrect because the culture component of the EVP encourages the entire organization to understand the overarching goals and objectives, including the values of trust, support, teamwork, collaboration, and social responsibility. Choice *B* is incorrect because the work environment component of the EVP includes the recognition of performance, balancing work life and home life, and encouraging engagement and involvement across all levels of the organization. Choice *D* is incorrect because the benefits component of the EVP includes the retirement programs, health insurance programs, time off, holiday schedule, telecommuting options, and educational reimbursements.

29. D: Choice *D* is the correct answer because this statement is incorrect in defining talent acquisition. Talent acquisition does not only deal with the initial hiring of an employee, but it also looks beyond to the promotional opportunities and the future development of the workforce. Choices *A, B,* and *C* are incorrect answers because they are all accurate statements regarding talent acquisition. Talent acquisition is the entire process from when a vacancy occurs to when the new employee joins the organization. It is a strategic process that also includes assessing the needs of the workforce and recruiting the best talent to fill those needs. Additionally, talent acquisition works to acquire the talent needed to align with the needs of the organization.

30. B: The SMART methodology should be used to ensure that success can be accurately defined and described when writing goals and objectives. SMART methodology requires the objectives to be specific, measurable, achievable, realistic, and time-targeted. Choice *A* is incorrect as the SWOT method is an analysis that defines the strengths, weaknesses, opportunities, and threats that an organization or department is experiencing. Choice *C* is incorrect because the 7 C's refer to the components of effective communication—clear, concise, correct, complete, considerate, concrete, and courteous. Choice *D* is incorrect because EVP is the acronym for the employee value proposition, or the brand the organization creates for current and future employees of the priorities and values regarding the employee experience.

Organization

31. A: An organization chart is a tool that presents how an organization, department, or group is designed. An organization chart shows how work is assigned and how positions report to each other. Choice *B* is incorrect because an organization structure is the actual design which is presented in the organization chart. Choice *C* is incorrect because the term organization design is another way to communicate the organization structure, which again is presented in the organization chart. Choice *D* is incorrect because organization function is a term that describes the work that is being done.

32. D: Darcie's new organization chart that provides in-depth and detailed information can be used as a tool to educate departments and employees on the appropriate contacts for specific topics. This can be extremely helpful to employees or managers who are looking for an answer to a specific question. By providing the organization chart as a tool, Darcie can realize a benefit to having more streamlined communications and increased efficiency and customer service. Choice *A* is incorrect because an organization chart should simply reflect how the organization is structured and not be used to communicate roles and scope of duties to employees. Job descriptions and strategic plans are the tools that should be used for this purpose. Choice *B* is incorrect because using an organization chart for budget preparation is not necessarily a benefit in having this tool. It may be a component that can be used, but there would not be a benefit gained in this circumstance. Choice *C* is incorrect because, as discussed, there is a benefit to having an organization chart with specific details, and it is not a good use of resources or time to create an organization chart simply to file it away.

33. C: The difference between a decentralized and centralized organizational structure is that a decentralized model allows for HR staff to report to external department leaders while a centralized model allows for all HR staff to report to the HR department. Both structures have positive and negative attributes, and organizations should select the model most appropriate for the customers being served. Choice *A* is incorrect because the definitions of the models are backwards. Choices *B* and *D* incorrectly state that both models allow for HR staff to report to the HR department. Additionally, these structures do not indicate an external or internal customer, but rather where the staff reports to and the departments being served by each position.

34. A: The SPOC methodology, or single point of contact, eliminates the need for a customer to search for the right person to call for a specific question. The SPOC methodology assigns a specific employee to customers so that the customer can call one person for all issues and concerns. Choice *B* is incorrect because SWOT stands for strengths, weaknesses, opportunities, and threats and is an analysis conducted to prepare information when making business decisions. Choice *C* is incorrect because SMART is used when establishing goals and objectives to ensure that success can be measured. SMART stands for specific, measurable, achievable, realistic, and time-targeted. Choice *D* is incorrect because ADR stands for alternative dispute resolution and refers to the processes and techniques used to assist in resolving issues prior to lawsuits and claims being filed.

35. B: If Amelia cannot meet the HR policy timeframe of a twenty-four-hour response, she should communicate directly with Bob that she is working on his FMLA leave request and will need some additional time to prepare the final information and response. Choice *A* is incorrect because while Amelia should continue to research to provide accurate information, she should reach out to Bob to let him know that she will need additional time to provide the response. Choice *C* is incorrect because Amelia should be providing Bob with the organization's information specific to the FMLA leave. While the state offices may be able to provide information related to coordinated benefits such as disability or paid family leave, Amelia should manage the response directly. Choice *D* is incorrect because Amelia should manage the request unless she is not able to due to workload or a lack of understanding in the process and subject matter. If this is the case, she must find someone to take over the request. She must then communicate this with Bob so he understands that he has a new point of contact for this request.

36. D: Organizational development is a process that includes three factors. Choice *D* is the correct answer because the organizational development process is NOT managed within each department. Choices *A, B* and *C* are incorrect answers because they are the three factors that Richard Beckhard identified within the organizational development process: organization-wide, managed from top levels of leadership, and planned.

37. C: When a department maintains a separate employee file, one concern may be that the documents are unsecured or filed in a confidential manner that protects the information and privacy for the employee. Choice *A* is incorrect because having multiple files for employees will not create efficiencies. Multiple files will increase the time needed to locate specific documentation. Choice *B* is incorrect because all documents are subject to the same retention schedules, which must be adhered to. Choice *D* is incorrect because Human Resources should maintain the master employee file, not the individual departments.

38. C: Employee relations is defined as the organization's commitment to foster a positive working relationship with its employees. Choice *A* is incorrect because labor relations are the actual relationship between an organization's leadership and the employees, often through a bargaining union. Choice *B* is incorrect because workforce planning is the process used to align an organization's needs and priorities with the available workforce and skills. Choice *D* is incorrect because the mission statement is the short value statement that describes the fundamentals and goals of the organization.

39. A: Labor relations includes establishing, negotiating, and administering bargaining agreements and policies. Labor relations also includes managing grievances and disagreements. Choice *B* is incorrect because workforce planning is the process used to align an organization's needs and priorities with the available workforce and skills. Choice *C* is incorrect because employee relations is defined as the organization's commitment to foster a positive working relationship with its employees. Choice *D* is incorrect because mediation is a facilitated negotiation that works out a solution between two parties with a neutral third party.

40. A: ADR processes progress from less formal to more formal. Choice *A* is the correct answer because it presents the process backwards. Choices *B, C,* and *D* are incorrect answers because they are all accurate statements about the alternative dispute resolution processes. ADR includes negotiation, mediation, conciliation, and arbitration. ADR includes both formal and informal processes to resolve issues. ADR works to expedite the exchange of information and decision-making for both parties.

41. B: Lisa can best be described as the SPOC—single point of contact—for all benefits and leave administration issue. A SPOC is the individual assigned to manage specifically identified areas so that customers know who to contact. Choice *A* is incorrect because customer service is a general term that describes the overall relationship between the customer and service provider. SPOC is considered a form of customer service. Choice *C* is incorrect because the term *HR representative* is generic and does not specifically define Lisa's role. Choice *D* is incorrect because CSR is the acronym for corporate social responsibility.

42. D: Technology management is a significant tool that provides numerous solutions to an organization. These solutions can include self-service portals, accessibility to employee information, filing electronic documents, and internal websites. Choice *A* is incorrect because an HR management system is a platform that specifically manages the HR function of an organization. HR management system is a solution that can be provided by technology management. Choice *B* is incorrect because policies and procedures communicate process, practice, and expectations regarding numerous topics. Choice *C* is inaccurate because a recordkeeping program is a platform that specifically manages the records of an organization such as employee files or payroll. A recordkeeping program is a solution that can be provided by technology management.

43. B: Harry should work to update the policies and procedures to accurately reflect new technology, including social media. Harry should also incorporate guidelines so that employees understand the expectations of the organization and know what would be considered inappropriate. Choice *A* is incorrect because the current policy is outdated and may not accurately reflect the current expectations. Harry should first work to update the policies and procedures and then provide all employees with a newly revised and updated policy manual. Choice *C* is incorrect because the employee has received an official counseling session, admitted responsibility, and indicated that their behavior would change. Additionally, since the policies are outdated, moving directly to formal discipline may be excessive and could be overturned in a grievance hearing. Choice *D* is incorrect because it is an overreaction to restrict full internet access to all employees because of one employee's excessive internet use. Additionally, many employees utilize the internet for resources and information in the course of their regular job. Moving to this type of reaction could negatively impact the productivity of employees.

44. A: Workplace technology policies should have several standard components, but having a specific daily usage limit should not be one of them. While it may seem that a specific limit may be a good idea to implement, placing an arbitrary number on usage could prove difficult to manage and administer. Instead, guidelines and expectations should be provided for employees to understand what would be considered inappropriate. Choices *B, C,* and *D* are incorrect because including a code of conduct, examples of ethical use, and appropriate guidelines in a workplace technology policy would all be appropriate. These standards would allow employees to understand the expectations of the organization toward internet usage and the ramifications of not adhering to these expectations.

45. C: Michael should continue to attend annual conferences to stay up to date with the new technology and programs available to Human Resources. Typically, conferences have vendors available to show new products, software, and resources that can provide better services and results to an organization. If Michael is aware of the products available, he can convey to his department and organization if the current programs being used are the best services available at the most competitive price. Choice *A* is incorrect because price shopping and switching vendors for only this reason is not appropriate. Systems that support HR are typically complex and, in order to switch platforms, it takes a large amount of resources and time to ensure accuracy.

These changes are not considered on an annual basis simply to save on cost. Choice *B* is incorrect because while free tutorials may be something that an organization can benefit from, using the services from another vendor simply to pull out resources for the organization to use would be considered unethical. Choice *D* is incorrect because the purpose of attending a conference and keeping abreast of the current technology is to ensure that the organization is meeting their needs with the technology being used. Meeting with vendors in this capacity should not be used to source a new job.

46. C: If inaccurate data is entered into the system, the report that is generated will NOT be useful or informative because it is based on bad data. Bad data in equals bad information out. Choices *A, B,* and *D* are incorrect because they are all accurate statements regarding data, data storage, and reporting. Depending on the need, Microsoft Excel® may be a more useful tool than an expensive program. Additionally, the technology and tools needed should be specific to the end user, or customer, as well as the needs of the organization. Finally, effective technology platforms should be able to hold numerous pieces of information in an organized and effective manner while also providing reports that can identify trends and issues.

47. D: The process of conciliation is the alternative dispute resolution technique that is a non-binding formal process. In the conciliation process, a negotiator explains the law and provides the two parties with a non-binding recommendation to resolve the issue. Choice *A* is incorrect because arbitration is a formal process in which an arbitrator considers evidence presented by each party and determines a solution that is binding and final. Choice *B* is incorrect because negotiation is a voluntary agreement that works out a solution directly between the two parties involved. Choice *C* is incorrect because medication is a facilitated negotiation technique that works out a solution between the two parties through a neutral third party.

48. B: The process of negotiation is a voluntary agreement that works out a solution directly between the two parties involved. Choice *A* is incorrect because arbitration is a formal process in which an arbitrator considers evidence presented by each party and determines a solution that is binding and final. Choice *C* is incorrect because mediation is a facilitated negotiation process that works out a solution between the two parties through a neutral third party. Choice *D* is incorrect because conciliation is a non-binding formal process in which a negotiator explains the law and provides the two parties with a non-binding recommendation to resolve the issue.

49. B: It is important to communicate an organization's mission, values, goals, and objectives to an outside vendor who is providing a technology platform because it will ensure alignment between the services offered and the strategic plan, which will then support the overall organizational goals. Choice *A* is incorrect because the pricing schedule will not be reliant on an organization's affordability, but rather the services and offerings provided. Choice *C* is incorrect because the organizational structure of a vendor may warrant discussion to ensure awareness and understanding of how services will be delivered; however, it is not necessary that a vendor structures their organization in the same manner as a customer. Choice *D* is incorrect because it is important to communicate this information to ensure alignment of goals and objectives. While outside vendors will have their own separate organizational identity (which will include a mission, vision, and goals), it is important to ensure that these items support or are in alignment with the customer so there is no conflict in the services provided.

50. A: When organizational development and effectiveness are not being realized within an organization, it could be due to many factors, such as lack of resources, ineffective technology, low motivation, mental fatigue, or increased workload. These factors are known as barriers. HR should work to identify the barrier and define a plan to address them. Choices *B, C,* and *D* are incorrect because they are all elements to a SWOT analysis: strengths, weaknesses, opportunities, and threats. These terms are not used to describe the factors presented.

51. C: When all HR employees report to the HR leader and provide services to assigned customers, the department is structured in a centralized manner. Choice *A* is incorrect because a decentralized structure would have certain HR employees reporting to external departments and providing services within those departments. Choice *B* is incorrect because a SPOC is a single point of contact, not a structural organization style. Choice *D* is incorrect because SMART is a methodology used to ensure that objectives and goals are structured to adequately define success.

52. A: Human Resources data is typically organized in six specific areas. Technology management is NOT one of these areas. Technology management is a tool that can deliver programs and services to the organization that can provide the necessary data to review. Choices *B, C,* and *D* are incorrect because employee data and job history, training, growth and development, and operational and departmental information are all areas of data that HR traditionally reviews to ensure that issues are addressed and trends are identified.

53. D: Lucille should recommend the implementation of a new standard. This change should be communicated to the departments, and all current files should be updated to reflect the new standard and ensure compliance. Having paperwork handled differently and stored in different places can cause confusion, inefficiencies, and security risks. Choice *A* is incorrect because the current practice should not continue until a new electronic system is put in place; the current practice should end immediately to end any potential risk to the organization.

The current program may be sufficient to handle the paperwork, and a purely electronic system may not be appropriate based on the organizational needs. Choice *B* is incorrect because an ineffective process should not be continued based on when employees will retire or leave an organization. If a process is ineffective or causes concerns or liability for an organization, it should be changed immediately. Choice *C* is incorrect because while implementing training in change is not inappropriate, it does not address the current issue regarding the process of new employee paperwork. This training may be necessary once a new process is implemented and may assist employees in this change, but it does not address the immediate need.

54. D: An organization can help ensure that employees feel protected regarding their personal information by enabling the most recent and powerful security protocols and safety features. Personal information such as home addresses, social security numbers, and dates of birth should be protected with the highest level of security as possible. Ensuring that employees know this is also key to making sure there is an awareness of this security. Choice *A* is incorrect because allowing an employee to review their personnel file regularly will not have an impact on the security and protection of the actual file. Choice *B* is incorrect because regardless of where the files are located, the security measures should reflect a high level of protection and confidentiality. If anything, there could be additional security risks in having master personnel files off-site. Choice *C* is incorrect because even with a paperless filing system, appropriate security measures should be put in place.

55. C: It is important to automate as many processes and tasks as possible in order to minimize the risks associated with providing inaccurate information. Choice *A* is incorrect because automated processes would actually minimize the risks associated with hackers and data leaks. Choice *B* is incorrect because even automated processes will need the data to be entered into the system, and audits will need to be conducted. Automation does not eliminate this need. Choice *D* is incorrect because the system will not locate, identify, and manage trends. While an automated process may provide reports that can assist with these items, an automated program will not perform these specific tasks.

56. B: Human Resources has an integral role in organizational development during the entire lifecycle of an employee. The lifecycle includes all steps within an employee's experience with an organization from the hiring and selection of the employee to when they depart the organization. Choice *A* is incorrect because the role that HR plays extends beyond just career planning and training of an employee. Choice *C* is incorrect because the role that HR plays extends beyond the hiring and selection of an employee. Choice *D* is incorrect because the role that HR plays extends beyond the recognition and promotion of an employee. HR participates in the organizational development and effectiveness of an organization by being involved in the entire lifecycle of an employee.

57. C: Courtney is engaging in the mediation process by contracting with a neutral third party to work with the two employees and resolve the issue. Mediation is a facilitated negotiation that works out a solution between the two parties through a neutral third party. Choice *A* is incorrect because conciliation is a non-binding formal process in which a mediator explains the law and provides the two parties with a non-binding recommendation to resolve the issue. Choice *B* is incorrect because arbitration is a formal process in which an arbitrator considers evidence presented by each party and determines a binding and final solution. Choice *D* is incorrect because negotiation is the voluntary agreement process that works out a solution between the two parties directly.

58. D: A robust and advanced technology platform that delivers information has numerous benefits. The benefit that is NOT included with advanced technology is incorporating external market data for trend analysis. This function would need to be performed outside of the platform, although the data the platform provides could be used to analyze against the external data. Choices *A, B,* and *C* are incorrect because they are all benefits realized with an advanced technology platform. Benefits include saving time, increasing proficiency, organizing information, providing a standard of data entry, maintaining confidentiality, and eliminating bias. Additionally, technology platforms offer better recordkeeping and improved accuracy.

59. A: The organization structure describes how a department is designed and how work is assigned. Additionally, the structure communicates how positions report to each other. Choice *B* is incorrect because an organization chart is the tool that presents the organization structure. Choice *C* is incorrect because an organization policy is a general term for any document that provides the process, expectations, or information related to a specific topic. Choice *D* is incorrect because organization system is a general term that could represent any system or program that an organization implements.

60. A: The most effective technology platforms are able to hold multiple pieces of information and provide reports to perform in-depth analysis. Choice *B* is incorrect because a technology platform is an automated system that should meet the needs of an organization. A technology platform will not be able to understand specific audiences and recommendations; the HR representative should perform these needs. Choice *C* is incorrect because an automated technology platform will most likely not be able to identify whether a piece of data is incorrect. The reports provided by the platform may be able to identify the outlier so that it can be corrected, but a technology platform holds the data that is entered. Choice *D* is incorrect because the cost does not correlate to how effective or efficient a system is.

Workplace

61. B: When an organization is operating in a global context, it is vital to ensure that employees have an awareness and understanding of the cultural differences and language barriers that may exist in each country. Choices *A, C,* and *D* are incorrect answers to this question because employees in any organization, regardless of having a global context and operating in other countries, should be informed in these areas. All employees should be aware of and fully understand the organizational structure, leadership, and mission; corporate policy, practices, and procedures; and compensation, benefits, and training.

62. A: The PESTLE tool analyzes six specific factors: political, economic, social, technological, legal, and environmental. This analysis can provide insight into gaps that an organization may have when operating in two different countries. It can also allow for specific and strategic plans to be implemented to address the areas of concern. Choices *B, C,* and *D* are incorrect because each answer provides elements that are not included in the PESTLE tool. While process, equipment, lawsuits, ergonomics, structure, and teamwork are all important, they are not factors included in the overall PESTLE analysis. With that said, it is important to note that they may arise as issues when working through the analysis under one of the overall factors. An example would be when conducting the legal review, lawsuits would potentially be an area to address; however, reviewing only lawsuits would not provide a holistic view of the organization's legal status.

63. B: Karen has identified the social factor as the one needing recommendations prior to establishing a satellite office in a new country. The social factor of the PESTLE tool includes the workforce demographics, career attitudes, training, development, and other elements specific to the employees working in the new office. Choice *A* is incorrect because the economic factor reviews items such as exchange rates, inflation rates, and other elements specific to the economy of the new country. Choice *C* is incorrect because the environmental factor reviews items such as climate change and other elements that an organization would need to be aware of before physically operating a location in a new country. Choice *D* is incorrect because the technological factor reviews items such as automation, research, development, and the systems that work to provide information and data to employees and customers.

64. D: There are three specific goals to achieve when auditing policies, systems, procedures, and documentation. Finalizing the audit as quickly as possible is NOT one of the goals; instead, the audit should take an appropriate amount of time to ensure that the audit is accurate. Choices *A, B,* and *C* are incorrect because these choices are specific goals to be achieved when conducting an HR audit. The goal of an HR audit should be to determine if policies, systems, procedures, and documentation provide a positive and healthy work environment, align with the organizational strategy and values. and comply with legal requirements and statutes.

65. C: Standardization works to ensure consistent, transparent, effective, efficient, and equitable practices. Choice *A* is incorrect because localization works to respect the local culture and traditions, understand the educational system, and adapt to the legislation and government. Choice *B* is incorrect because compliance works to ensure that process aligns with legal and regulatory statutes. Choice *D* is incorrect because adaptation works to ensure that appropriate changes are implemented, that employees accept these changes, and that they work to ensure the success of the change.

66. A: Localization works to respect the local culture and traditions, understand the educational system, and adapt to the legislation and government. Choice *B* is incorrect because compliance works to ensure that process aligns with legal and regulatory statutes. Choice *C* is incorrect because standardization works to ensure consistent, transparent, effective, efficient, and equitable practices. Choice *D* is incorrect because adaptation works to ensure that appropriate changes are implemented, that employees accept these changes, and that they work to ensure the success of the change.

67. D: Miguel will NOT assist Emily in recruiting new employees for the service center. Emily and the staff at the new location will perform this function. While recruiting is a function of HR, Miguel's role is working with Emily in her expatriate assignment. Choices *A, B,* and *C* are incorrect because these three choices are all examples of functions that Miguel will assist Emily with as she works on her expatriation assignment. Miguel will assist Emily's spouse in finding employment in the new country, locating medical facilities and short-term housing options, and repatriating back to the United States when the assignment has been completed. Additionally, Miguel will assist Emily with completing paperwork, moving household goods, and traveling to and from the Philippines. Miguel is Emily's single point of contact, or SPOC, for all of her needs while she is on this international assignment.

68. D: Diversity refers to the identities of the employees within a workforce. Choice *A* is incorrect because demographics refer to data that describe the workforce. Demographics include age, years of service, salary, position, and other descriptive pieces of data. Choice *B* is incorrect because integration refers to incorporating elements into a process or policy. Choice *C* is incorrect because inclusion refers to the acceptance of thoughts, ideas, and perspectives from every employee.

69. C: Inclusion refers to the acceptance of thoughts, ideas, and perspectives from every employee. Choice *A* is incorrect because demographics refer to data that describe the workforce. Demographics include age, years of service, salary, position, and other descriptive pieces of data. Choice *B* is incorrect because integration refers to incorporating elements into a process or policy. Choice *D* is incorrect because diversity refers to the identities of the employees within a workforce.

70. B: Creating a new job and role for an employee as a workplace accommodation would be considered unreasonable. The Americans with Disabilities Act (ADA) requires employers to make reasonable accommodations to support employees in the workplace; however, these accommodations should not create an undue hardship on the organization. Creating a role that has not existed before would be considered an unreasonable accommodation. Choice *A* is incorrect because interpretation software, while having a cost associated, could be considered reasonable based on the need of the employee. Choice *C* is incorrect because reassigning the employee to a new job is an appropriate request; if it does not displace or negatively affect another employee, then it should be considered a viable option. Choice *D* is incorrect because workplace accommodations often include acquiring new office equipment and special devices. As long as the cost is not substantial, employers should consider these options to assist an employee in the workplace.

71. C: An employer should make every effort to provide reasonable accommodations for an employee; however, modifying the work schedule to allow for unlimited paid breaks would be considered unreasonable. Employees still have a responsibility to complete their work and adhere to the work schedules and legal standards regarding breaks. Allowing an employee to take as many paid breaks as possible would not be appropriate. If there is medical documentation that substantiates this request, it may be appropriate to discuss a limited work schedule or a different position versus allowing the employee to take unlimited paid breaks.

Choice *A* is incorrect because providing access to the workplace for an employee who is utilizing a wheelchair is a completely reasonable and appropriate request under the ADA. It may be necessary to discuss options to ensure cost is not prohibitive. Choice *B* is incorrect because a telecommuting arrangement for an injured employee would be considered reasonable and appropriate. This arrangement could be temporary until the employee can return to work with no restrictions and have specific deliverables and expectations outlined as well. Choice *D* is incorrect because providing additional breaks and private areas for nursing mothers to lactate is not only reasonable and appropriate, but it is also mandated by law in several states.

72. A: Rita is working through the risk management process by identifying, addressing, and eliminating any challenges and threats that the HR department may encounter. Choice *B* is incorrect because a SWOT analysis is a tool that is used to define strengths, weaknesses, opportunities, and threats to an organization. It is important to note that this tool may be used during the risk management process. Choice *C* is incorrect because the PESTLE analysis works to identify the political, economic, social, technological, legal, and environmental variables that may influence decisions. Choice *D* is incorrect because a root cause analysis is a process to determine why a certain issue is occurring so that a recommendation can be made to correct the specific and underlying concern.

73. B: HR should identify risks when a specific incident occurs, or in a reactive setting. However, HR should also identify risks in a proactive manner. Choice *A* is incorrect because it is a factual statement; every policy and practice within an organization should focus on supporting the workplace and minimizing risk. Choice *C* is an incorrect answer because HR should work to be proactive in minimizing and eliminating risk with strong documentation and process. This can include job descriptions, policies, safety procedures, complaints procedures, and investigations. Choice *D* is an incorrect answer because HR should conduct regular audits to ensure compliance with laws and updates. Being proactive is vital in ensuring a solid and robust risk management process.

74. C: Brandon should implement the current emergency management plan to address the immediate needs of the organization and employees. He should also recommend modifications that address the current needs of the organization and the employees. Choice *A* is incorrect because while the emergency plan should be implemented immediately, Brandon should make recommendations for change as needed and not wait until the disaster is over. It would be appropriate to update the emergency plan after the disaster is over for formal inclusion of the new changes and recommendations.

Choice *B* is incorrect because implementing a policy that is not already included in the emergency plan may be inappropriate at the time. While this recommendation may be appropriate or may already be in the plan, Brandon should first assess what actions are included in the plan and what new actions would be appropriate to initiate that would address the current needs. Choice *D* is incorrect because when a disaster occurs, the emergency plan that is approved and prepared should be implemented. There may be a need to request information as to what other agencies are initiating to work through current issues, but the emergency management plan that is already prepared should be enacted immediately without waiting for other organizations to provide insight and then prepare a new plan.

75. A: A due diligence investigation is a detailed risk assessment that provides insight and information regarding a specific concern or issue. Due diligence investigations provide insight into the issues, root cause of the concern, and a direction for recommendations. They should be thorough, extensive, and fully assess the situation. Choice *B* is incorrect because a policy audit is a process to specifically review and assess a policy and make recommendations to update. Choice *C* is incorrect because a workplace safety investigation is a process to specifically investigate a safety issue or an incident in which an injury occurred. Choice *D* is incorrect because a benefit audit is a process to specifically review and assess the benefits being offered to employees or to ensure that the appropriate paperwork is completed and filed with HR.

76. B: The first priority when an accident or injury occurs in the workplace should be to ensure that the employee who has been injured receives the appropriate care needed to treat the injury. This could include first aid or calling for an ambulance to deliver emergency care. Choice *A* is incorrect because an investigation should only begin after ensuring that the injured employee has received care for their injury. Choice *C* is incorrect because while this is a focus after an injury occurs, ensuring that safety violations are resolved can only occur after an investigation is conducted. Choice *D* is incorrect because taking photographs, while important to the investigation, should not supersede caring for the injured employee first.

77. D: The three standard steps in an audit process are planning, execution, and finalizing. These three steps are vital to ensuring that a robust and strategic audit is conducted. Choices *A, B,* and *C* are incorrect because each of these choices do not indicate the standard audit steps required. There will be elements of each of these terms contained within the standard steps of planning, execution, and finalizing, but on their own, the elements of review, assessment, results, discussion, evaluation, and analyzing do not fully encompass a complete audit.

78. B: The planning step in a risk management audit would include mapping out the scope of the investigation and defining the objective. Choice *A* is incorrect because preparation is not an actual step within the risk management audit process. Choice *C* is incorrect because the execution step includes interviewing individuals, gathering and reviewing reports and procedures, and conducting the actual audit. Choice *D* is incorrect because the finalizing step includes preparing a report that summarizes the findings, highlights strengths, identifies weaknesses, and provides recommendations.

79. D: The finalizing step in a risk management audit would include preparing a report that summarizes the findings, highlights strengths, identifies weaknesses, and provides recommendations. Choice *A* is incorrect because preparation is not an actual step within the risk management audit process. Choice *B* is incorrect because the planning step would include mapping out the scope of the investigation and defining the objective. Choice *C* is incorrect because the execution step includes interviewing individuals, gathering and reviewing reports and procedures, and conducting the actual audit.

80. A: By incorporating elements of social awareness regarding the environment, community, marketplace, and workplace, Rosalie is ensuring that the organization's policies reflect corporate social responsibility, or CSR. CSR is a sustainable, operational strategy which ensures that the business operates in a socially acceptable manner. Choice *B* is incorrect because environmental programs are not a holistic strategy, but rather one element of CSR that is vital to the success of the strategy. Choice *C* is incorrect because a sustainable strategy could be any strategy for any specified topic. CSR is in fact a sustainable strategy that can be incorporated on various levels within an organization. Choice *D* is incorrect because social justice practices continue to evolve regarding the equity and fair treatment of others.

81. A: The appropriate alignment, or order, of the four responsibilities of corporate social responsibility are economic, legal, ethical, and philanthropic. The foundation of economics must be solid to then allow the CSR to expand to the next level of legal, then ethical, and finally philanthropic. Choices *B, C,* and *D* are incorrect because they are not representative of the appropriate alignment of the CSR responsibilities. Without a solid economic foundation, the organization will not be able to continue to build further into the other responsibilities.

82. C: Communication is not an easy task, and most individuals will NOT hear the same information and then have the same understanding of the message. Individuals hear things differently, interpret words differently, and may have a completely different understanding of the same message. Choice *A* is incorrect because this statement is true about communication. It should be practiced, and managers should be coached frequently on effective techniques. Choice *B* is incorrect because this statement is also true. Many individuals hear different information, interpret words differently, and may have separate understandings of the same message. Choice *D* is incorrect because this statement about communication is accurate. It is a critical need within an organization, and managers should be trained and educated on how best to communicate with employees.

83. C: The Department of Justice (DOJ) is responsible for enforcing the laws regarding employee privacy. Choice *A* is incorrect because the Occupational Safety and Health Administration (OSHA) is responsible for enforcing the laws regarding workplace safety. Choice *B* is incorrect because the Equal Employment Opportunity Commission (EEOC) is responsible for enforcing the laws regarding discrimination. Choice *D* is incorrect because the Department of Labor (DOL) is responsible for enforcing the laws regarding compensation.

84. A: An organization can offer a benefit to employees that is different from the federal or state requirement only if the offered benefit is more lucrative or greater than the requirements in the law. An example would be regarding FMLA and maternity leave. It would be possible for the agency to extend additional paid time off if they wanted to as long as the requirements within the laws are met. Choice *B* is incorrect because an organization cannot offer a less lucrative benefit to employees. Choice *C* is incorrect because under no circumstances can an organization reduce a federal or state entitlement to an employee, even due to finances. Choice *D* is incorrect because employees cannot sign away their rights under the law with a waiver.

85. B: An inappropriate reason to contract with an outside legal service would be due to the current staff not wanting to audit the safety practices just because they are uninteresting. Choice *A* is incorrect because negotiating a contract with a union can be a difficult and consuming process. Additionally, if the staff does not have this experience, it would be in the organization's best interest to bring in expertise to assist with this task. Choice *C* is incorrect because resolving conflict by a third party may be appropriate based on the previous attempts. This would be another good example of when to bring in an outside legal service. Choice *D* is incorrect because bringing in legal expertise specific to updated legislation when reviewing and updating policies is a vital component to ensuring that the policies comply with the new regulations.

Greetings!

First, we would like to give a huge "thank you" for choosing us and this study guide for your SHRM-CP exam. We hope that it will lead you to success on this exam and for your years to come.

Our team has tried to make your preparations as thorough as possible by covering all of the topics you should be expected to know. In addition, our writers attempted to create practice questions identical to what you will see on the day of your actual test. We have also included many test-taking strategies to help you learn the material, maintain the knowledge, and take the test with confidence.

We strive for excellence in our products, and if you have any comments or concerns over the quality of something in this study guide, please send us an email so that we may improve.

As you continue forward in life, we would like to remain alongside you with other books and study guides in our library. We are continually producing and updating study guides in several different subjects. If you are looking for something in particular, all of our products are available on Amazon. You may also send us an email!

Sincerely,
APEX Test Prep
info@apexprep.com

FREE

Free Study Tips Videos/DVD

In addition to this guide, we have created a FREE set of videos with helpful study tips. **These FREE videos provide you with top-notch tips to conquer your exam and reach your goals.**

Our simple request is that you give us feedback about the book in exchange for these strategy-packed videos. We would love to hear what you thought about the book, whether positive, negative, or neutral. It is our #1 goal to provide you with quality products and customer service.

To receive your **FREE Study Tips Videos**, scan the QR code or email freevideos@apexprep.com. Please put "FREE Videos" in the subject line and include the following in the email:

 a. The title of the book

 b. Your rating of the book on a scale of 1-5, with 5 being the highest score

 c. Any thoughts or feedback about the book

Thank you!